East Anglian Studies

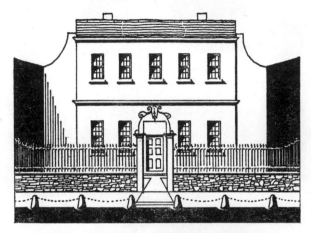

Harbour House at the Hythe, Colchester,
based on an illustration of Robert Tabor's house
in a volume of family letters compiled *c.* 1815.
The house still stands

Drawn by Christopher Wright
from the original in the
Essex Record Office

East Anglian Studies

Edited by Lionel M. Munby

ESSAYS BY

J. C. Barringer

D. P. Dymond

J. A. Alexander

P. Eden

J. R. Ravensdale

L. M. Munby

A. F. J. Brown

R. E. Pahl

W. Heffer & Sons Ltd
Cambridge

Printed in Great Britain by
W. Heffer & Sons Ltd, Cambridge
and published by them in 1968 for the
Board of Extra-mural Studies of
the University of Cambridge

To Geoffrey Fletcher Hickson

Contents

References are given at the end of each essay

The Contributors

J. A. ALEXANDER, M.A., PH.D., Staff Tutor, 1957–64; Lecturer in Archaeology, Department of Extra-mural Studies, University of London, 1964–

J. C. BARRINGER, M.A., Senior Geography Master, Lancaster Royal Grammar School, 1953–65; Resident Tutor in Norfolk, 1966–

A. F. J. BROWN, B.A., Master at Colchester Royal Grammar School, 1939–40, 1946–7, 1951– ; W.E.A. Organising Tutor for Essex, 1948–51

D. P. DYMOND, B.A., Senior Investigator, Royal Commission on Historical Monuments, 1957–64; Resident Tutor in Suffolk, 1964– .

P. EDEN, M.A., PH.D., Principal Investigator, Royal Commission on Historical Monuments, 1948–65; Senior Lecturer in English Topography in the Department of English Local History at the University of Leicester, 1966–

L. M. MUNBY, M.A., Staff Tutor, 1946–

R. E. PAHL, M.A., PH.D., Resident Tutor in Hertfordshire, 1959–65; Lecturer in Sociology in the University of Kent at Canterbury, 1965–

J. R. RAVENSDALE, M.A., Adult Tutor and other posts at Impington Village College, 1953–66; Lecturer at Homerton College, 1966–

Illustrations

* Drawings by Avril Henry   † Drawings by Jane Holmes

Introduction

When Mrs Gaskell portrayed Job Legh in *Mary Barton* as an outstanding local naturalist and collector of specimens, she was copying her character from life. Many nineteenth-century working men made such remarkable collections of local fauna and flora that they laid the foundations on which local museum collections were built and studies of local ecology developed. In the same period the local gentry, squires and parsons in the main, were promoting the study of local antiquities through antiquarian and archaeological societies. In the twentieth century these hobbies have become professionalised. But the enquiring and observant native has retained one advantage over the professional when his own neighbourhood is the subject matter of academic study: he knows the neighbourhood as a living whole. Modern developments in various kinds of local studies have tended to focus on the relation between the subject matter under observation and its environment. The native starts with natural advantages in investigating any kind of ecology, whether the enquiry is formally biological, historical or sociological. It is, therefore, no accident that the development of local studies has been so marked in adult education. Here the specialist meets the intelligent and interested local inhabitant in a genuine partnership, for the intellectual pursuit which brings them together is one to which they can both contribute.

The University of Cambridge Board of Extra-mural Studies has been fostering this development for over a third of a century. The late W. P. Baker, who began teaching for the Board in 1927, became its first full-time tutor in 1931. Not only did he stimulate the study of local history all over the fenland and its surrounding country, but he played an important part in founding the Cambridgeshire Cottage Improvement Society. Ever since this time local studies have been an important element in extra-mural teaching. The contributors to this volume have all worked for the Board in the post-war years, either as full-time or part-time tutors; they have been continuing and, they hope, developing a

Introduction

worthwhile tradition. There are many reasons why examples of the knowledge acquired in extra-mural teaching should be put before a wider public. The studies brought together in this volume are presented as examples of some of the varied fields of knowledge which are being illuminated by taking the locality, community, county or region, as the object of research. They have developed out of teaching experience with adult students and have been stimulated by the interests of such students.

In the whole of education, from the schools to the new universities, there has been a recent marked growth in teaching which breaks out of the bounds of traditional academic disciplines. One of the more effective ways in which traditional 'subjects' can be fruitfully combined into new disciplines is by making a given locality the object of study and investigating it with different specialisms. The essays in this volume, in some cases at any rate, suggest such an approach, though the book is in no sense intended as a model of this kind. The experience being developed in teaching for the Certificate of Secondary Education, in Colleges of Education, and in courses in local studies for schoolteachers organised by the Board of Extra-mural Studies, should produce such models in the next few years. What we do hope to demonstrate in a small way in this volume is that this approach is not necessarily parochial. The study of a locality may throw new light on national developments. While the authors have been writing primarily about the localities they know and for local people, it will be obvious that many of the contributions have a much wider significance.

The time for publishing such a collection is in a general sense opportune. Eastern England is a region unduly neglected by government agencies and by planners. It is a rapidly growing area with a varied character of its own. Its geography and history, the factors which explain the modern community, need to be better known and appreciated. Some of the experience accumulated in a third of a century of extra-mural teaching in the region can profitably be put before a wider public. While most of the book will be of primary interest to teachers, adult students and the growing serious reading public, some parts may interest perceptive businessmen and members of local authorities. Mr Dymond and Dr Eden, in different ways, discuss the changing physical environment in which we live. Mr Brown has given us a model of the changes produced in a town by the decay of an industry and its replacement by other economic influences. Dr Pahl discusses the impact of somewhat similar modern changes on different types of communities.

There is, however, a particular and personal reason why this collection of essays is published at this time for the University of Cambridge Board of Extra-mural Studies by Heffers of Cambridge. Geoffrey Hickson, to whom this book is dedicated, retired on 30th September 1967 after over forty years' service to the University of Cambridge, to adult education, and to local government. He became Assistant Secretary to the Board of Extra-mural Studies in 1925 and Secretary in 1928, Secretary to the Regional Committee for Adult Education in H.M. Forces in 1940, a University member of the Cambridge City Council in 1943, and has twice served as Mayor of Cambridge. For sixteen years he was a member of the Council of the Senate of the University and from 1964 to 1966 he served on Sir George Mallaby's Committee on the Staffing of Local Government.

This book has been produced by its authors not only as a tribute to a distinguished public life, in the region and nationally, but also in gratitude for personal qualities which they have learned to appreciate in a colleague and friend. In an age in which the brasher elements of those admirable qualities of go-ahead, drive and efficiency have penetrated deeply into the educational world to its detriment in terms of human relationships at least, it is refreshing to find dignity without arrogance, kindliness and helpfulness without ulterior motives. For the teacher who knows what he or she wants to teach and how, it is better to be left to find one's own way than to be driven down someone else's path at someone else's speed. Geoffrey Hickson has not been directly responsible for the developments in local studies in the Cambridge extra-mural region in any ordinary sense, but he has made possible this and other significant developments because he has left his staff alone while supporting them in whatever they achieved. To some this may seem a strange virtue in the modern world, but it is one badly needed in education as those teachers at every level who have been driven before the storm will readily appreciate. It is, above all, in gratitude for this quality that the present book is published.

L. M. M.

The Rivers of Norfolk and North Suffolk

J. C. Barringer

It is strange that our knowledge of the physiography of East Anglia is still in many respects in a rudimentary state [1].

East Anglia and adjoining districts, with their wealth of glacial deposits and monotonous relief, have stimulated research into problems of drift geology, but the development of relief has been largely neglected [2].

These two views upon the state of knowledge of the evolution of the relief of East Anglia, although written in 1942 and 1957 respectively, are still broadly true. The aims of this short commentary are to indicate what seem to be some of the most interesting points about the map of the river systems in the area of North Suffolk and Norfolk, and to air some of the ideas put forward in papers that may not be generally accessible. It must be stressed that this is meant to be a provocative starting-point from which it is hoped field examination may stem: map evidence is the primary source of material for this article and scattered field observations of a purely visual order form a secondary source.

A study of the map suggests that the following points about the relief of the area are of interest:*

Land over 200 ft. above O.D. lies mainly in north-west Norfolk to the north of Watton; also between Fakenham and Sheringham and lastly along an almost east-to-west line south of Bury St Edmunds. The relief map does not show a continuous ridge of highland to tally with the concept of 'the East Anglian Heights'.

Land below 50 ft. O.D. forms a very clear-cut boundary on the west of the area: this is of course the eastern edge of the Fenland. In the east the pattern is much less clear and many small islands of over 50 ft. O.D. show up; Flegg and Lothingland are perhaps the most distinctive of these. The 50 ft. contour, shows a high degree of indentation, for example downstream of Aylsham in

* See maps listed at end of References.

the Bure Valley. The 25 ft. contour shows better than the 50 ft. contour the involved pattern of lowland and upland in the eastern part of Norfolk. There are many tongues of *upland* which stretch eastwards, yet they are below 50 ft.; one example will suffice. It is that of a distinctive low plateau reaching about 40 ft. O.D. between the Bure and the Ant Valleys in the Hoveton, Horning, Neatishead triangle; Ludham too lies on a similar area between the Ant and the Thurne.

Between the lowland and the highland there is a large area which is sometimes called High Norfolk and High Suffolk and is also termed the boulder clay plateau. The bulk of this area is in fact over 100 ft. O.D.; considerable areas are over 150 ft. O.D. and scattered points just top the 200 ft. mark (see Map 1). Both in the west, east of a line from Lynn to Downham Market, and in the east, to the north-east of Norwich, there are considerable areas between 50 and 100 ft. O.D. Maps 1 and 2 show contrasting sample areas. In Map 2 it is seen that the Rivers Wensum and Tud are sharply incised into what appears to be a 125 ft. plateau surface. Map 1 on the other hand shows a rather more undulating relief and the spot heights show that the divides are not flattened.

*   *   *

The existence of considerable stretches of land at particular heights such as 125 ft. and 40 ft. must raise the question of whether this is purely accidental or whether these level areas are of significance in the evolution of the East Anglian landscape. Such levels may possibly reflect pre-glacial erosion surfaces upon which the glacial deposits are evenly enough spread to echo the sub-glacial relief, or alternatively the glacial deposits may themselves be almost flat over wide areas. In that fluvio-glacial gravels occupy considerable areas of the surface to the north and north-east of Norwich it may well be that these surfaces are in fact portions of gently sloping outwash zones. Careful analysis of the highest points of watersheds may give some answer to this problem and yet further collection of borehole information would answer the query with references to the chalk surface and possible bevelling thereon. Clayton's paper on southern Essex points the way towards the analysis of immediately post-glacial relief forms upon which drainage would be consequent [3].

The two sample areas already referred to (Maps 1 and 2) show that the monotonous relief mentioned by Sparks in the second of the two initial quotations would be better termed small-scale relief. There are contrasts within this broadly low-lying area that pose many interesting physiographical problems. Detailed morphological mapping of the type suggested by Waters in his work on the south-east Pennines [4] might be a worthwhile exercise, though the system of mapping would have to be adjusted to the less dramatic relief of Norfolk. The work of Clayton in south Essex offers an interesting morphological map from a neighbouring region with which comparison should be possible and his use of 10 ft. contour interval mapping of the Springfield Till surface in south Essex is also a technique that has much to recommend it in an area such as that of Norfolk. The 25 ft. contour interval can miss relief elements of considerable significance in a region in which the maximum relief may only be of an order of 40 ft. A traditional method of geological and geomorphological study has been that of argument by analogy. Mention has already been made of the existence of fluvio-glacial deposits to the north and east of Norwich, and Sparks and West have studied two examples of such deposits near Holt, the Kelling and Salthouse outwash plains, in great detail [5]. The nature of the surface relief and the order of gradients recorded upon the great spreads of gravels, the sandur, to the south of the Vatnajokull in the south-east of Iceland, may well provide a comparison, since this is an area that is analogous to much of north-east Norfolk as it was at the end of the Gipping glaciation and perhaps even during the Hunstanton glaciation also (Table 1).

Sufficient has been said to show that the relief of Norfolk and north Suffolk has many interesting features. It is probably artificial to consider relief as a facet of the landscape separate from that of its drainage. It is, however, a useful device for the purpose of description. The following points have been selected as being of particular interest in the drainage pattern of the area shown on Sheet 14 of the Fifth Series of the Ordnance Survey Quarter Inch Map:

Breydon Water and its outlet take the run-off of a very large part of the area under discussion. Indeed the greater part of this commentary is about the streams that drain to it.

A corollary to this is that no other streams now flow to the Norfolk Coast between Mundesley Beck and Yarmouth although

3   B

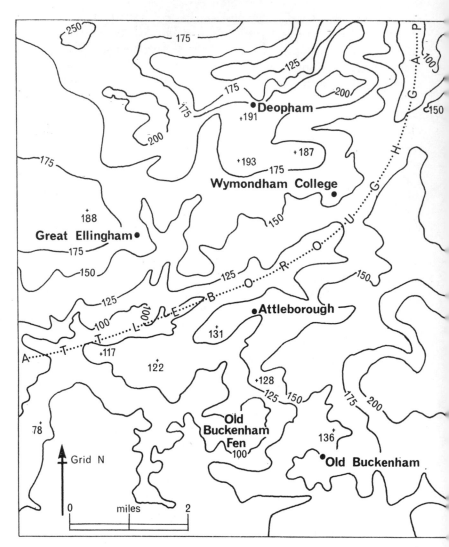

Map 1.   The Attleborough Gap
Crown Copyright reserved

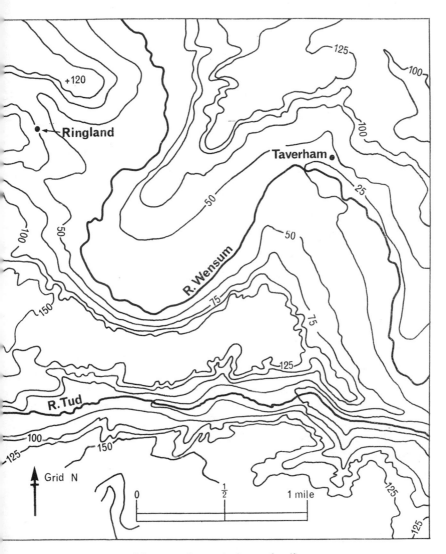

Map 2.   Some drainage details
Crown Copyright reserved

the Hundred Stream (Horsey Gap) route and the Cockle Water (Caister on Sea) gap have both carried drainage in historic time. Whilst it is suggested that the latter took the Bure water, or some of it, until 1347 [6] it is not clear how much drainage would be taken by the former. Discussion of the evolution of the Norfolk coast, especially by Steers [7], and of the development of the Broads [8,9,6] has been full. It is, therefore, merely necessary to underline the point that it is not possible to understand the evolution of the lower courses of Norfolk's main east-flowing rivers without considering the marine processes at work in modifying the coastline which consists of largely unconsolidated glacial and post-glacial materials.

The courses of the Bure/Ant systems and that of the Waveney system are particularly interesting in that they do not echo the flow pattern that is the generalised direction of flow of the east-flowing rivers of Great Britain. Further, the two systems show no agreement as to their eccentricity of direction. A very clear secondary watershed exists to the south and the south-east of the Waveney and it is this watershed which forms the southern boundary to the area under discussion.

The well-known through valley of the Little Ouse/Waveney system needs little emphasis; it shows up clearly on the map.† An interesting situation is revealed between Thetford and the Yare Valley. Map 1 shows the central part of that zone at a scale of one mile to one inch. This has been termed the Attleborough gap on Map 1 but the whole sub-region might be termed the Thetford/Attleborough zone of shallow valleys. This gap's highest point is at 132 ft. O.D. (Ref. TM 074975) as opposed to that of the Little Ouse/Waveney at 80 ft. O.D. (South Lopham Fen), and it is occupied by an indeterminate drainage system which finally becomes the River Thet to the west and the River Tiffey to the east. The major East Anglian watershed here lies well to the east of any chalk cuesta* crest that may once have existed and it follows a tortuous course. Whilst the meres of Breckland form a topic meriting a particular study, the tentative suggestion is put forward that these meres show a marked relationship to this intricate shallow valley system to the north and east of Thetford.

The west-flowing rivers draining towards the Fens and occupying

* A ridge with a steep scarp slope and gentler back-slope.
† See maps listed at end of references.

an obsequent* position show a more uniform drainage pattern than do those of the eastern (dip) slope. Even here, however, the courses of the Blackwater northwards to Thetford, the Thet to the north-east of Thetford, and the Wissey from the south-east of Swaffham, all show irregularities that are not typical of chalkland valleys. Some analogy may be possible between these irregularities and that of the Bain in East Lincolnshire [10].

*   *   *

An attempt to summarise the main points of the relief and drainage of the area is made in the two block-diagrams (Figs. 1 and 2). Fig. 1 is an attempt to consider the area in terms of traditional (i.e. Davisian) theory [11]. It is treated as an embayed cuesta with the maximum embayment in the Brandon area. On such a structure near-parallel secondary consequent streams would flow to the east and each stream would develop its associated tributary pattern. This hypothetical diagram begs the question of the lack of a chalk scarp in the region between Thetford and Swaffham. Boswell, in his valuable paper 'On the Surface and Dip of the Chalk in Norfolk' [12], points out, from the evidence of 142 boreholes in Norfolk, that the chalk surface beneath the glacial cover is much more complex than that suggested by Fig. 1. He did not suggest to what extent he considered glaciation was responsible for this irregular chalk surface. The detailed map of the chalk zones in *The Geology of Norfolk* [13] shows that the chalk zones outcrop almost due north to south, and suggests no evidence of any local variations in dip that might explain the basin-like drainage pattern of east Norfolk. It seems reasonable to theorise that the pre-glacial (Pliocene and early Pleistocene) eastward-flowing drainage was of a pattern similar to that suggested in Fig. 1. It is suggested in this figure that the Little Ouse/Waveney gap may well have its origin in the line of an early consequent stream of mid-Tertiary times, comparable with the breaks in the chalk cut by the Thames and the stream which carved the Wash Gap. Work by Wooldridge and Henderson on 'Some Aspects of the Physiography of the Eastern Part of the London Basin' [14] throws doubt on a pre-glacial age for the Goring Gap, however, and also suggests that the Pliocene sea at 600 ft. O.D. resulted in

---

* A scarp-face stream flowing against the angle of dip of the cuesta.

consequence of rivers in this post-Pliocene surface. In this broad setting the Little Ouse/Waveney gap must clearly pose a number of problems still.

Fig. 2 is an attempt to show some of the present surface features of relief and drainage in Norfolk. The Cromer Ridge is the best-known relief feature. The diagram shows how this eastward-curving mass of glacial deposits forms the present coast between Sheringham and Mundesley. It is clearly this feature that is in broad plan responsible for the general direction of the courses of the Wensum, Bure and Ant to the south and those of the Burn, Stiffkey and Glaven to the north. It is the very complex detailed relief of this ridge that controls the confused courses of the upper Wensum, the Stiffkey and the Glaven. An interesting additional irregularity is that of the lower course of the Stiffkey: the eastward deflection of this stretch of the river is not the result of a marine process and may well be related to the last ice advance, that of the Hunstanton glaciation. It is only in the course of the Yare and its smaller northern neighbour, the Tud, that any reflection of the original drainage pattern suggested in Fig. 1 appears. Even here, however, the headstreams of these two rivers lie some way to the east of the western limits of the chalk outcrop and rise on the drift watershed well to the east of the western edge of the chalk.

The Waveney system provides the southern limit to the area under consideration. Boswell provides no suggestion of a subsidiary chalk watershed to the south and east of the Waveney. It seems likely therefore that the course of the Waveney is controlled by a drift ridge and that the river may in fact be occupying some form of glacial *or* fluvio-glacial depression. As Fig. 2 shows, the River Tas, a south bank tributary of the Yare, parallels both the course of the Waveney and that of the Waveney/Tas watershed to the south-east of the Waveney. Much more evidence is needed before the true nature of these two ridges is fully known but on the basis of Boswell's work it seems reasonable to presume that they are drift areas in depth as well as in plan.

This raises the question of whether there is similarity of alignment in the area under consideration to that found in Jutland and the North German Plain with its pattern of terminal moraines and urstromtäler.* Whether the zone of shallow valleys near Thetford,

---

* Broad shallow valleys eroded by glacial meltwater which flowed parallel to the front of the ice sheets.

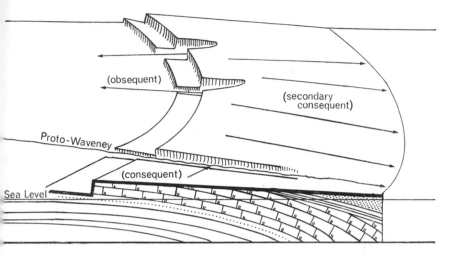

Fig. 1. Theoretical sketch block-diagram of pre-glacial conditions in the area

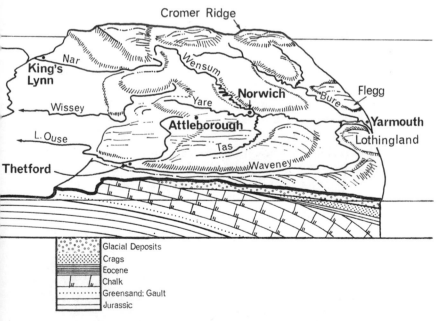

Fig. 2. Sketch block-diagram of the post-glacial relief and drainage of the area

9

already referred to, and the Attleborough Gap may also fit into such a system is a question for further examination. The solid chalk which forms the cuesta is visualised as having been breached by east-west glacial meltwater streams. These streams followed either the lines of the ice margins or those of the natural depressions which were created between a series of east-west lines of terminal moraine deposited by the ice as it melted. The collection of much more borehole information and of observations from any excavations in the drifts and in the shallow, often peaty, depressions within them is clearly a practical exercise of value in any further discussion of the development of the river system of the area, as also is more careful mapping of the small-scale relief features of the area.

So far discussion has been on a broad basis, that of ridges and of the alignment of river systems. There is also much interesting detail within the individual valleys and in the courses of the particular streams. The traditional tool of valley analysis is that of the examinations of the river profile (down valley) and of the valley cross-section. There are considerable differences within the valleys and along the rivers of the area. The long profiles show much variety: in the case of the larger rivers it may well be that the profiles are the results of a very complex series of events. However, such features as the south slope of the Cromer Ridge (Bure), the drift-covered dip slope of the chalk (Wensum), and the Little Ouse/Waveney Gap (Waveney), all show up. The smaller streams are probably younger and less complex in their history. The small river Tud not only shows a steeper gradient than do the larger rivers but it shows a marked steepening in its long profile near its confluence with the Wensum. Other breaks of slope not revealed by a 25 ft. contour interval are also observable on the ground upstream of this major break in slope. This last point emphasises that careful levelling may well reveal breaks in the long profiles. The siting of mills along the courses of these rivers may also offer a human response to localised changes in river gradient and therefore reflect physical events. It should be noticed that the present highest point of ordinary tides is well up the main rivers, e.g. Wroxham Bridge on the Bure and Trowse Bridge on the Yare.

Cross-sections of the valleys show that there is a considerable degree of dissection in the low plateau country to the north and east of Norwich. The Bure valley at Acle (Ref. TG 415115) shows evidence of considerable lateral cutting and at Saxthorpe (Ref. TG 115303) it shows dissection of the upland to the extent of 75 ft. The valleys of the Yare at Bickerston (Ref. TG 085087) and the Tud at Honingham (Ref. TG 090122) show a similar order of vertical dissection. The upper valleys, for example that of the Bure at Melton Constable (Ref. TG 040325), show a depth that appears too great in relation to the size of the existing streams. The degree to which these valleys show a true river terrace development is far from satisfactorily established. Map evidence is just not accurate enough for this analysis. It is important to distinguish between drift shoulders below which valleys have been cut, meander terraces and properly paired terraces left by the rivers in former flood plains. The material in which early palaeolithic finds were made at Keswick (Ref. TG 213051) near Norwich on the south bank of the Yare has been termed a river terrace deposit. If this is valid physiographically then this terrace stands some 30 ft. above the present flood plain of the river. Funnell and Larwood record a fluvio-glacial terrace on the Waveney between Harleston and Beccles [15]. Here again, only much careful mapping and collection of material will provide the basis for a real description of the Norfolk river valleys. Explanation cannot really begin until much more accurate information has accumulated: the Keswick find reminds us that archaeology and geomorphology may be mutually helpful also.

The actual nature of the courses of the rivers is a subject upon which, as far as the author is aware, no work has yet been done in Norfolk. The outstanding features of interest show well on the map. The huge meanders on the middle sections of the Bure, Wensum and Yare are clearly of a very different order from the much smaller (present?) meanders that lie within the large ones. Map 2 shows this double pattern of meandering on the Wensum at Taverham. Dury has discussed the problem of misfit streams and, using his terminology, it would seem that these three rivers are manifestly underfit streams [16,17]. Whether the smaller meanders are in fact forming now is also an interesting problem. It must be remembered that many of Norfolk's rivers have been heavily modified by man and that parish boundaries, such as the eastern boundary of North Walsham, are much better guides to natural river courses than are those provided by the canalised rivers of the present day.

Map 2 also shows the final feature of valley detail to be stressed. It is that of the marked degree of dissection of valley sides by tributary valleys which are now, in the main, dry. A good example of this is seen at Ringland on Map 2 and another to the south of the Tud. In that the geological sequence of these valley sides is glacial sands, brickearth, crag and then chalk; a mainly porous and rather arid *upland* surface exists and produces very little run off. It seems reasonable to assume that many of these minor valley slope dry valleys are peri-glacial in origin. Whether the dry valleys result from a single origin is also doubtful: Sloughbottom (Ref. TG 212110) to the north-west of Norwich, for example, is much larger than the examples illustrated on Map 2. The relationship of these valleys to the geology is an obvious first point for examination.

These features of valley detail suggest that run-off conditions in the area must have been very different from those now effective. It would seem that Norfolk's rivers are only actively modifying their valleys either vertically or laterally at a few points or on a few short sections of their courses: for example the Yare is cutting laterally into its south bank at Colney Church (Ref. TG 180081). The correlation of such points of erosion with the sequence of sea-level fluctuations is a very important task remaining to be carried out in this area. The dominant visual impression is one of valleys that are becoming shallower by the combined influences of infilling by silt deposition (both marine and fluvial) and peat growth and the process of valley-side soil creep.

It has been suggested that the drainage of this area of Norfolk and North Suffolk shows features of interest in terms of its overall plan and in terms of its detail of valley cross-section, long profile and river plan. The Quaternary glaciations provide an almost endless permutation of variables that may help to explain the anomalies of drainage pattern that have been discussed. The possible impact of these glaciations may be summarised in general terms as follows:

Actual changes of pre-glacial drainage lines by the deposition of drift.

Modifications of pre-glacial drainage lines by glacial, sub-glacial, fluvial or fluvio/glacial action: Boswell suggests evidence for this in Suffolk [18] and Funnell for the Yare valley at Trowse just to the south of Norwich [19].

The Rivers of Norfolk and North Suffolk

Significant changes in river regime in areas outside the ice limits; these changes may stem from both variations in run off and load.

Fluctuations of land/sea-levels which would in turn influence the extent to which the extra ice-sheet drainage systems would dissect the area.

Regional crustal movements that might stem from isostatic readjustments to the existence of large masses of ice.

It might also be added that it seems likely that the North Sea Basin is undergoing long-term changes of a geosynclinal* nature too.

The generalised picture of the phases of the Quaternary glaciations in Norfolk is shown in Table 1. Column three shows in a hypothetical way how each of these phases may have influenced the drainage conditions in East Anglia. Clayton in South Essex [3] and Straw in East Lincolnshire [10] have both suggested sequences as the results of very detailed studies that might offer bases for comparison with events in Suffolk and Norfolk. This paper has purposely emphasised drainage features; the literature on the glacial deposits of Norfolk and their interpretation is now large and highly specialised [20], but it is hoped that, if only in very broad outline, some of the problems that remain in the attempt to reach a further understanding of the physical landscape of the area under discussion have been highlighted. The state of understanding of the physical evolution of the area is still much as the opening quotations suggested. It is clear that only the accumulation of a great deal more information [21] will provide the material from which further progress can be made.

Acknowledgement. The author wishes to thank A. R. Cartwright for many valuable points raised in discussion of the draft of this paper, but of course accepts full responsibility for all the opinions expressed.

---

* A geosyncline is a major depression formed by an actual sagging of the earth's crust in which sediment is accumulating.

Table 1

THE PLEISTOCENE IN NORFOLK AND NORTH SUFFOLK

The first two columns are based on Larwood and Funnell [13] and in *Norwich and its Region* [15]

Stage	Deposits	Possible drainage forms	Sea-level
Post-glacial	Coastal dune and spits. Broadland and Fenland deposits	Establishment of present system. Deflection by split growth	Rising
Glaciation 3 Hunstanton Glaciation	Hunstanton Till and Outwash	Most of the area's rivers in existence but ratio of load to flow different from present	Low?
Interglacial 3 Ipswichian Interglacial	Morston Raised Beach	Present river system largely established	High?
Glaciation 2 Gipping Glaciation	Gipping Till and Outwash Cromer Ridge	Drainage obscured in N.W. Norfolk, the Breckland and W. Suffolk. Fluvio-glacial spread in N.E. Norfolk	Low?
Interglacial 2 Hoxne Interglacial	Nar Valley Beds Hoxne Lake Deposits	Long period of erosion by drainage system consequent to Lowestoft and Cromer Till Surfaces	High
Glaciation 1	Lowestoft Till: Suffolk and S. and S.W. Norfolk Corton Beds	Pre-glacial drainage system obscured by drift	Low
Lowestoft glaciation	Cromer Till: central, northern and N.E. Norfolk		
Interglacial 1 Cromerian Interglacial	Arctic Freshwater Beds Cromer Forest Bed series	Drainage system consequent to chalk, eocene and crags established	
Icenian Pliocene	Crags	Long period of Post-Eocene erosion	Falling? ?

14

REFERENCES

TNNNS = *Transactions of the Norfolk and Norwich Naturalists' Society*
IBG   = *Transactions of the Institute of British Geographers*
GJ   = *Geographical Journal*

1. J. A. Steers, 'Physiography of East Anglia', *TNNNS* 15 (1942), p. 231.
2. B. W. Sparks, 'Evolution of the Relief of the Cam Valley', *GJ* 123 (June 1957), p. 188.
3. K. M. Clayton, 'The Landforms of Parts of Southern Essex', *IBG* 28 (1960).
4. R. S. Waters, 'Morphological Mapping', *Geography* (January 1958), p. 10.
5. B. W. Sparks and R. G. West, 'The Drift Landforms around Holt in Norfolk', *IBG* 35 (1964), p. 27.
6. E. A. Ellis, *The Broads* (1965); also a valuable bibliography to the Geology and Physiography section.
7. J. A. Steers, *The Sea Coast* (1953), especially chapters 6 and 8 and the bibliography.
8. J. N. Jennings, *The Origins of the Broads* (Royal Geographical Society Research Series, no. 2, 1952). Valuable bibliography.
9. Lambert, Jennings, Smith, Green and Hutchinson, *The Making of the Broads* (Royal Geographical Society Research Series, no. 3, 1960). Very full bibliography.
10. A. Straw, 'The Development of the Middle and Lower Bain Valleys. East Lincolnshire', *IBG* 40 (1966).
11. R. J. Small, 'Morphology of Chalk Escarpments. A Critical Discussion', *IBG* 29 (1961). A discussion of the problems of chalkland landscape development relevant to this figure.
12. P. G. A. Boswell, 'On the Surface and Dip of the Chalk in Norfolk', *TNNNS* 11 (1919–24), p. 22.
13. G. P. Larwood and B. M. Funnell in *TNNNS* 19, pt. 6 (1961), facing p. 340.
14. S. W. Wooldridge and H. C. K. Henderson in *IBG* 21 (1955).
15. *Norwich and its Region* (British Association for the Advancement of Science, 1961), p. 29.
16. G. H. Dury, 'Test of a General Theory of Misfit Streams', *IBG* 25 (1958), p. 105.
17. G. H. Dury, 'Underfit Streams in relation to Capture. A Reassessment of the Ideas of W. M. Davis', *IBG* 32 (1963), p. 83.
18. P. G. H. Boswell, 'The Age of Suffolk Valleys with notes on the Buried Channels of the Drift', *Quarterly Journal Geological Society* 69 (1913), p. 581.
19. B. M. Funnell, 'A Yare Valley Buried Channel', *TNNNS* 18 (1958), p. 10.
20. Larwood and Funnell, op. cit., bibliography.

21. The following by F. Debenham are useful for those wishing to map and record features in the field: *Map Making* (3rd ed. 1955); 'A Simple Water Level', *GJ* 130 (December 1964); with A. R. Cartwright, *Simple Surveying* (1967).

Ordnance Survey Maps

Quarter Inch, Fifth Series, Sheet 14.
Half Inch, Sheet 39 (Norwich).
One Inch, Seventh Series, Sheets 126 (Norwich), 125 (Fakenham), 136 (Bury St Edmunds), 137 (Lowestoft), 124 (King's Lynn), 135 (Cambridge).

Geological Survey

Quarter Inch, Drift Editions, Sheet 12, 1964 (1906 Survey, Amendments 1953 and 1964).
One Inch, Old Series, Sheets 68, 66, 69, 65, 67 (all out of print).

The Suffolk Landscape

D. P. Dymond

Although it is not one of the largest English counties, and has no really dramatic scenery, Suffolk has a great variety of landscape features. The natural or physical landscape may not be varied in relief, but it has a wide range of rocks, soils and vegetation. These have clearly influenced human settlement and exploitation from prehistoric times to the present day, so that the cultural or man-made landscape is as varied as the physical. The purpose of this essay is two-fold. Firstly to point out the essential features of the present-day landscape, and secondly to suggest how they have evolved historically. Little detailed work has been published so far on the second subject, and in many cases one can only pose problems and suggest how they may be tackled. However, several individuals and groups have recently begun research on various aspects of the Suffolk landscape, and this seems a good opportunity to review the present state of knowledge [1].

The county has three major natural divisions [2]. In the northwest is an extensive area of light soils, which includes the Breckland and the chalk downland around Newmarket. This is the area which John Kirby in his *Suffolk Traveller* of 1735 called the Fielding, presumably because there were in his day large areas of arable land in the form of open fields. There was also a great amount of open heath and downland, some of which survives today. The term 'Breckland' was coined in 1894 by W. G. Clarke, though the first element 'breck' had been used in the area since medieval times to describe temporary arable or out-field. On the west the Breckland meets the Fens, but its eastern and southern boundaries are harder to draw. There the Breckland almost fades into High Suffolk, but roughly speaking the road from Garboldisham on the Little Ouse to Ixworth (B1111), the main road from Ixworth to Bury St Edmunds (A143), and the main road from Bury to Newmarket (A45), mark its limits. The chalk downland is a narrow corridor approximately six miles wide, which runs

17

south-west to north-east between the Fens and the heavy clay; only a small length of it lies in West Suffolk, merging with the Breckland in the vicinity of Barton Mills.

The central two-thirds of Suffolk consists of much heavier loam and clay, which forms a broad belt across the county from south-west to north-east. It is continuous with similar country in Essex to the south and in Norfolk to the north and for centuries has been called High Suffolk [3]. Although in absolute terms it is not high, it nevertheless gives the impression of height and exposure, particularly on the flat boulder-clay plateaux between the main river-systems [4]. Kirby's term for the region, the Woodland, no longer seems appropriate, as most of the woodland and forest which did exist has been cleared. However his description of the area as 'Dirty and Fruitful' is as accurate and economical as anyone could devise, and applies as much now as it did in the eighteenth century.

The coastal strip of lighter soils from Lowestoft in the north down to Felixstowe and Ipswich in the south forms the third major division. This Kirby described as the Sandland (later Sandlings), because it consists of glacial sands and gravels with the sandy loams of the famous Crag series. His term is apt and still in use today. Along this coast and in the river valleys and estuaries, there are considerable acreages of marshland, which have been drained and embanked since medieval times. The medieval high road from Ipswich to Great Yarmouth, now the A12, is roughly the boundary between the Sandlings and High Suffolk.

There are, of course, smaller areas in the county which do not fall into the three divisions described. For example, in the very north-west tip of the county is an area of fen, which in its history has more in common with Cambridgeshire. There is also the 'island' of Lothingland in the north-east corner, where the county boundary follows the winding estuary of the River Waveney; it too has a distinctive landscape and history, and much in common with the Broadland of Norfolk.

A glance at a modern Ordnance Survey map will reveal striking differences between the man-made aspects of the major regions. As obvious examples, parishes have distinctive shapes and sizes, field-systems and farming practices vary, villages differ in shape and character, and there are contrasts in the road-system. These are characteristics which exist today, but their origins and evolution are a matter of historical enquiry.

THE SUFFOLK BRECKLAND

In the Breckland, which is the driest and most arid part of the British Isles, it is not surprising to find a distinctive pattern of settlement and land-use. This pattern may be breaking down now, but it is still discernible behind the new agricultural techniques, forestry, housing developments and air-bases. Villages vary enormously in size and population, but they tend to be much more tight and nucleated than in High Suffolk. Houses are usually strung along a single street as at Icklingham, or arranged around a crossroads or other road junction as at Fornham All Saints and Ingham. Sometimes they are grouped around a green, as at Flempton, or around an enclosed green as at Honington. The main point is that they are as nucleated as East Anglian villages ever become; houses do not usually abut directly against each other, and there are many sizeable gaps between them, but the village is nevertheless a recognisable, single entity. In addition, the church is usually securely embedded in the village. Geographically this corner of Suffolk is the easternmost limit of an area of predominantly nucleated settlement, centring on the east Midlands.

As water supply is a vital consideration in deciding the site of any settlement, the Breckland villages tend to congregate in the river valleys or on the edge of the fen. In the valleys of the Lark and Blackbourn, in particular, there is a striking pattern. Villages are spaced out at intervals of approximately one to two miles, usually on both sides of the river but sometimes alternately on opposite sides. Along the edge of the fen, the interval lengthens to two or three miles. In the Little Ouse valley, an area of very light soils, the spacing of villages is far less frequent, and on both the Suffolk and Norfolk banks there are large, infertile parishes. Only Elveden sits in the central wastes of the Suffolk Breckland, but even it is carefully sited beside the small 'fairy valley' from which it takes its name [5]. A favourite spot for valley settlements was a low gravel terrace, just above the floodplain of the river. As there is plenty of archaeological evidence to show that such sites were occupied in Romano-British and prehistoric times, [6] it is theoretically quite possible that some living villages have been

c

occupied continuously ever since. This possibility should be borne in mind, even if it remains impossible to prove archaeologically or otherwise [7].

In some parishes, the pattern is complicated by the existence of subsidiary settlements. As well as the primary settlement (usually recognisable as containing the church and bearing the name of the parish), there are apparently later ones. These may take the form of hamlets or be quite large villages in themselves. A good example are the Rows of Mildenhall, where a great arc of hamlets and villages seems to have grown up in medieval times around greens or commons on the edge of the open fields. Certainly Holywell Row and Holmsey Green were inhabited by the twelfth century [8]. Lackford parish provides another variation. Here the modern village is associated with the green, enclosed after 1843 [9]. It seems that population has shifted from the old centre near the church half a mile to the east, where there are distinct archaeological traces, to a secondary settlement growing up around the green.

As in the rest of Suffolk and East Anglia generally, the vast majority of Breckland villages seem, from their place-names, to have been Anglo-Saxon foundations. The most common suffixes are *-ham* and *-tun* (ton); others with a much smaller incidence are *-ford*, *-wella* (well) and *-halh* (hall). There is only one name which is really early in type, and this is Icklingham (*Ecclingaham* in Domesday Book). This is rather surprising because there is in the Lark and Blackbourn valleys a notable concentration of early Anglo-Saxon cemeteries [10]. In date they are mainly fifth and sixth century. Clearly these people must have lived in local settlements, and one would have therefore expected to find more early names. This kind of discrepancy between the place-name and archaeological evidence has been remarked on by C. Green for the Flegg area of east Norfolk [11]. In Suffolk certainly the majority of the early *-ingas* and *-ingaham* names are in the central belt, and only overlap the distribution of pagan burials to a small extent. It is of course perfectly possible that some Breckland names, for example ending in *-ham*, *-ford* and *-tun*, go back to the fifth and sixth centuries, but it is strange that names regarded by philologists as characteristically early do not appear.

In the middle of the Lark valley around Icklingham is a particularly striking concentration of pagan burials. This may well be connected with the site of a large Roman villa south-east of

Icklingham [12] and the nearby crossing of the River Lark by the Icknield Way. It is tempting to speculate that early Anglo-Saxon colonists, making their way by boat up the valley or on foot along the Icknield Way, were attracted to the large estate belonging to the villa. They were characteristically uninterested in the villa itself, but the estate would surely have been irresistible. It may even have been a going concern, with a working-force of slaves. One mid-fifth century and later Anglo-Saxon settlement has already been found just over one mile to the south-east of the villa, and is currently being excavated [13]. There were clearly others in the area, indicated by the high number of burials; these are either on subsequently abandoned sites or under living settlements, such as Icklingham itself.

For many years it has been recognised that the Breckland area has seen the desertion and shrinkage of a high proportion of settlements [14]. Several former villages now consist of no more than a church, a farm and perhaps a row of cottages. There are sometimes earthworks visible, but these are never as impressive as the deserted villages of, say, the Midlands or the Yorkshire Wolds. It is rare to find an earthwork which appears to mark a house; only the occasional levelled platform, where a house once stood, and croft boundaries survive. Churches apart, the buildings seem to have consisted of a material, probably wood, which does not produce firm earthworks. Sometimes there is a series of hollow-ways representing the road-system of the village. Unfortunately several of these sites are now regularly ploughed, and any original earthworks will only be recovered by aerial photography if at all. As an example of a severely shrunken village, one could quote Wangford near Lakenheath. Here there is a small, basically Norman church, which survives intact, a hall-farm and a few nine-teenth century cottages. There are also earthworks, particularly to the south of the church, which have never been assessed and survey-ed. Wordwell, which had twenty taxpayers in 1327, has shrunk to a church, a hall-farm and four nineteenth- and twentieth-century cottages; the area around is intensively ploughed, but extensive earthworks survive east of the main road. Finally, Little Livermere is now a single farm and a ruined church, but air-photographs show the main street and a few house-sites [15].

As J. Saltmarsh pointed out, on such marginal land as the Breckland, agriculture and village life are very vulnerable to economic depression. The relatively high number of simple, unaisled churches suggests that these villages were never greatly prosperous or populous. Many were on the decline in the late Middle Ages, though few actually disappear; usually the church and the parish survived with a few farms and cottages. Also there was frequently some recovery of population in the nineteenth century. Several villages were either destroyed or shifted to make way for parks from the sixteenth to the eighteenth centuries. In these cases the church was usually allowed to remain within the new park. Good examples of emparked villages are Hengrave, Culford and Fornham St Genevieve.

The whole subject of the retreat of population in the Suffolk Breckland needs further study. Documentary research should be integrated with the survey of surviving earthworks, the use of air-photographs and the scientific excavation of selected sites. It should never be overlooked that the living villages also have been subject to the same pressures. They too have contracted and expanded at different periods, and several village streets, for example in Icklingham, have gaps in them which have certainly contained houses in the past [16]. Recent work at Chippenham in east Cambridgeshire near the Suffolk boundary has reconstructed the full size of the village before the Black Death. This showed that as a result of the plague not only the extremities of the village died, but that even the main street developed gaps as houses decayed [17].

The parishes of the Breckland are noticeably larger than those of High Suffolk, a feature which is common in areas of marginal land. Mildenhall, for example, is the largest parish in the county. Quite often, boundaries run straight for long distances, undoubtedly across areas of originally waste land. Several such boundaries appear to have banks and ditches along them, for example the Icklingham–West Stow boundary along the Icknield Way, but none of these has been properly investigated. Sometimes, however, parish boundaries are indented with many right-angled bends; enclosure maps and other sources often show that in these cases the boundary fits around former blocks of strips in the open-fields [18]. There have clearly been some later revisions of parish boundaries. The most common is when a settlement has decayed, and a neighbouring parish has taken over its territory. The extraordinary shape of Bardwell parish, for example, is undoubtedly due to its having swallowed the Domesday vill of Wyken. In the early fourteenth century it seems that Mildenhall seized 500 acres of fen and heath from Eriswell, and the parish boundaries were accordingly redrawn [19].

At Rymer Point on the Bury St Edmunds–Thetford road is one of the most remarkable convergences of parish boundaries in Britain (see Fig. 1). Today nine, originally perhaps ten, parishes converged on an area 300 yards long [20]. At this spot there is a rather stagnant choked pond, which seems to be the remains of a once large mere. In the Middle Ages this was called Ringmere ('the round mere'), now corrupted into Rymer. As late as the eighteenth century, the area around the mere was largely open heathland notable only for heather and rabbits [21]. Each parish having flocks and herds on the heath wanted access to the pond, because it was the only possible watering-place for some distance. So, whenever the boundaries were drawn (probably in the tenth or eleventh century), each parish received a long, tapering finger of land leading to the edge of the mere. The villages themselves and the arable land were lower down in the valleys, particularly to the south and east, and this meant that most of these parishes were wedge-shaped, with the base in the valley and the apex at the mere.

There is one other piece of evidence concerning Rymer. Several early maps show that the tip of land, which now belongs to Fakenham Magna parish, was in fact extra-parochial [22]. This could mean that the whole area was originally intercommoned, but more likely it is a relic of a medieval monastic farm called Ringmere Grange, which belonged to the Cistercian priory of Tilty in Essex [23]. The radiating boundaries suggest that the extra-parochial grange had originally been carved from Fakenham Magna. In 1881 it was officially re-absorbed into that parish.

Warren lodges are an interesting phenomenon. These occur widely in Suffolk, where various lords in the Middle Ages had rights of free warren or hunting. A warrener was employed to guard the game. In the large, central Breckland parishes, his job was sufficiently dangerous and lonely to warrant the provision of a semi-defensive tower house. The best preserved is in Thetford parish, and appears to be fifteenth century in date; it is now maintained by the Ministry of Public Building and Works. In a forgotten corner of Mildenhall parish is a similar structure of

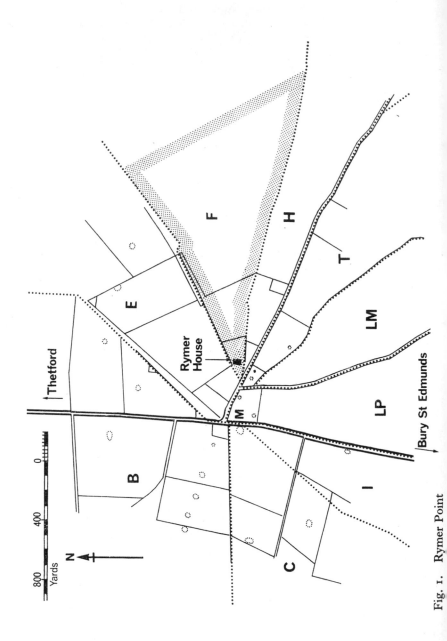

Fig. 1. Rymer Point

apparently the same date, and there are distinct archaeological traces of others at Eriswell and Lakenheath [24]. Of the warrens themselves, the earthen boundary banks are a common survival.

The type of open-field agriculture which prevailed in the Breckland has been described by M. R. Postgate [25]. The shift system, fold-courses, in-field and out-field, brecks and other features meant that this was 'champion' land with a difference. The basic reason for these peculiarities is undoubtedly the light, hungry soil, which demanded special treatment if it was to be productive. Occasionally on the ground, and more frequently on air-photographs, one can see fragments of the open-field landscape still surviving, in the shape of meer-balks, boundary banks and abandoned tracks. Most of the medieval landscape has however been obliterated, and can only be reconstructed from maps and written surveys. Several early manuscripts maps survive, covering for example Ampton (1629), Honington (1667) and Sapiston (1667) [26].

Some enclosure of the open fields took place in the Middle Ages, but it affected only small acreages. In the seventeenth and eighteenth centuries, some parishes were enclosed 'by agreement' and without Act of Parliament; this was particularly likely to happen where there was a single powerful landlord. For example the parish of Sapiston seems to have been enclosed in 1758 by the Duke of Grafton [27]. The main period of enclosure was however the nineteenth century, when the majority of Breckland parishes and large acreages of arable land were transformed into the familiar landscape of today—the large, rectangular fields; thorn hedges; windbreaks and game coverts mainly of Scots Pine; long, straight roads and tracks; nineteenth-century farmhouses and outbuildings

---

Fig. 1 (*opposite*).   Rymer Point (seven miles north of Bury St Edmunds). The site of a shrunken mere, where nine parish boundaries converge. The dried-up remnant of the mere is marked M. The parishes are as follows: Barnham (B), Euston (E), Fakenham Magna (F), Honington (H), Troston (T), Livermere Magna (LM), Livermere Parva (LP), Ingham (I) and Culford (C). The formerly extra-parochial Rymer is shown with a stippled outline; this has now been absorbed into Fakenham Magna, from which it was probably carved originally. Rymer House is the probable site of the grange buildings. The relatively modern pattern of hedged fields and marl-pits is also shown

The Suffolk Landscape

There is a great amount of unstudied material relating to Parliamentary enclosure. For example, minute-books of enclosure commissioners are said to be rare, but ten survive for West Suffolk alone and Cambridgeshire has at least forty [28]. There is also a considerable amount of official and unofficial correspondence which throws light on the way local enclosures were mooted and carried through. For example, there are 603 items, mainly papers of the Commissioners covering the years 1806–15 for the parish of Exning, which was enclosed in 1812 [29].

It is obvious that the Lark and Blackbourn valleys have been centres of human settlement since at least Neolithic times. Scattered remains of most periods have been found. Although much has been found accidentally during farming operations and gravel-digging, aerial photography has recently yielded striking results. In particular there is the great complex of crop-marks around Fornham All Saints, photographed by J. K. St Joseph; this appears to represent a number of ritual or religious monuments of Neolithic–Bronze Age date [30]. The main feature is a *cursus* or processional way which is at least three-quarters of a mile long, roughly parallel with the course of the river. Such crop-marks vividly underline how the Suffolk landscape, like others, is a palimpsest which the topographical historian has to decipher. The present landscape is mainly the creation of a single period, short or long, recent or ancient, but through it fragments of earlier landscapes show up. In the case of Fornham All Saints, the basic agrarian landscape is the result of Parliamentary enclosure in 1804. It was then that most of the present fields, hedges and tracks were laid out. But the church and the shape of the village remain as a direct legacy of the Middle Ages, and there are fragments of the open field system to be seen. Under all this are the substantial remains of the prehistoric landscape of the third and second millennia B.C.

HIGH SUFFOLK

This is a very different landscape, consisting of much heavier, sticky land, which was covered originally by woodland and forest. It therefore presented a much greater problem of clearance than the scrub of the lighter soils. Nevertheless by the Norman Conquest, High Suffolk was fully settled, and carried with central Norfolk a population denser than anywhere else in England [31].

Place-names show that the Anglo-Saxon colonisation of High Suffolk began early, in the fifth to seventh centuries [32]. Names involving the element *-ingas*, particularly -ing and -ingham, are found near the east coast but also penetrate deeply into the interior of the county, and it is noticeable that they often fall in and near the major river valleys such as the upper Deben and Gipping. Examples of this early group are Barking, Cowlinge, Letheringham and Mettingham.

A very common place-name element is *-ham*, which generally denoted a proper community rather than an isolated farm or homestead. This again is usually accepted as fairly early, with a limited life, so that it indicates the main weight of early settlement. O. K. Schramm has pointed out that places bearing the genuine *-ham* suffix (as opposed to *-hamm* meaning meadow) seem in the main to be important and successful locally, with few failures [33]. This is in direct contrast to places ending in *-tun*, which are often of minor importance or have decayed. In Suffolk the suffixes *-tun* and *-ingatun* are even more numerous than *-ham*, but they do not have the same early significance as a group.

The remaining names seem to be characteristic of later Anglo-Saxon settlement, probably seventh to tenth century in the main, and must mark the steady colonisation of the woodland after the original invasion and settlement. The most common suffixes are *-leah* (-ley), *-feld* (-field), *-denu* (-den), *-worth*, *-stede* (stead), and *-set*. Some of these, like -ley, and -field, generally imply the clearance of woodland. Others like -worth, -stead, and -set probably applied to no more than isolated homesteads and enclosures, though by 1086 they often represented sizeable vills. This kind of development is implied at Onehouse, a parish near Stowmarket; the name means 'a single house' but by Norman times it represented at least thirty-six households. Miss J. Mitchell has shown in map form how this tide of later Anglo-Saxon settlement spread over the south-western corner of the county [34]; no doubt this was largely typical of the rest of High Suffolk.

The main problem about settlement in High Suffolk concerns its shape and character. Admittedly there are many fairly tightly knit villages, a proportion of which turn out to be former market towns and cloth-making centres. Whether or not such places exist, most parishes as a whole have a very dispersed appearance with several small hamlets, usually with names ending in Green, Tye, End or Street, and many isolated farms and cottages. For example the parish of Cockfield consists of eight hamlets each grouped loosely around a green. Worlingworth has houses and farms peppered around the parish, some forming loose-knit hamlets and others isolated. Even where the map shows a tighter settlement, houses do not usually abut directly against one another, but straggle along a street or the edges of a green, with gaps of varying sizes in between. In such an area, the word 'village' is often meaningless; only the names of the hamlet and farm have any directional value. Important elements in this centrifugal pattern are isolated churches, greens and commons, and moated sites.

Theoretically there seem to be four possible explanations for isolated churches. Firstly, it may be thought that the church had been left behind by a village which has either died or moved. The Black Death is commonly supposed to have been the cause, but in practice this is rarely or never proved [35]. There is no evidence to prove that the landscape of High Suffolk was created or even seriously modified by the Black Death; indeed the main elements all seem to be older that that period. This is not to say of course that the plague had no effect. Miss F. G. Davenport's work on Forncett, Norfolk, which is an area of scattered settlement, proved that half the population either died or fled the manor, that houses and tenements fell vacant, and that manorial life was transformed [36]. But except in detail, the settlement pattern was not greatly effected; the two parishes remained collections of scattered hamlets and farms.

The possibility must therefore be faced that most of these churches have always been isolated. For example, Depden near Bury St Edmunds is listed by M. W. Beresford as a possible deserted medieval village [37]. Good air-photographs taken by J. K. St Joseph do not however show the slightest trace of an early village around the isolated church [38]; the main settlement lies a quarter of a mile away around a forty-three acre green, and may always have been there.

Secondly, the site of a church may have been chosen, not because it was adjacent to a village, but because it was roughly central to a dispersed parish. For example, it is tempting to regard Cockfield church in this light; it is roughly equidistant from its eight hamlets.

Thirdly, as W. G. Hoskins has suggested, the site of a church may have been determined by a pre-existing pagan site, which it was intended to 'christen' [39]. There are no obvious cases in Suffolk like Knowlton, Dorset or Harrow, Middlesex, but there are persistent legends of holy wells and springs which ought to be considered. The church at Ellough, near Beccles, may well be built on top of the 'heathen temple' which is implied in the place-name [40]. It is quite certain that a few churches, like for example Burgh near Woodbridge, Stowlangtoft and Kedington, are built on Roman sites, but not necessarily religious ones [41].

Lastly, the site of a church may have been determined by the wishes of the local lord or thegn, and the site of his hall. Domesday Book makes it clear that not only was the parish system of Suffolk largely complete by 1086, but that the founders and patrons of the new churches were generally secular lords and sometimes groups of freemen. It seems significant that out of fifty-two 'isolated' churches in West Suffolk, thirty-six are beside either existing halls or empty moated sites [42]. For example Bildeston church and hall lie together half a mile west of the town, and Brockley church lies wedged between two moats three-quarters of a mile north of Brockley Green, the main settlement of the parish. In East Suffolk also there are of course many examples of this relationship. Syleham near Hoxne is an interesting though extreme case, where the church and a moated site lie on a small knoll in the marshy bottom of the valley. There could never have been room for a village on this site. The church is connected with the rising ground to the south by a raised causeway. Providing the dispersed type of settlement is pre-Conquest, which hardly seems in doubt, the siting of the church beside the lord's hall and within his demesne is logical and without mystery.

Greens and commons, ranging from large heaths to roadside verges, are still a striking feature of the map of High Suffolk. Originally, they were much more numerous and extensive, for enclosure has been going on for centuries [43]. Many were effected by Parliamentary enclosure in the late eighteenth and nineteenth centuries. For example, the Great Green at Thrandeston, which covered about fifty acres, was enclosed in 1857; even so, one can still reconstruct its original layout, because of the pre-nineteenth century buildings scattered along its former bounds. Like so many of these commons, it had attracted settlement to it. There are many hamlets dotted around such open spaces, and they often bear the name of Green or Tye (a dialect word meaning a 'large common pasture' which is found in the southern part of the county and Essex). There is a distinct tendency for the largest greens to be in the far north of the county, for example Mellis, Wortham and Wingfield, but no good historical explanation for this has ever been given.

When a large village was grouped around a green, and this was subsequently enclosed, the physical effect is curious. Again, all the older houses lie well back from the roads, often with long tracks and gardens approaching them. The former green is chopped up into small fields, paddocks, gardens and lanes. Any houses near the road or against it are patently late in date and modern. Good examples of this kind of village are Elmswell, where the green was enclosed in 1814 (see Fig. 2), and Hinderclay, where a large green disappeared in 1819 [44].

More research is needed into the origin of these commons and greens. Their main function in the past was of course to pasture animals. Domesday Book shows that there were many plough-teams at work in High Suffolk, and the acreage of arable land must have been considerable. Up to the mid-fourteenth century, even more land became arable as assarts were made from the woodland and waste. As well as the highly priced meadows, the greens and commons which survived were vital for the draught-animals and other stock of the parish. It seems that the Anglo-Saxon and medieval economy of this area was a mixed one, which necessitated the provision of substantial acreages of permanent pasture. D. Charman has already commented on the apparent lack in East Suffolk of references to the pasturing of arable after harvest and in the fallow year. If it indeed never became the custom to use such land as pasture, it is probably because of the original provision of these permanent pastures [45]. Finally it should be noted that the names of greens, and the hamlets that sometimes surround them, change frequently over the centuries; this Miss Davenport demonstrated long ago at Forncett, and it is equally evident in Suffolk. For example Earl's Green, Bacton was known as Alice Green in the eighteenth century.

High Suffolk and Essex have the greatest concentration of moated sites in the country. There are estimated to be between five and six hundred in central Suffolk alone. Every year a few get

Fig. 2. Elmswell. This composite map shows the village as it was in 1903, with gardens, orchards, paddocks and relatively modern houses where the green was until enclosure in 1814. The area of the former green is stippled. Other modern houses have been built over the green since 1903. The railway was built *c.* 1846. The older buildings (pre-1814) are all set well back from the road, often approached by long drives and front gardens. In many Suffolk villages and hamlets the edge of the former green is marked by a deep ditch and hedge

destroyed, because of their inconvenience to modern farmers. So far, however, none has been fully and scientifically excavated, and this is one of the most urgent tasks for qualified archaeologists to undertake [46]. Any such work would need to be integrated with against the background of local medieval colonisation.

In the main, moated sites are assumed to be twelfth- to fifteenth-century, the majority before 1350 [47]. This however does not mean to say that there are none earlier or later. There is no reason

31

why some should not be pre-Conquest, and it is certain that some can be as late as seventeenth century when they were fashionable garden features [48]. As their distribution on the heavy land suggests, the most important function of a moat was drainage, to provide a raised, dry platform for a timber-framed house. It would have the added advantage of protecting the household and stock from wild animals and occasional marauders, but only in rare instances, such as at Wingfield Castle, where the moat is broad and extensive can it be regarded as militarily defensible.

Sometimes moats are in, or adjacent to, a village, but many are scattered in isolation. Some lie towards the edges of the parish, suggesting that they were part of the colonisation of waste and woodland. For example, the parish of Cotton near Stowmarket, as well as two central moats, has no fewer than six towards the edges of the parish. A proportion must be manor-house sites; sixteenth-century surveys sometimes describe already abandoned moats as *citum manerii de . . . cum quodum mota circum . . . nuper aedificatum* [49]. Others were probably no more than ordinary farms, though belonging to the wealthier classes. The occasional medieval parsonage house may also have been moated. It has been plausibly suggested that some of the slightest moats may never have contained buildings, and may be no more than ditched orchards and similar enclosures. Careful surveys are urgently needed of all the various shapes and sizes which occur.

No references in the manorial records of medieval Suffolk seem to have been found, which refer indisputably to moats. The most likely Latin word is probably *mota*, but some may be hiding behind words like *piscarium* or *vivarium* because they were undoubtedly used as fish-ponds [50].

It is surely likely that some at least of these moated farmsteads created their own enclosed fields, held in severalty. Maps of all sorts, old and new, printed and manuscript, could well show fragments of such dependent field-systems, particularly any original perimeter hedges appearing to centre on the moat.

The parish boundaries of High Suffolk are very different from those of the Breckland. In general parishes are smaller in area with complicated and irregular outlines. They frequently inter-lock with one another in a very tortuous way. Frequently the boundaries follow natural features like streams, watersheds and scarps, but equally often they follow man-made features like roads and hedges. This suggests that by the time that the boundaries were first drawn, probably in the tenth and eleventh centuries, the land was already heavily colonised and farmed, and that the boundaries often had to weave around existing fields and tracks. The frequent irregularity of the fields also suggests that they were enclosed and not open-field. The boundary between Stansfield and Poslingford is a good example, as it follows a most involved course around numbers of small irregular fields and lanes, which still partly exist to the south of Assington Green [51]. Although some original boundaries are known to have been revised in medieval and later times, the majority seem stable enough. This is supported by the fact that Suffolk has at least two examples, at Bury and Chelsworth, of the almost exact coincidence of parish boundaries and earlier Anglo-Saxon estate boundaries [52].

It has been said in the recent past that there were probably no open-fields in High Suffolk. This is clearly wrong. There is abundant evidence in a variety of sources, some quite late, that open-fields did exist. Medieval sources like charters and extents imply the system, while manuscripts maps from the seventeenth to nineteenth centuries show substantial acreages still being farmed in the medieval manner [53]. Even modern Ordnance Survey maps show areas which, although now enclosed, were clearly open-field strips originally. An example is the western end of Wyverstone parish against the county boundary [54]. Moreover in the Gipping valley, the parish of Baylham had strips, which were only consolidated and enclosed in the late 1950s [55].

The essential difference from the Breckland is that open-fields here were subject to consolidation and enclosure at a much earlier date. Certainly, as writers like Tusser show, enclosure was usually well advanced by the sixteenth century and the emphasis was by then largely on dairy-farming [56]. A further difference is that there was probably a higher proportion of originally enclosed land, even from the earliest period of colonisation. It would be interesting to know the proportion of medieval assarts or new intakes that were in the form of open-fields, and the proportion enclosed from the start.

Everywhere in this area fields are associated with deep ditches, forming a complicated system of artificial drainage, eventually linked to the natural. These ditches in origin must be as old as the fields they serve. They were probably as necessary in the former open-fields, and by providing physical boundaries within which strips could be usefully consolidated, they may have contributed to steady, piecemeal enclosure.

The road system of High Suffolk is worth comment. It is a remarkably complex, intricate network, which no doubt grew up to serve the numerous hamlets, farms, cottages, fields and greens as they were created from the natural woodland. So intricate is the pattern that signposts cannot possibly bear the names of all the places that could be reached, and so they are often lamely labelled-'by-roads'. The system is very similar to that of central Devon. In the Breckland and the Sandlings the contrast is immediate, for roads there tend to be much straighter first as a result of crossing much open heathland and secondly the conventions of Parliamentary enclosure; for example, there are the straight roads converging on the east end of Newmarket, or the south end of Wilford bridge, near Woodbridge, in each case crossing a large expanse of originally open country [57].

The extent of the early woodland and forest is indicated by place-names and by Domesday Book [58]. In the twelfth and thirteenth centuries there are frequent references to assarts. It is of course no accident that they are often mentioned in the same breath as woodland, for example *ij acras in sarto sub bosco* [59]. Early field-names, such as *Redinge* and *Stubbing* which both mean a clearing show the same process going on [60]. Even today, after centuries of attrition, there are many patches of woodland left. These often bear the name of the parish, and are against the boundary, for example Woolpit Wood and Gosbeck Wood. Occasionally such places are called 'Thicks' and even in one case 'Wield' (OE. *wald* meaning 'woodland'). Although they are not primeval, natural woods, and are now completely private property, they are relics of the manorial woodland of the Middle Ages. It is noticeable that most of these survivors are in the southern part of High Suffolk; the northern part, although it apparently had the greatest stocks in 1086, now has very little.

But woodland was not just a nuisance which had to be cleared. It had important, even vital uses in the medieval economy. Villagers had a variety of customary rights, which were jealously guarded. For example in 1214 several rights were exercised in woodland at Sotterley [61]; there was *husbote* whereby timber was obtained for house-building, and *heibote* which was the right of taking wood for making hedges and fences. In addition it could be gathered for fuel and for selling, *excepto quercu et pomerio*, and there were rights of pasturing draught-beasts and no doubt swine as well.

Vast quantities of wood must have been used to construct the timber-framed houses, barns and church-roofs of the county. For example, in the eleventh century the Abbey of Bury St Edmunds acquired Chippenhall in Fressingfield. The monks chose it 'because it abounded in woods' [62]. In the first half of the twelfth century Chippenhall was used to obtain timber for the great Norman rebuilding of the abbey; Abbot Anselm granted a certain wood *ad opus ecclesie ut sumatur materia* [63].

By the early seventeenth century, Reyce could say that the timber resources of Suffolk were 'nothing so plentifull as of late dayes'. He blamed a 'multiplicity of curious buildings' and a 'variety of costly shipping' for the situation [64]. Even so, surveys show that there were still considerable areas of woodland which have since disappeared; the great number of 'Wood Farms' and other suggestive names shows that clearance has gone on to the present day, and no doubt is still going on [65]. It is ironical that today, because of the activities of the Forestry Commission, it is the Breckland and the Sandlings which are mainly associated with woodland.

Just how old is the cultural landscape of High Suffolk? Most of the church sites can be accepted as at least eleventh century, and it has already been argued than many manor-house sites are probably older, although the moats themselves may be later additions. The hamlet system is certainly implied in Domesday Book, and is therefore Anglo-Saxon in origin. As H. C. Darby pointed out in the entries for Great and Little Bradley, the frequent mention of several groups of villeins and freemen suggests a dispersed settlement pattern [66]. In addition a considerable number of now subsidiary hamlets are mentioned specifically in Domesday, for example Chickering near Hoxne, and Stone Street near Hadleigh. Others like *Chilton* Street, Clare and *Thorington* Street, Stoke-by-Nayland have Anglo-Saxon names which are very likely to be pre-conquest. Miss Davenport's work suggested that there may well be differences in status between hamlets; some may be predominantly bond, others predonimantly free [67]. Place-names also suggest that there may be racial differences as well—

there are several cases where parishes with Anglo-Saxon names contain hamlets with Scandinavian names, for example Upthorpe in the parish of Stanton.

Many Domesday vills are now only identifiable as isolated farms and halls. For example, *Martlega* is now Martley Hall, Easton, and *Ciltuna* is Chilton Hall near Stowmarket. From their recorded populations it is obvious that these were substantial settlements which have decayed, but at the other end of the scale others may always have been nothing more than isolated farms, worked by single families [68]. After all, the word *tun* originally meant no more than an enclosure or farmstead. A good example is *Colestuna*, now Colston Hall near Framlingham; in 1086 it had a recorded population of only one freeman and three bordars.

Although Domesday Book makes no specific reference to greens, around which so many hamlets are gathered, there seems no reason to doubt that they existed. From the twelfth century onwards, mention of them in charters becomes frequent; for example, in the cartulary of St John's Abbey, Colchester, there is mentioned *cheminium quod ducit a Wichamgrene versus Skeith* [69]. The hamlet of Wyvermarsh Green near Polstead, which is grouped around a green, features as *Withermers* in Domesday Book and as *Hwifer(mer)sce* in a tenth-century land charter [70]; surely the green already existed at these dates. Again it must be stressed that all greens need not necessarily be pre-Conquest; in the twelfth and thirteenth centuries, for example, numbers may have been created from the woodland, especially towards the edges of parishes.

All this evidence, scrappy though it is, implies that the pattern of dispersed settlement was established by the Norman Conquest. This does not mean that all the details of today were there; there have been new creations and there have been losses. No doubt new hamlets, like new villages and towns, have been created since 1086, particularly in periods of population pressure like the thirteenth, sixteenth and early nineteenth centuries; others that were mentioned in Domesday have since decayed and disappeared. The balance of settlement and its detail are constantly changing, but the type was surely established in Anglo-Saxon times.

In High Suffolk and other dispersed areas, concepts like the Deserted Medieval Village are inapplicable. If one wants to study the rise and fall of population, and consequent expansion and contraction of settlement, the details have to be worked out laboriously from manorial and other documents, and the results checked by fieldwork on scores of scattered sites. In place of a compact village, leaving behind a unified series of earthworks, one has to identify many scattered house-sites, mentioned in manorial records by such formulae as *messuagia vacua* and *messuagia aedificata*. Moreover in a dispersed parish, desertion is rarely complete, and some early sites at least will still be occupied today. There is no doubt, incidentally, that hamlets expand, contract and move, like nucleated villages. Early maps usually show some shift of settlement if only in small detail, and archaeological evidence is frequently visible. At Monk Soham Green, to quote a single example, there are clear archaeological traces of abandoned house-sites.

If the basic framework of the landscape of High Suffolk is Anglo-Saxon in origin, it should not be overlooked that, as in the case of the Breckland, elements of earlier landscapes may survive. Certain place-names like Brettenham, Walsham and Walpole imply that occasionally pockets of Romano-Celtic people survived among Anglo-Saxon and Danish neighbours. Although there is as yet no proof, it seems a reasonable working hypothesis that the South Elmham-Ilketshall area has a pattern based on some form of Roman land-division. For several square miles, roads, tracks and fields show a marked rectangularity; the main axis is an accepted Roman road, called Stone Street [71].

THE SANDLINGS

The main purpose of this essay has been to compare High Suffolk with the Breckland, but for the sake of completeness some mention must be made of the third major region. The settlement pattern of the Sandlings resembles the Breckland. Again there is a tendency for villages to be more nucleated, in spite of the frequent desertion and shrinkage of sites. Parishes tend to be larger, and their boundaries less tortuous than on the heavy land. Roads are noticeably straighter particularly across the original open heath-land.

The deserted and shrunken villages of this part of the county are being currently studied by Miss G. Dyke [72]. There is evidence of desertion, shrinkage and shift of settlement over many centuries. Certainly Alston or Trimley St John was abandoned by

1362 soon after the Black Death, when its parish was consolidated with Trimley St Martin. This may be a rare example of the plague completely depopulating a place. Once again there was a gradual decline in late medieval times effecting particularly the marginal parishes like Wantisden, Hazlewood and Dunningworth. Emparking also took place at this end of the county, at Loudham near Wickham Market for example. Finally the influence of roads has been important, and accounts for example for the rise of Wickham Market and the shifting of Melton near Woodbridge.

The hundred of Colneis between the Orwell and the Deben estuaries is particularly interesting for its population history and settlement pattern. It had a remarkably high density of population and plough-teams in 1086, undoubtedly the result of its attractive coastal position and patches of fertile soil. As well as many Anglo-Saxon place-names, there is a concentration of Scandinavian names and hybrids like Grimston and Nacton. This suggests a later wave of settlers in the ninth and tenth centuries. However, since 1086 many settlements have declined and even disappeared. For example there are several unidentifiable Domesday vills in the Trimley area. This early concentration of population and its later decline would surely repay detailed study.

One of the great fascinations of the Sandlings is the eventful history of its ports. Dunwich, once the seat of the East Anglian bishopric and later a town with nine parish churches, has lost its thousand-year battle with the sea and has largely disappeared. Aldeburgh similarly has lost several streets to the sea. Orford by contrast has been left high and dry, silted up and cut off from the sea by the great shingle barrier of Orford Ness. All three towns were important medieval ports, and have declined since the sixteenth century. It is a topographer's delight to walk around these places today, with reproductions of the good early maps that have survived [73]; for example one can trace the original harbour at Orford, now silted up and built over, or identify a small length of the defences at Dunwich, and follow the extra-mural road system, now largely overgrown and forgotten.

In 1600–1 John Norden did a detailed survey of the estate of Sir Michael Stanhope, covering several parishes in the Orford area [74]. These detailed maps give a wealth of topographical details large and small. It is obvious, for instance, that open-fields were widespread, but it is equally obvious that enclosure was well advanced by this date. It is interesting that the parishes of Orford, Sudborne and Iken had small acreages of open-field not fully enclosed until the nineteenth century. The same picture is visible in the far north-east of the county in Lothingland: a manuscript map of 1652 covering the Wentworth estates in Somerleyton, Ashby and Flixton shows considerable open-field, many enclosures, and incidentally several smaller topographical details such as ornamental gardens and duck decoys [75]. In this area also, small acreages of open-field survived until the early nineteenth century.

One other feature of the Sandlings must be mentioned. This is a coast which has been invaded and threatened with invasion since prehistoric times. For example in the Roman period it was part of the heavily defended 'Saxon Shore'. Only Burgh Castle near Yarmouth survives, but there was another fort at Walton, near Felixstowe, and perhaps other stations in the Dunwich and Aldeburgh areas [76]. Ironically, at least one wave of the Anglian invasions landed here, and the Rendlesham area and the nearby Sutton Hoo barrow-cemetery became the focus of the new East Anglian kingdom. One of the greatest challenges in Suffolk archaeology is the whereabouts at Rendlesham of the royal palace of the Wuffingas dynasty, which Bede briefly mentions. Several places are suspected as the possible site, but none has yet been excavated [77]. In more recent times, this coast has been threatened by invasion by the French under Napoleon and by the Germans in the two World Wars; a chain of martello towers from Aldeburgh to Felixstowe, and a tangle of pill-boxes and gun-emplacements, remain as visible reminders.

FUTURE RESEARCH AND RECORDING

There are many aspects of the Suffolk landscape which have not been mentioned. For example, there are a great number of buildings covering many centuries, but these have not yet received the attention they deserve. The church architecture of Suffolk is outstanding in its range of sizes and styles [78]. At one end of the scale are simple, unaisled Norman churches, while at the other are some of the largest and most famous Perpendicular churches in Britain, for example Southwold, Blythburgh, Lavenham and Long Melford. Unfortunately detailed architectural analyses and reliable plans are rare, and the Historical Monuments Commission have not yet tackled this county. Even the outstanding churches are not fully studied; a recent and unpublished survey of Blythburgh by E. A. Gee has brought to light considerable evidence concerning the Perpendicular rebuilding, and even the earlier church, which has been completely overlooked in the past.

The timber-framed domestic architecture of the county is even less studied, though work has now begun under the direction of various members of the Vernacular Architecture Group [79]. Although many of these buildings have been endlessly photographed, they have only rarely been subjected to serious archaeological analysis. For example, until recently no medieval aisled-halls were known, yet in neighbouring Essex, through the work of the Historical Monuments Commission, several were already published. Since 1955 however, at least three such buildings have been recognised and recorded in Suffolk, and doubtless more will be discovered [80]. Evidence of this kind will obviously be of great help to the topographer in his study of the changing pattern of settlement. For example, Mr and Mrs Colman's discovery of an apparently late thirteenth-century aisled hall at Purton Green, Stansfield, gives tangible proof of dispersed settlement; it is associated with a small strip of green, over half a mile north of the parish church.

Although it is not an outstanding industrial county, Suffolk also has a number of industrial buildings and structures. The post windmill—which in East Suffolk was, in the words of R. Wailes, 'brought to the highest pitch of perfection anywhere in the world' —is an obvious example [81]. But there are other more mundane and less attractive structures which have so far not been investigated. For example there are the abundant remains at Woolpit of the brick-making industry which was so important during the eighteenth and nineteenth centuries but which had at least sixteenth-century origins [82]. It is encouraging that a group has been recently formed to study the industrial archaeology of the county [83].

The study of urban origins is also in its infancy. By far the largest and most important town in the county is Ipswich; its growth has been most rapid since the early nineteenth century and it is about to absorb an overspill population of 70,000. Here there has been some documentary and archaeological research in recent years, which has thrown light on the important industrial status of the town in Anglo-Saxon times, and the development of its defences [84].

The smaller towns, however, with the partial exceptions of Clare and Bury [85], have as yet received little attention. Yet there are intriguing problems concerning their plans, growth, markets, defences and other features, and little evidence has been sought. As an example of the way documentary and physical evidence could be co-ordinated, one could take the market-place at Gorleston. The Hundred Rolls of the late thirteenth century mention that the market had been encroached upon by thirty feet on all sides; the modern Ordnance Survey map shows a long thin triangular market-place, with fragments of an earlier frontage twenty to forty feet behind the present one [86]. Fragments of the defences at Bury St Edmunds are still recognisable and ought to be surveyed and excavated before they are destroyed [87]. Even more urgent is the excavation of the short length of rampart left on the cliff-edge at Dunwich. At Sudbury, rapid modern development makes the excavation of selected sites most desirable: the street pattern strongly suggests the outline of the Anglo-Saxon town inside the larger medieval one. The detailed identification of burgage-plots would be possible in Suffolk, particularly in Bury, where rentals and wills contain a wealth of topographical information [88]. At the other end of the time-scale, the nineteenth-century growth of towns like Felixstowe, Leiston and Haverhill also deserves detailed explanation in social and economic terms.

It is clear from a rapid search that the custom of several adjacent parishes 'intercommoning' on rough pastures was by no means unusual in Suffolk, though it is usually associated with the Fenland and the North of England. An Intercommon Heath at Cavenham was probably originally shared with Risby and Lackford parishes. In a survey of 1581 for Hawstead parish, an 'Intercommon' shared with Great Horringer is mentioned [89]. In the same source, two other intercommons belonging to Hawstead manor cover certain parts of the open-field lands and meadows of Bury St Edmunds; they were only available therefore at certain times of year. Until its enclosure in 1814, Button Haugh Green, a permanent pasture of 600 acres, was being carefully regulated on a joint basis by the parishes of Elmswell, Ashfield, Hunston and Norton. The number of animals allowed on the heath was rated according to the sizes of the parishes [90]. Special pinders and drivers were appointed to administer the rules. A strip of inter-common between the parishes of Fornham St Genevieve and Culford is shown on an eighteenth-century map, but was similarly enclosed in the early nineteenth century [91]. Until the nineteenth century there was an extra-parochial place at Thorington called No-Where House. This and No-Where Farm at Wyverstone also look and sound suspiciously like original intercommons. A careful examination of enclosed commons, converging parish boundaries and extra-parochial places could well produce other examples of this early practice [92].

If Suffolk had considerable areas of open field, why is it that no ridge-and-furrow, such as abounds in the Midlands, can be seen now? There is no simple answer to this problem, and insufficient evidence has been collected. However, there is no doubt that standard ridge-and-furrow did exist. The use of the word *reugiatus* in Lothingland during the thirteenth century implies a ridging technique [93]. At West Stow near Bury St Edmunds, ridge-and-furrow, dated thirteenth century and earlier, has actually been found on a stratified site in an area of surprisingly light soil [94]. The real problem is therefore not, did it exist, but how widespread was this technique, and to what extent has it been obliterated by later ploughing? Compared with the Midlands, Suffolk farming has had much greater emphasis on arable since the eighteenth century, and this may have resulted in the destruction of earlier ridges. One would have expected that on the heavy soils in particular, ridging would have been a valuable means of drainage. On the other hand, it is perfectly possible that in some parts of Suffolk, other methods of demarcating strips may have been employed. For instance the enclosure map of Barrow parish (1849) shows hundreds of grass balks and small lynchets between strips [95]. In any search for physical survivals, it should be remembered that this problem relates to broad ridge-and-furrow. Narrower and straighter ridges tend to be later in date [96] and can be seen, for example, in parkland which was ploughed up during the Napoleonic Wars [97] or in out-of-the-way places like the Dingle, Westleton.

Another important element of the Suffolk landscape which may well leave traces, particularly in the form of earthwork banks and ditches, is the medieval park. This was an area of private demesne, usually completely enclosed by an earthwork, within which the lord hunted deer. The purpose of the earthwork was partly to keep in deer, and partly to keep out poachers and unwanted wild animals. In Domesday Book, three parks are already mentioned, at Ixworth, Dennington and Bentley, and scores more were created in the twelfth to fifteenth centuries [98]. The large, medieval park at Framlingham, for example, was enclosed by a bank and paling, of which the former was still traceable in the nineteenth century, even though the area had long since been disparked and cultivated [99].

The more modern park has of course no necessary connexion with hunting, though deer were often an ornamental feature, and is a landscaped area around a large house or mansion. Its impact on the Suffolk scene since the sixteenth century is obvious, and can be seen in practically all parts of the county. It is on a particularly grand scale at places like Euston, Ickworth and Henham, with the usual features like lakes, tree belts and clumps, drives, lodges, temples, orangeries and icehouses.

It has only been possible to indicate the main characteristics of the Suffolk scene, and a tremendous amount of work remains to be done before even they can be properly explained in terms of social and economic history. Why for example did enclosure take place so early in High Suffolk? Was it the result of weak manorial control, or absence of common rights over arable, or an early drift towards dairy farming, or a combination of these? Again, what is the effect on a landscape of different inheritance customs, or of racial differences? On some of these issues work has already started, but little has so far been published.

Every county is a unique blend of natural and man-made elements. In an age of increasing standardisation and change, we specially need to understand the essential qualities of the area we live in, and its long, slow evolution over centuries. If this basic knowledge and appreciation were widespread among planners, local authorities and the general public, there would be some guarantee that the inevitable changes of the next few years will be planned sensitively and responsibly. In Suffolk the next twenty-five years are critical. A landscape, which has evolved over centuries and millennia, could, if badly treated, become an extension of the metropolitan jungle further south. On the other hand, with careful and wise planning, it can absorb increased population, traffic and industry and even add to its attractions and individuality.

1. For their advice and kind co-operation I would particularly like to thank Mr Norman Scarfe, and the archivists of E. and W. Suffolk, Mr D. Charman and Mr M. Statham, and their staffs.

2. D.S.I.R., *British Regional Geology, East Anglia* (1961); Geological Survey, ¼-in. maps, Drift Edition, Nos. 12 & 16. There is a useful summary in H. C. Darby, *Domesday Geography of Eastern England*, pp. 204 ff.

3. R. Reyce, *Suffolk in the 17th century* (1902), p. 37.

4. The highest point in the county, 420 ft. in the parish of Depden, S.W. of Bury St Edmunds, falls in High Suffolk.

5. A. H. Smith, *English Place-name Elements*, I, p. 149.

6. Grimston End, Pakenham, *P.S.I.A.* xxv (1954), p. 189; XXVIII (1959), p. 166; XXIX (1961), p. 100. Honington, *P.C.A.S.* XLV (1951), p. 30. Ixworth Thorpe, *P.S.I.A.* xxv (1951), p. 213. Barnham, *P.S.I.A.* xxv (1951), p. 207.

7. See H. P. R. Finberg, 'Continuity or Cataclysm', in *Lucerna* (1964).

8. R. H. C. Davis, *Kalendar of Abbot Samson* (1954), charter 106. The *antiquum castellum* referred to in this charter is quite possibly the Roman 'villa' at Thistley Green, near which the Mildenhall Treasure was found.

9. Lackford Tithe Map, 1843, Bury and West Suffolk Record Office (hereafter B. & W.S.R.O.), T 49/2.

10. See A. Meaney, *Early Anglo-Saxon Burial Sites* (1964); O.S. map, *Britain in the Dark Ages* (1966).

11. Lambert, Jennings, *et al.*, *The Making of the Broads* (1960), 120n, figs. 5 & 8. See also J. M. Dodgson, *Med. Arch.* x (1966), p. 1.

12. V.C.H., *Suffolk*, vol. I, p. 309.

13. By S. E. West for the Ministry of Public Building and Works.

14. J. Saltmarsh, 'Plague and Economic Decline in England in the later Middle Ages', *Cambridge Historical Journal* 7–8 (1941–6), p. 23.

15. Cambridge University Collection, AGX 18 & 19.

16. In the battle-area N. of Thetford is a perhaps unique opportunity of seeking what lies under the average *living* village. When this area was taken over in the Second World War, villages like Tottington and Stanford were abandoned and are now ruinous. Information from sites of this kind would be a valuable check on that obtained from anciently deserted and shrunken villages.

17. M. Spufford, *A Cambridgeshire Community*, Leic. U.P. (1965).

18. Map of Sapiston (1667), B. & W.S.R.O., TEM. 293/12.

19. J. T. Munday, *Early Medieval Eriswell* (1965), p. 5.

20. The tenth parish which may have converged on Rymer is Barnham St Martin, which was consolidated with Barnham St Gregory in 1639.

21. Translated by S. C. Roberts, *A Frenchman in England 1784* (1933), p. 210.

22. See Greenwood, map of Suffolk (1824); also map of Rymer Farm (1810), B. & W.S.R.O., TEM. 293/12. The remains of the mere are in the angle between A134 and the road to Honington (TL 86647576), and should not be confused with the small, post-enclosure quarry-pits in the area.
23. W. Dugdale, *Monasticon Anglicanum* (1846 Edition) v, p. 624. Also C. G. Holland, *Suff. Rev.* 3, 4, p. 122.
24. *Ex inf.*, J. T. Munday; Mildenhall, TL 74077556; Eriswell, TL 76157909; Lakenheath, TL 75208071.
25. M. R. Postgate, 'Field Systems of Breckland', *Agric. Hist. Review* (1962), p. 80.
26. All in B. & W.S.R.O.; Ampton 778/1, Honington TEM. 293/8, Sapiston TEM. 293/12.
27. B. & W.S.R.O., TEM. 293/13: working map of enclosure, Sapiston (1758). See also 1028/7.
28. The W. Suffolk examples are in the B. & W.S.R.O., with exception of those for Barningham and Eriswell; for Cambridgeshire, see *List of Enclosure Records*, Cambridgeshire Record Office.
29. Cambridge University Library, 632.
30. Dr J. K. St Joseph, *Antiquity* XXXVIII, no. 152, Dec. 1964, p. 290.
31. See H. C. Darby, *Historical Geography of England before 1800* (1936), pp. 209 ff.
32. Unfortunately the English Place-name Society has not yet published its Suffolk volume. In the meantime, local students must use with caution W. Skeat, 'Place-names of Suffolk', *P.C.A.S.* (1913), supplemented by the standard work, A. H. Smith, *English Place-name Elements* (1956).
33. *Norwich and its Region* (1961), p. 145.
34. J. B. Mitchell, *Historical Geography* (1954), figs. 14 & 15.
35. N. Scarfe, *Suffolk Review* 1, 4, p. 82.
36. F. G. Davenport, *The Economic Development of a Norfolk Manor 1086–1565* (1906).
37. M. Beresford, *Lost Villages of England* (1965), p. 386.
38. Cambridge University Collection, AHG 93 & 94.
39. W. G. Hoskins, *Local History in England* (1959), p. 155.
40. A. H. Smith, *English Place-name Elements* (1956), I, p. 150.
41. *Ex inf.* N. Scarfe.
42. This survey was based on the 1st Edition O.S. 6 in.
43. See W. Tye, *Suff. Rev.* 1, 5, p. 97. In East Suffolk between 1787 and 1864, 16,000 acres of commons were enclosed (includes Sandlings).
44. For details of enclosures and further references, see W. E. Tate, *P.S.I.A.* xxv (1951), p. 225.
45. Mr Charman is working on this subject and will be publishing shortly.
46. Since this was written, Mr S. E. West has just completed (May, 1967) the excavation of a moated site at Brome near Eye.
47. B. K. Roberts, *Medieval Archaeology* VIII (1964), p. 219. Contains distribution map. Also F. V. Emery, 'Moated Settlements in England', *Geography* 47 (1962), p. 378.

48. *Ex inf.* R.C.H.M. (Eng.). See forthcoming inventory on S.W. Cambridgeshire.
49. For example, Survey of manors of Cotton Hempnalls, Cotton Bresworth and Wickham Skeith (1564), B. & W.S.R.O., E7/6/2; Extent or Survey and Rental of manors of Thrandeston with Terrier (1579–80), Ipswich and East Suffolk Record Office (hereafter I. & E.S.R.O.), VII/3/3,
50. Sometimes separate, rectangular fish-tanks can be found near a moat (e.g. Cotton Hall or Aspal Hall, Mildenhall).
51. O.S., 6 in. map, TL 75 S.E. See also boundaries of Barking and Willisham, TM 05 S.E.
52. See C. R. Hart, *The Early Charters of Eastern England* (1966), p. 54; G. Pocklington, *Chelsworth* (1956), p. 7.
53. E.g. D. C. Douglas, *Social Structure of Medieval East Anglia* (1927), p. 238, charter no. 29: description of a scattered holding at Rougham. Also map of Elmswell (1627), B. & W.S.R.O., E7/8/11: shows area of open field in E. of parish.
54. O.S., 6 in. map, TM 06 N.W.
55. *Ex inf.* D. Charman.
56. T. Tusser, *Comparison of Champion and Severall* (reprint 1878), p. 141. See also for useful summary of this evidence Tate, *P.S.I.A.* xxv (1951), p. 240.
57. For Newmarket, see I. Chapman's printed map of 1787; for Wilford Bridge and area, see Greenwood's map of Suffolk (1824).
58. See H. C. Darby, *Domesday Geography of Eastern England* (1952), p. 179 & fig. 45.
59. D. C. Douglas, *Feudal Documents . . . of Bury St Edmunds* (1932), p. 128.
60. See the many early field-names indexed in B. Dodwell, *Feet of Fines . . . for Suffolk . . . 1199–1214* (1958).
61. Dodwell, *op. cit.*, p. 269, no. 562.
62. C. R. Hart, *Early Charters of Eastern England* (1966), p. 249.
63. Douglas, *Feudal Documents . . .* p. 113, no. 112.
64. Reyce, *Suffolk in the 17th Century* (1902), p. 33.
65. For the creation of one Wood Farm, with the boundaries of the former wood almost exactly preserved as field-hedges, see maps of Barrow parish, B. & W.S.R.O., 862/2 (1597, copied in 1779) and 862/2 (1849).
66. H. C. Darby, *Geog. J.* 85 (1935), p. 432. See also G. Ryan & L. Redstone, *Timperley of Hintlesham* (1931), p. 114.
67. F. G. Davenport, *Economic Development of a Norfolk Manor* (1906).
68. W. G. Hoskins, 'The Highland Zone in Domesday Book', *Provincial England* (1963).
69. *Cartulary of St John's Abbey, Colchester*, Roxburghe Club, 1, p. 145.
70. C. Hart, *The Early Charters of Eastern England* (1966), p. 60.
71. J. Ridgard is now collecting evidence for this area.
72. I am indebted to Miss Dyke for the loan of an unpublished paper.
73. For printed versions, see *inter alia* T. Gardner, *An Historical*

Account of Dunwich (1754), W. G. Arnott, *Alde Estuary* (1952), and *Orford Ness, A Selection of Maps . . . presented to J. A. Steers* (1966).

74. John Norden's survey of the estate of Sir Michael Stanhope (1600–1), I. & E.S.R.O., V5/22/1 (the separate key-map is HD 88).
75. I. & E.S.R.O., HD 86:707.
76. See O.S. map of Roman Britain (1956). The roads converging on Peasenhall clearly proceeded beyond to the coast.
77. R. L. S. Bruce-Mitford, *P.S.I.A.* XXIV, p. 228.
78. For a good summary, particularly useful for fittings, see Munro Cautley, *Suffolk Churches and their Treasures* (1954).
79. S. Colman, *P.S.I.A.* XXIX (1963), p. 336; P. Hill & D. Penrose, *Suff. Rev.* 3, 2, p. 3.
80. Edgar's Farm, Stowmarket, J. T. Smith, *P.S.I.A.* XXVIII (1958), p. 54; Purton Green, Stansfield, G. & S. Colman, *P.S.I.A.* XXX (1965), p. 149; Abbas Hall, Gt Cornard, publication forthcoming by G. & S. Colman.
81. R. Wailes, *Arch. J.* CVIII (1952), p. 154, and *Windmills in England* (1948). Also H. E. Wilton, *Suff. Rev.* 1, 7, p. 151.
82. See maps in B. & W.S.R.O., 608.
83. By the Suffolk Local History Council. Secretary: Mr P. Northeast (Rattlesden).
84. S. West, *P.S.I.A.* XXIX (1963), p. 233; N. Smedley & E. Owles, *ibid*, p. 304.
85. G. A. Thornton, *A History of Clare, Suffolk* (1928); M. D. Lobel, *The Borough of Bury St Edmunds* (1935). Both these books have sections on topography.
86. J. Hervey, *Hundred Rolls, Lothingland* (1902), p. 72.
87. The most important stretch is immediately south of the town centring on TL 85386350, where a low bank and ditch can be clearly seen.
88. Mr A. Allan is now collecting evidence for the topography of medieval Bury.
89. B. & W.S.R.O., E2/12/1.
90. B. & W.S.R.O., E3/10/106.2; Tate, *op. cit.*, p. 257.
91. B. & W.S.R.O., 373/23.
92. Mr Charman informs me that intercommoning was certainly practised in the S. Elmham area.
93. J. Hervey, *Hundred Rolls, Lothingland* (1902), p. 62.
94. *Ex inf.* S. E. West.
95. B. & W.S.R.O., 862/3.
96. See H. C. Bowen, *Ancient Fields*, British Association for Advancement of Science (1961).
97. I. & E.S.R.O., HA 11/C9/25.1: Henham Park was ploughed during the Napoleonic Wars. Is there narrow ridge-and-furrow?
98. W. Farrer, *Deer Parks of East Anglia* (1923), Ipswich Pub. Library S/9 and Bury St Edmunds Borough Library.
99. R. Green, *Hist., Topography & Antiquities of Framlingham and Saxstead* (1834), p. 17.

Clopton: the life-cycle of
a Cambridgeshire village

J. A. Alexander

The site of the deserted village of Clopton lies on a hillside over-looking the Cambridge-Biggleswade road two miles west of Croydon, with which, since it officially ceased to exist in 1561, it has formed a single parish. From the slope, for neither it nor its neighbours were built on the crest, it looks south to the Hertfordshire hills across the valley of the River Rhee, as the young Cam is here named. The village was built on the springline, for halfway up the hillside is the junction of the chalk and gault clay, and a prolific spring still rises in the centre of the village.

Today only a single strip from the crest to the valley remains pasture [1]; the rest has been regularly ploughed for many years and the archaeological evidence has been largely destroyed. Much information about the village has been learnt in recent years, most of it through research carried out under the Board of Extra-mural Studies.

Three kinds of evidence are available: Field Surveys both aerial and ground; Archaeological from excavations carried out in 1961, 1962 and 1964; and Documentary. These complement each other and enable a more complete understanding of the village than was possible when a history was last attempted thirty-three years ago [2].

The aerial survey, undertaken by the Director in Aerial Photography in the University, produced some oblique shadow photographs (LM 45 147/303387) (see Fig. 3) which enabled the unploughed strip to be studied as a whole. Here when the grass was short and the shadows long, terraces, banks, ditches, hollows and mounds had been seen, but only from the air could many of them be interpreted. Of especial importance was the establishment of the road pattern and the full north/south extent of the village,

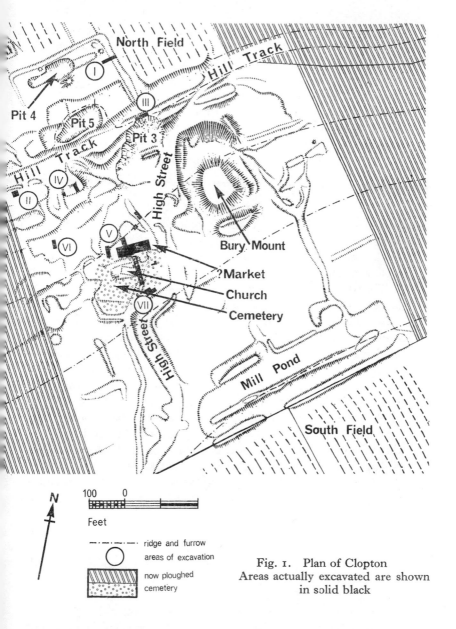

North Field

Hill Track

Pit 4

Pit 5

①

③

Pit 3

Track

Hill

④

②

⑥

⑤

High Street

Bury Mount

?Market

Church

Cemetery

⑦

High Street

Mill Pond

South Field

N

100   0

Feet

— · — · — ridge and furrow

◯ areas of excavation

now ploughed

cemetery

Fig. 1.   Plan of Clopton
Areas actually excavated are shown
in solid black

Note. References in the text to numbered and lettered Trenches, Enclosures,
etc., which are not shown in Figs. 1 or 2, are designed to make cross-reference
to the full archaeological report easier.

49

for fortunately the unploughed strip contains the centre of the settlement. A detailed ground survey was also undertaken, in 1962, by the Investigators of the Royal Commission on Historical Monuments, and their measured plan [3] contained the features visible in the aerial photograph as well as a pattern of terraces, ancient fields, streams and ponds. This plan was supplemented in 1961, 1962 and 1964 by large-scale plans of areas selected for excavation. During those three years other kinds of survey were carried out. The fields round the unploughed strip were systematically walked after ploughing, and concentrations of occupation debris planned; all sherds were collected, and distribution maps made and studied; from this the west/east extent of the village was determined. Within the unploughed strip, a number of surface profiles of terraces, hollow-ways and other features were made and some of them tested by probe, auger and electrical-resistivity surveys.

The documentary histories of Jones [4] and Palmer [2] are largely manorial, genealogical and ecclesiastical, but much miscellaneous information from public and private records is brought together, and from them an outline history of the medieval village and its desertion exists. They also preserved some of the oral traditions concerning the site which were still current at the end of the nineteenth century. Their work made Clopton the best-documented deserted village in the county [5].

Archaeological evidence of the village was lacking before 1961. An excavation had taken place in 1933 on a low oval mound in the North Field of the village to test an oral tradition that a vault and graves had been found there, but Mr Lethbridge found neither buildings nor burials [6]. The ten weeks of excavation in 1961–4 were used to test seven areas (see plan, Fig. 1), and in three of them grids covering considerable areas were laid down. The excavation [7] was carried out with the permission and active help of Mr Randall the landowner, to whom we are most indebted, and with the permission and encouragement of the Inspectorate of Ancient Monuments, the Ministry of Public Building and Works.

The evidence from all sources will be considered together and in chronological order, for the history of Clopton falls conveniently into four periods covering the last 1,800 years.

Clopton

The first indications of this period were the finding of some 700 small worn sherds of Romano-British, second-to-fourth-century, forms and wares. These came from all the areas tested by excavation and from the plough-soil of the fields on the east and west of the unploughed strip. From the field to the east also came a coin of Antoninus Pius.

The pottery was commonest at the eastern end of Area V (plan, Fig. 1), the natural terrace on the springline, where it outnumbered the sherds of all later periods. Here the sherds included products of the Horningsea and Cherry Hinton kilns in the Cambridge area, of the kilns of the Nene valley in Northamptonshire, and imported wares from the Rhineland and Central France [8].

Extensive gridding in Area V revealed two areas where, at a depth of about 4 ft., the surface of the clay terrace with its original soil, a clayey 9 in.-thick loam, was intact. In Trench G, 20 sq. ft. were sealed by the bank of the terrace (Fig. 2) of either this period or or of Period II, and beneath it forty-two large, unweathered, Romano-British sherds and many oyster shells lay horizontally in the clayey loam, with animal bones and charcoal fragments. In Trench 4 a similar area of 18 sq. ft. was found cut through, and so sealed, by a Period II pit. Within this sealed area, ninety Romano-British sherds with oyster shells, much charcoal and a bronze bangle of Romano-British type were found. This concentration of pottery and occupation debris suggested a settlement near by and evidence of it was found in Trenches G, H, and I.

The Settlement (plan, Fig. 2)

Sealed beneath the bank already mentioned, in Trench G, was a small U-profiled ditch (No. 1) 1 ft. wide and cut 9 in. into bedrock. It ran, as far as could be judged in the 4 ft. exposed, north/south and had silted up naturally, Romano-British sherds being found in the silt. On its eastern side were three possible stake-holes 4 in. in diameter and 4 to 6 in. deep.

Six feet further south was a large ditch (No. 2). The spoil from the ditch formed a bank on the north side of the ditch sealing a soil which contained only Romano-British debris.

No trace of any palisade was found in it and the few sherds found were all of Romano-British type. The ditch was V-profiled, about 10 ft. wide at its contemporary ground surface and 5 ft. deep. It was traced in a curved/continuous line for 60 ft. through Trenches G, H and I and probably bounded a large enclosure later destroyed by the making of the church terrace. It was approximately at right-angles to Ditch 1. Ditch 2 had silted up slowly and naturally, but two different fillings could be seen. The lower, a heavy clay, contained only a few sherds, all Romano-British: the upper which was lighter in texture and colour contained many Late Saxon sherds and must belong to Period II (Fig. 2).

Conclusions

Romano-British remains have been found previously within a few miles of the site [9] particularly along the River Rhee, and a possible road close to the river has been suggested by Fox [10]. It is equally likely that the track along the hillside, which was to be the main road until the nineteenth century A.D., was already in use, although Fox describes it as 'certainly late Saxon'. The settlement was on the natural terrace at the springline and close to a still existing and never-failing spring. It would seem on the present limited evidence to have lasted from the second to the fourth century A.D. and if the big enclosure really belongs here, rather than to the next period, it must have been a substantial affair. Since the enclosure bank seals the earlier ditch at least two phases of settlement were present.

PERIOD II (SEVENTH TO TWELFTH CENTURIES)

Early and Middle Saxon (seventh to ninth centuries)

No certain structural or stratified remains of this period were found but from the limited amount of excavation undertaken there are hints that the village may have begun before the tenth century. Five sherds, found with those of later periods, were quite different from them. They were hand-made of thick shell-tempered ware and two were decorated with lines of stamped ornament of the kind found on Early Saxon pottery [11].

The big enclosure surrounded by Ditch 2 which was described under Period I could equally well belong here. Although the lower silting contained only Romano-British sherds these would

Clopton

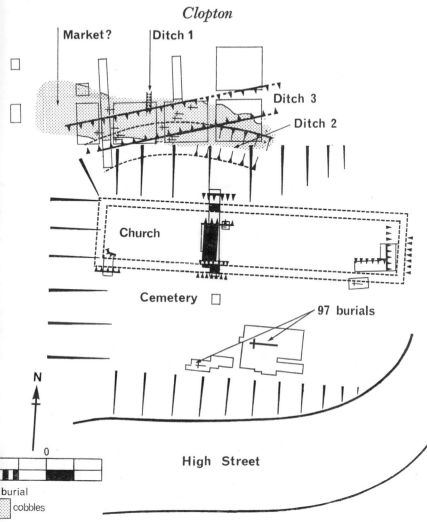

Fig. 2.   Plan of Areas V and VII showing Roman, Saxo-Norman and
Medieval features. Crosses mark graves and stippling cobbles.
Hachures mark banks outlining the terrace

always have been numerous here, and no change in the ditch
silting, to mark the long period (fourth to twelfth centuries)
when it would have lain derelict, was noted. If the enclosure was
a Middle Saxon one, the two siltings are more easily explained.

Late Saxon (tenth to eleventh centuries)

The evidence of Domesday Book shows that the village was

already well established in the eleventh century [12]. It was divided into two manors which were farmed in 1068 by at least nineteen households [13]. An estimated total of 840 acres of arable land, enclosed meadow for fifty-six oxen, and pasture for a large flock of sheep (293) and an unspecified number of cattle, shows that much of the available land was being used, for the modern parish including Croydon had an area of only 2,711 acres [14]. Only a minimal amount of woodland was recorded. An interesting Late Saxon service-holding provided a man for duty at the burgh at Cambridge [15]. Similar services were recorded at nearby East Hatley. The village had been rated at five hides in the Armingford Hundred [16].

From the distribution of finds, the village was already well spread out over perhaps 30 acres, for sherds of this period came not only from all the areas excavated but also from the fields immediately west of the unploughed strip. Especially interesting was the scatter through Great Sales field (map, Fig. 4). The greatest concentration of sherds was, as for Period I, on the natural terrace on the springline. Here in Area V, they were commoner than those of any later period, and here at least one structure was contemporary with them.

As has already been mentioned, the upper silting of Ditch 2 was accumulating during this time. The conditions must have differed from earlier ones, for the silt was much looser and darker and contained large numbers of shell-tempered St Neots ware sherds, many animal bones and much charcoal. It seems likely that there was habitation near by and that Ditch 2 was out of use. This habitation was probably connected with a new Ditch 3 which cut obliquely across the earlier one. *Enclosure 3* was defined by a bank and this ditch aligned north-east/south-west, and was thus not parallel to the hillside in the way the older one was. The ditch was traced in a straight line for 80 ft., in Trenches F, G, H and I. It was V-profiled, 10 ft. wide at the contemporary ground level and 5 ft. deep. The spoil from it had been piled on the northern lip to make a bank but this had later been removed and only the bottom 9 in. remained. No trace of a palisade was found. The ditch had silted up slowly, the lower fill being a stiff clay which contained St Neots ware sherds only. The upper fill contained twelfth-century sherds and so belongs to the next period (Fig. 2).

Clopton

Early Norman (late eleventh century)

The history of this period has been interpreted by Palmer [17]. The larger manor (600 acres) fell sharply in value after the Conquest and by the end of the century, although improving, had not returned to its 1066 value. The smaller (240 acres) had doubled in value possibly because of the large flock of sheep which belonged to it.

It is likely that *Enclosure 3* was in use at this time and was the boundary ditch of one of the crofts.

Conclusions

The village, possibly established in Early Saxon times on land which had been farmed in the fourth century, was making use of most of its available land in the eleventh century. Little woodland was left, both the chalk and the clay lands being exploited, and the population was probably more than half that of its period of maximum prosperity. It was linked to its neighbours by the Hilltrack, which connected with the 'Old North Road' (Ermine Street); and it was well spread out, most but not all of the houses being south of the track. Near the spring on the natural terrace was one certain and one possible enclosure of this period, well embanked and ditched.

PERIOD III (TWELFTH TO FIFTEENTH CENTURIES)

During these centuries the village first flourished and then decayed. The basis of the economy was arable farming and the acreage increased, possibly by linking Clopton with East Hatley. It was divided into several manors, and while parts were kept in hand by great non-resident families, several families of substantial under-tenants have been recognised.

Twelfth Century

Little of the documentary evidence relates to this period, but the archaeological evidence is helpful. The pottery is generally different from earlier periods and the distribution of sherds shows that the village extended into the fields west but not east of the unploughed strip. They were also found in Great Sales Field north of the track (map, Fig. 4), suggesting that the village was a straggling one.

Enclosure 3, made in the eleventh century, was still in use, the upper silting of the ditch containing quite a different range of forms and fabrics from the lower. The quantities of animal bones, pottery and charcoal, here and in the interior of the enclosure, suggest that a house stood nearby.

Thirteenth Century

In this century the village was thriving and even beginning to outstrip its neighbours. A rector was in residence and a church existed; a substantial family who took their name from the village were living there and at least one manor house was fit to receive a bishop. By the end of the century a weekly market had been licensed.

That the pattern of settlement visible in the aerial photographs belongs to this period was confirmed by excavation. Linked with the rest of the world by the Hilltrack, the heart of the village with its church and graveyard, principal manor house and market lay on both sides of a High Street which meandered down through the village from the Hilltrack to the South Field at the foot of the hill. No crofts lay immediately north of the Hilltrack where the North Field stretched over the crest. The village did not extend far east beyond the present unploughed strip but lay on both sides of the Hilltrack to the west. A number of features of this period are examined in detail.

The Church and Graveyard of St Mary. The site of the church had been forgotten, for both the area assigned to it by local oral tradition [18] and by the Ordnance Survey [19] were wrong. It was found by chance when exploring Area VII (plan, Fig. 1), the terrace next below the natural one on the springline. This terrace proved to be an artificial one; it had been cut into the hillside destroying part of the older higher one (Area V) and *Enclosures 2* and *3* upon it. The spoil was dumped to extend the new terrace to the south and an area of about 3,000 sq. yd. created. Here a church was erected and the dead buried. Some suggestion of when this took place can be made. The new terrace destroyed Ditch 3 (see p. 54) which had silted up completely in the twelfth century. No glazed sherds came from its upper fill although they did from the stratum above. The earliest graves on the new terrace, which could be distinguished on stratigraphical evidence, contained thirteenth-century sherds including glazed ware, so that it is likely that the terrace was made fairly early in the thirteenth century. Any building earlier than the thirteenth century was either elsewhere or was destroyed when the terrace was made. The church, as discussed on pp. 58–9, may be of fourteenth-century date, but no trace of an earlier building was found.

North of the church, on the next terrace up the hill (Area V), a few graves were also found. The earliest, on stratigraphical grounds again, might belong to this period since they lie beneath thirteenth-century cobbling and contained only Period II sherds. These might well be unsanctified graves (see pp. 60–1).

The Rectory is first mentioned in 1265 and probably stood where it did two centuries later, beside the High Street and opposite the principal manor house. The site of this, *Bury Mount*, has survived in oral tradition until today; it is mentioned in this period [20]. It lay facing the High Street and in the fourteenth century was a house of some consequence. No excavation of it has yet been carried out.

It is possible that the area north of the church, on the natural terrace (Area V), was left open and used as a *Market* from 1292 when a Friday market was licensed. For two centuries it was cobbled and recobbled. The earliest layer of cobbling, an area about 16 ft. wide by 50 ft. long (plan, Fig. 2), was aligned to the church below and lay intact above the final silting of Ditch 3. It also sealed two graves which had been cut into the ditch silt and contained twelfth-century sherds. Above the cobbling a stratum containing only thirteenth-century sherds was found. It is possible therefore that the first cobbling of this area belongs to this century and that the market may have been close to the church [21].

The High Street was not identified by Jones or Palmer but shows very clearly on the aerial photograph and was preserved in the boundary of Canal and Walnut Tree Closes (map, Fig. 4). It was traced on the ground as a hollow-way 20 to 50 ft. wide and auger surveys across it showed that it was metalled. In its present form it must date to this century for it makes a double right-angled turn round the churchyard terrace. This rather awkward arrangement suggests that it was diverted to enlarge the area of the graveyard and that in the twelfth century it ran straighter, but this has not yet been tested by excavation.

The main road of the settlement, the *Hilltrack*, was twice

sectioned, and in one place (Area III) showed evidence of this period. Here it ran on a 40 ft.-wide artificial terrace in the chalk and a ditch which followed the hillside contour seems to have been a drainage ditch for the road. It was 2 ft. 6 in. wide and 8 in. deep and had silted up slowly. No finds came from it but the loam from which it had been cut contained one thirteenth-century sherd. Three shallow scoops (Pits A3, G, H and I) without dating evidence were cut through it and were themselves sealed by the fourteenth-century cobbling.

Conclusions. The village had, by the late thirteenth century, settled into the pattern which was to survive to the end. The creation of the church terrace with its possible diversion of the High Street must have been a major event.

Fourteenth Century

In this century the village was at its largest and most prosperous. A series of tax returns [22] shows a population which reached its highest recorded figure in 1377 with 104 taxpayers over the age of fourteen. At this time it was larger than any of its neighbours. The pattern of the village shows clearly from the aerial and ground surveys. It lay obliquely across the Hilltrack (plan, Fig. 1) with its centre on both sides of the High Street as in the previous century. Crofts, presumably twenty to thirty of them, and several manor houses were scattered, on the evidence of the finds and surveys, along the hillside mostly west of the High Street. Open fields lay immediately north and south of the village on the chalk and clay respectively, with accommodation roads leading into them.

The Church. Documentary evidence shows that a new church was dedicated in 1352 [23], and the church found and partially excavated in Area VII (Trenches S1, 2, 5 and 10) was this one. No trace of it showed in either ground or aerial surveys. It was built at the northern edge of the terrace, was 20 ft. wide and probably 80 ft. long and was oriented west-south-west/east-north-east. The foundation trenches of four walls were found (plan, Fig. 2), probably those of the nave, the chancel and the tower. The nave and chancel walls had foundation trenches about 4 ft. 6 in. wide and 5 ft. deep. Within them were footings made of large water-horn cobbles and flint nodules, neither of which are found locally. Nothing remains standing above ground, but over the whole area round the church was a scatter of flint nodules with mortar adhering, mortar lumps, and fragments of squared limestone. These suggest that the walls were similar to those of the still-standing church of East Hatley which was dedicated in the same year and which is built of flint with limestone quoins. Scraps of clear window glass and lead glazing-bars suggest some of the limestone framed windows. The only large limestone block found stratified had been re-used in a Period IV house nearby (see p. 67), but another lay in a hedgerow on the site and others were removed to Tadlow in the early twentieth century [24]. The fourth wall, a cross-wall, was found intact so that its footings could be better studied than the others. The vertically sided foundation trench was as wide as those of the main nave walls but only 2 ft. 6 in. deep, and was filled with tightly rammed flint nodules and cobbles. These were intact to the floor level so that the wall must have been placed on them without further foundation.

The floor was destroyed, but the debris left included fourteenth-century glazed and unglazed floor tile fragments. Scattered over the whole terrace, but with concentrations just outside the nave walls, were broken ceramic pegtiles which had formed the roof of the church.

The Churchyard occupied the whole width of the terrace and was only sampled by excavation (Trenches S4, 6, 7, 8 and 9) [25]. One hundred and ten graves were found within an area of 800 sq. ft. No gravestones were found and no mounds distinguished the graves. The graveyard had been intensively used throughout this and the succeeding century, up to four successive layers of burials being found. The earliest, some of which as already mentioned contained only thirteenth-century sherds, were dug 9 in. into the clay bedrock and at the southern edge of the terrace were nearly 6 ft. deep. Nearer the church even the oldest were only 3 ft. 6 in. deep. Later burials were dug down to the level of the earlier but rarely disturbed them. This meant that the latest burials were only 2 ft. 6 in. below the surface. With the exception of one grave close to the chancel, all were buried in simple pits cut to the size of the body and without coffins. They were all oriented east-north-east/west-south-west, parallel to the axis of the church. The bodies were extended, the arms, with one exception, being placed by the sides or on the pelvis. The position of the feet in some cases suggested shrouds. The sherds from most of the grave-pits were of the fourteenth to fifteenth centuries. The study of the skeletons which has now been completed [26] throws much light on a late medieval population. Some grouping of the graves took place, for a concentration of children's and infants' burials was found on the extreme south edge of the graveyard. The only burial of any elaboration was close to the wall of the chancel (Trench S5). This 4 ft.-deep grave contained a wooden coffin the outline of which, with its six iron nails, survived; thirteenth- and fourteenth-century sherds came from the infillings.

An extension of the cemetery on the next terrace north of the church has already been mentioned, and this was in use in this as in the thirteenth and fifteenth centuries. Six graves probably belong to this century since they were cut through the lowest cobbling but were sealed by a fourteenth- to fifteenth-century one. They were similar in all respects to the ones on the lower terrace. It may be concluded that, since the churchyard was restricted, the favoured southern part of it was systematically re-used a number of times, and that perhaps a thousand burials are present on the terrace. At least four complete strata of burial seem likely, suggesting that grave-plots were assigned for perhaps two generations. The pits were probably shallow because those dug into the clay soon fill, and remain filled, with water, a problem still present in some local cemeteries. The concentration of infant graves at the edge could mean that some officially denied the Christian burial were allowed to rest there.

Now that the site of the church as well as that of the Bury Mount Manor House is known, the *Rectory* site can be suggested with some certainty, for it was opposite the gate to the manor across the High Street. A Period 4 house (pp. 66–7) might well be on the site of it, but no definite evidence was found in excavation.

Two roads of this century have been studied. The *Hilltrack* was tested in two places (Areas II and III). In Area II the 40 ft.-wide road terrace present in the thirteenth century had been enlarged to 50 ft. and cobbled. Some 70 sq. ft. of it were exposed in Trench 1. It was cambered and its outer edge marked by an outwash of gravel and small stones. Towards the centre of the road it was made of close-set cobbles and at least two remetallings could be seen. From its surface came many sherds of the thirteenth to fourteenth centuries. A second section was exposed in Area III at the top of a Period 4 marl-pit. Trench 3 showed that the chalk here was hard and that the road terrace had not been metalled. No ruts were noted on the area exposed.

The *North Field Road* showed both on the aerial photograph and on the ground as a hollow-way. It was sectioned in Area I, Trench 1 (plan, Fig. 1) where it was bounded on the west by a croft (No. 4) in the fourteenth to fifteenth centuries. The hollow-way was found to be 14 ft. wide and only 1 ft. deep. The track itself was about 9 ft. wide, unmetalled but with a rutted surface in the hard chalk. Two inches of very stiff clay lay on it beneath the later humus. The 5 ft. nearest the croft had been roughly metalled (as a path?), with a scatter of flint nodules and cobbles but had been part of the track originally. In the path make-up were two thirteenth- to fourteenth-century sherds, iron, bone and brick fragments.

The 'Market Place'. During this century the cobbled area north of the church continued to serve its dual purpose. Above the first layer of cobbles already mentioned, one foot of clayey loam accumulated before a new layer of cobbles, larger and better matched than the earlier ones, was laid down. They covered an area about 15 by 60 ft., much of which was exposed in Trenches F, G, H and I. On its surface and in the humus above were fourteenth- and fifteenth-century sherds. Cut through it were one certain grave (No. 5) and three incompletely excavated pits which might have been graves. All contained fourteenth- to fifteenth-century sherds, oyster shells, animal bones and charcoal. As with earlier cobbling a layer of stones and gravel restored the level surface over the grave, confirming that the cobbling remained in use through this period. Although considerable areas of the edge of the cobbling were cleared and studied, no trace of any wall or other foundations was found. Several small breaks in the cobbling could have been post-holes but no pattern could be seen in them. The dual purpose of this area over two centuries makes it likely that this was the site of the market and that the few graves were those of suicides or other unfortunates not entitled to Christian burial [27]. The post-holes could have been for stalls.

The Watermill and the Fish Ponds. A watermill may have existed on the river at this time, but it is very likely that there was one in the village proper as well [28]. At the south-east corner of the village, at the bottom of the slope, two embanked rectangular depressions (plan, Fig. 1) 450 ft. long, one 30 ft., the other 50 ft. to 65 ft. wide, show clearly on the ground. They were full of water in 1750, when they were known as 'The Canal' (map, Fig. 4), and even today have water standing for much of the year. On both the aerial and ground surveys these parallel depressions are linked with a dry channel still bordered by ancient willows, which joins them near the north-eastern corner, and which flowed from the Bury Manor moat, itself fed from the spring. Another stream leaves the depression from near its south-east corner flowing in the direction of the river. The ground where this stream leaves the depression is disturbed, particularly on the west. This complex is interpreted by the Royal Commission on Historical Monuments [28] as a millpond with its feeder and overflow streams; the disturbed area mentioned might well be the site of the mill. The hypothesis has not yet been tested by excavation. A shallower rectangular area immediately north of the mill-pond and connected with it could well be a fishpond, presumably attached to one of the manors.

The Manor Houses. Three manors, Bury Mount, Rouses and Wakefields, are mentioned at this time; one of them can be certainly identified, and the sites of the others suggested. The form in which *Bury Mount Manor* has survived probably dates from this period. There is a reference to its moat in 1348 [29] and water still stands in the south-west corner of the nearly circular, 90 ft.-diameter, moat; it was shown on three sides of a rectangle in 1750 (map, Fig. 4). It was kept filled by the spring and the overflow was taken away by a stream at the south-east corner. There is no knowledge of the building which stood here except that a bishop stayed here in this period [29].

Wakefields might be either of the isolated but large rectangular, embanked enclosures (Nos. 4 and 6). No. 4 (230 by 170 ft.) is bounded by two ditches and the Hilltrack and North Field roads. It is the only enclosure north of the main road near the centre of the village (plan, Fig. 1). The east bank was sectioned (Area I, Trench 2) and proved to be a very minor feature; although 10 ft. wide it was only 1 ft. 4 in. high. There was no sign of a fence or wall. From the bank came a fourteenth-century sherd, a scrap of glazing-lead and brick particles. The interior has been much disturbed by later marl digging but the possible house-platforms lie near the main road at the south-west corner [28]. It has not been tested by excavation.

To the south of the village lie today, as they did in the eighteenth century, sub-rectangular ditched enclosures which might equally well be *Wakefields* [28]. The ditch of the one nearer the village (No. 6) still holds water for most of the year. It has not been tested by excavation. Further south, on the parish boundary in Rouses Wood, lies a complex of earthworks which might well mark *Rouses Manor*.

Croft/Enclosure No. 5. On the terrace immediately south of the Hilltrack two test trenches (Area II Trenches I and Ia) showed a ditch (No. 7) parallel to the road, which should belong either to the fourteenth or fifteenth century. Cut through earlier sterile pits (A2D and C), it was U-profiled, 6 ft. wide and 3 ft. deep, and had remained open for some time, probably with water standing in it. The upper fill, which looked a deliberate infilling, contained a fourteenth-century sherd. Part of the interior of the enclosure was found to be cobbled and fourteenth-century sherds came from the surface. This ditch seems to have been superseded in the fifteenth century or later by Ditch 8.

The Fields. Two of the great arable fields of the village are partially preserved in the unploughed strip. South Field is on the heavy clay of the valley and still preserves the deep rig and furrow needed to drain it; a possible manor-house enclosure (No. 6) projected into it. A strip of North Field on the chalk crest of the hill is also well preserved, its rig and furrow being shallower than those of the South Field; another possible manor-house enclosure (No. 4) projected into it.

Fifteenth Century

This was the last century of active life in the village for although at the beginning of the sixteenth century much of the land was still arable, the population had declined to six households. Enclosure for animal farming was already beginning about 1489 [30]. From the history of lawsuits and families unravelled by Palmer, it seems that the bulk of the land came, in this century, first into the hands of the Clopton and then the Fisher family, so that it was in effect a single lordship [31].

Clopton

The Church and Graveyard. The endowment of a Chantry Chapel and priest by Lord Justice Clopton in 1447 must have added to the importance of the church and it is probable that the five inscriptions and ten pictures [32] destroyed by the Puritans in 1643 were of this period. One of them was certainly to a Chantry priest, one of the two known to have been buried in the church. Within the church a grave was found close to the north wall of the nave; it was a simple pit-grave without a coffin. It is also likely that the two bells taken away in 1552 were given in this century, and that the vaults broken into and the gravestones taken for road-mending in the early twentieth century [33] would have belonged here rather than earlier. The latest graves in the churchyard contained fifteenth-century sherds. The latest grave in the terrace north of the church might also be as late as this century.

The latest sherds above the final cobbling of the *Market Place* were of the fourteenth and fifteenth centuries. *The Bury Mount Manor House* known as 'Clopton Bury' was lived in, in the later part of the century at least, by the lord of the manor, and was large enough for two gentle households in 1525 [34]. *Croft/ Enclosure* 5 was possibly re-ditched at this time. The older ditch (No. 7) was apparently deliberately filled in and what may have been the butt-end of another (No. 8) was found just south of it on a very similar alignment. It was also very similar in shape, being U-profiled and cut 4 ft. into bedrock, with a well-rounded butt. It had silted up slowly, first with clay and then loam from which came fifteenth- to sixteenth-century sherds, tiles, nails and a rowelled spur.

Other crofts and enclosures are suggested by the scatter of fourteenth- to fifteenth-century sherds in the fields west of the unploughed strip and by the patterns of trees and woods in that area (Grove Close) in 1750 (map, Fig. 4). In the aerial and ground surveys of the unploughed strip, at least four terraces appear west of the High Street and churchyard. These have not been tested and may belong to this period or earlier.

EARLY SIXTEENTH CENTURY (TO 1561)

This period was studied in some detail by Palmer for during it the village was finally enclosed for pasture. From the documents the manor house and the rectory were both inhabited but the

64

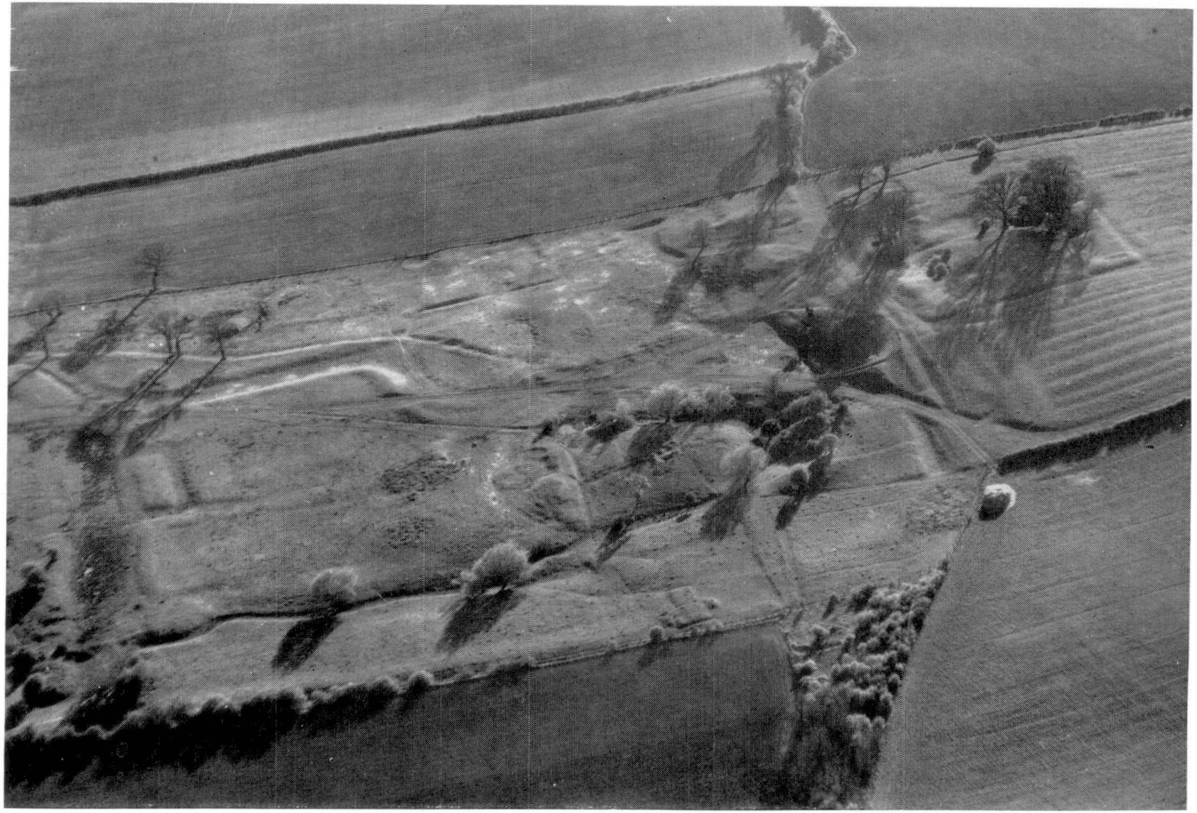

Fig. 3. Clopton today

→N

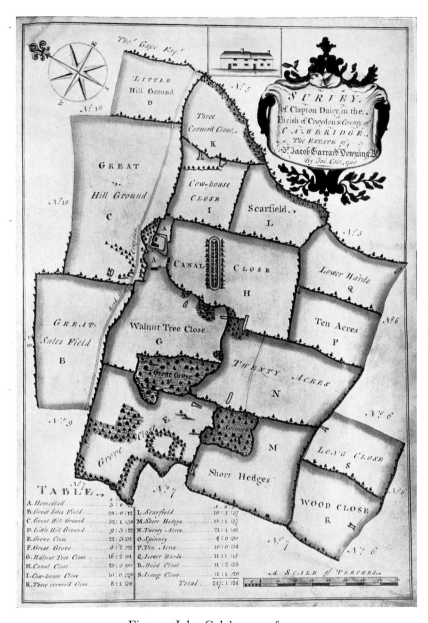

Fig. 4.   John Cole's map of 1750

By permission of the Master and Fellows of Downing College, Cambridge, and the Cambridge Antiquarian Society

assessed population in 1524 was only six households. Although the enclosure seems to have begun before 1500 there was still much arable land in the village in 1511. The process was complete by 1553 but cattle rather than sheep may have been the cause. No direct archaeological evidence of this period was found except for a scatter of sherds.

PERIOD IV (1561–)

At the extinction of the ecclesiastical parish in 1561 only two houses were reported. The estate had passed by descent to the St Johns of Bletsoe and it was to pass, before 1677, to the Howards of Effingham and the Earls of Bedford. Early in the seventeenth century it was described as 'wholly given over to pastures and feeding grounds' and only three or four houses remained [35]. In 1677 the 247 acres which included the village site were sold to Sir George Downing from whom, in 1717, it passed to the University of Cambridge under whose authority the first surviving map, that of J. Cole, was made in 1750 (Fig. 4). Entitled 'Clapton Dairy', it shows seven buildings: three within the manor-house moat, one on the probable site of the rectory, and three near by. In 1818 the estate passed to Downing College and from the College to its present owner. Six of the houses were still surviving in 1808 [36] but by 1886 (Ordnance Survey 6 in. map LII, N.E. and S.E.) all had gone except the larger building inside the manor-house moat now named 'Clapton Cottages'. These were abandoned and levelled early in the twentieth century, the last person to be born in them still being alive in 1961.

Excavation was able to add something to this summary.

The Destruction of the Church. After it ceased to be used in 1561, the church, already ruinous, was allowed to stand and decay for over 100 years. The accumulation of roof tiles found along the outside but not inside of the nave walls suggests that the roof was still standing when they slid from it [37]. The church was then deliberately destroyed sometime between 1685 and 1749. Not only were the standing walls removed but the footings were dug out to a depth of 4 ft., the robber-trenches being 8 ft. wide. The floor was also taken up but the crosswall footings were apparently overlooked. A farthing of Charles II from deep in a demolition trench and the absence of the church from the 1750 map date the destruction. Only a thin scatter of debris was left over the site and the churchyard, and all usable material must have been removed. Since there was no visible sign of the robber-trenches they must have been deliberately filled in and levelled [38]. The churchyard was probably levelled at the same time for no grave-mounds could be seen, but the graves had not been disturbed. A shallow diagonal ditch or hollow-way crosses the site and appeared from the aerial photograph to continue across the whole unploughed strip.

The Manor House and its Successors. The manor house of 'Clopton Bury' had been an important house in 1524. Although no longer the main residence of a gentleman it probably remained habitable through the seventeenth century, since from 1690 to 1718 a large house suitable for a substantial farmer (Conder the dissenter) existed in Clopton. From the inventory of his possessions made in 1718, after his death, it seems that it had at least four main rooms (kitchen, parlour, men's chamber and servants' chamber). There was a dairy, brewhouse and 'drinkhouse' in addition. It is indicative of how the land was farmed that his twenty-six cows and bull calf were worth over half his total estate, £104, while twenty-three 'couples and fifteen dry sheep' were worth only £18 and six hogs worth £7 [39].

In 1750 the moat still contained water on three sides and within it were two buildings set at right-angles to each other. The larger faced the bridge or causeway from the High Street, probably the original entrance, and appears to be a pair of cottages [40]. Both in plan, and in an inset elevation, it is composed of two blocks each two storeys high, with a door, four windows and a chimney. Since a building of similar size and position appears on both the 1839 and 1886 maps as 'Clapton Cottages', they were probably the same building. They were, when they were taken down in the present century, made of red brick and their foundations and much of the red brick are visible today. It seems likely that they were built between 1718 and 1750 by the University to house their dairymen, the bricks coming perhaps from the brick-kiln shown on a neighbouring farm (Lower Farm, Croydon) in 1747 [41].

The Rectory and its Successors. This was also one of the last surviving houses of the medieval village, for a rector was still in residence in 1560 [42]. In 1750 a building similar in size to the two cottages on the manor site existed beside the churchyard facing the manor, on the site of the rectory. This too had gone in 1886 but the red-brick ruin remembered by Mr A. Lee in the mid-nineteenth century, and wrongly thought by him to be the church [43], was probably it, and was excavated in 1962. This building, found in Area V, was more than 30 ft. long and had wall footings of handmade red bricks set in 8 in.-deep foundation trenches. Parts of two rooms were found: Room 1, more than 15 ft. wide, had a floor of red brick laid directly upon bedrock; Room 2 had no brick floor. In the 9 to 15 in. of humus which lay above both rooms were small fragments of bricks, but the bulk of the debris must have been removed. There were also fragments of ceramic pegtiles from the roof and a large block of squared limestone. Also lying in the humus were many sherds of the eighteenth to nineteenth centuries and many iron objects (nails, knives and a thimble), coal and charcoal. It seems likely that this building replaced the rectory early in the eighteenth century and was probably built by the University when it built the manor cottages.

The garden for these cottages must have stretched westwards and two pits and a ditch found in the area were probably connected with them. Ditch No. 9 was a wide north/south one which cut through the late medieval market-place cobbling and was parallel to the cottages. It might have marked the limit of the gardens. Two pits were dug through Period III levels and should, on stratigraphical grounds, belong here, although no late sherds came from them. They were not completely sectioned but were dug into the clay and so were probably rubbish pits.

A small ditch (No. 8) in the southern edge of Area II (Trench 1) might belong here. Its silting contained one eighteenth-century sherd. It seems to coincide with the boundary of Walnut Tree Close in the 1750 map and could have been the hedge drain. Three other buildings are shown on the 1750 map of which only one can be located today. *Two cottages or byres* are shown at the boundary of Homestall and Cowhouse Close and, although they had disappeared by 1886, show clearly on the aerial photographs and on the ground. Similar in size to the other cottages, these cottages have red brick visible on their surfaces today, and they might well have been a pair of cottages or a cowbyre built at the same time as the others. *Two cottages or cowbyres* lay beside the High Street and had both disappeared by 1886. Nothing further is yet known about them, but from their position they could have survived from the village.

Until the making of the valley turnpike on the line of a track to Biggleswade, in 1826, the hillroad remained in use [41]. The latest cobbled surface of the Hilltrack had sherds of seventeenth- to eighteenth-century type on it and was still the full width of its terrace. At some time later, probably after 1826, it was narrowed to 20 ft. by dumping soil near its southern edge, giving today the false impression of a hollow-way.

Marl Pits. A number of pits and scoops were dug into the chalk for marl in this period (plan, Fig. 1). Three pits (Nos. 1, 2 and 3 in Area III) cannot have been dug until the Hilltrack was reduced in width (after 1826?) for they are cut into the line of it. *Pit* 3 is a very large pit, 200 ft. wide and 25 ft. high, which today dominates the hillside. It was cut through the filled-in Pits 1 and 2. *Pits 4 and 5* are in the possible manor-house enclosure north of the road. No. 4 is shown on the 1750 map, No. 5 is not; neither were filled in. *Pit* 6. This, in Area VI, was more than 7 ft. deep and 10 ft. long and had been deliberately filled in.

REFERENCES

1. A scheduled Ancient Monument protected by the Inspectorate of Ancient Monuments, Ministry of Public Building and Works.
2. Dr W. Palmer, 'A History of Clopton', in *Proceedings of the Cambridge Antiquarian Society* XXXIII (1933), pp. 3–61.
3. Under publication by the Royal Commission on Historical Monuments. I am grateful for the use of the map in advance of publication.
4. Rev. W. Jones, *A History of Croydon cum Clopton*, Warner Bros., Royston (1904).
5. M. Spufford, *A Cambridgeshire Community—Chippenham from Settlement to Enclosure* (1965) is a modern model, though dealing with a shrunken rather than a deserted village.
6. Palmer, op. cit., p. 60. There is still no explanation for this mound.
7. The work was carried out by adult students, undergraduates, and senior scholars from many Cambridgeshire schools. I was assisted in all three years by Mr L. M. Munby and in 1963 by Dr D. Hughes. Preliminary reports were published in *Medieval Archaeology* V (1962), pp. 333–4, VI–VII (1962–3), p. 341, and Deserted Medieval Village Research Group, 12th *Annual Report* (1964), p. 13.
8. The pottery and other objects will be published in the archaeological report on the site.
9. From records kept in the Museum of Archaeology and Ethnology, Cambridge.

10. C. Fox, *Archaeology of the Cambridge Region* (1923). The village of Clopton is not shown in the text or maps.
11. I am grateful to Mr J. Hurst for examining the pottery of this period.
12. *Victoria County History of Cambridgeshire*, vol. I, p. 416, and Palmer, op. cit., pp. 5 and 12.
13. Following Palmer's interpretation.
14. Jones, op. cit., p. 2. Clopton would not have been more than half this total.
15. Palmer, p. 56. This service continued into the thirteenth century.
16. *V.C.H.*, op. cit., p. 415. This makes it one of the smaller villages in the Hundred.
17. Palmer, pp. 5–6 and 10–12.
18. Mr A. Lee, quoted by Palmer, p. 60.
19. O.S. (6 in.) LII, S.W.
20. Palmer, pp. 13–14.
21. A location for which there are many parallels, i.e. Norwich and King's Lynn.
22. Palmer, pp. 56–60.
23. Palmer, pp. 34–5.
24. Taken there by Dr Stephens. Palmer, p. 36.
25. By permission of the Rector of Croydon cum Clopton and the Bishop of Ely, from whom a Faculty was obtained.
26. By Mr L. Tattersall. I am indebted to him, to Mr Pilbeam and to Mr Denstone, all of the Duckworth Laboratory, for much help.
27. For use of the north side of the church for burials of this kind see the *Gentleman's Magazine* (1802) part I. Palmer, pp. 54–5, quotes examples of such deaths from the Plea Rolls.
28. R.C.H.M., *West Cambridgeshire* (1968), p. 78 I am indebted to the Commissioners for information in advance of publication.
29. Palmer, p. 35.
30. Sheep are usually assumed to have been the reason for enclosure but cattle seem equally possible here. Cattle and large quantities of hay are mentioned in the early sixteenth century. Palmer, pp. 30–1, 49–50 and 53.
31. Palmer, pp. 28–9.
32. Jones, p. 11.
33. A desecration stopped by the Bursar of Downing; Palmer, p. 36.
34. Fisher and Clopton.
35. Jones (p. 11) quoting an unspecified early seventeenth-century source. This would mean no change from the previous century.
36. Lysons, *Magna Britannia—Cambridgeshire* (1808), p. 172.
37. As is happening today to the derelict church of East Hatley.
38. This might well have been done by the University as part of the tidying up and rebuilding which went on early in the eighteenth century.

39. Jones, p. 11. The inventory is in the University Archives. I am grateful to Mr Munby for this information.

40. Elevation inset on Cole's map and Tithe Map of 1839. Red brick shows in the trench dug in 1944 as a practice bombing range. This is described as 'a farm' by the R.C.H.M. (loc. cit., p. 78).

41. Wing's Map in Cambridge County Record Office. I am grateful to the County Archivist for helping to locate this.

42. Cole, Brit. Mus. Add. MS. 5813, p. 78. Palmer, p. 47.

43. Palmer, p. 60.

Smaller Post-medieval Houses in Eastern England

P. Eden

Since the publication of the *Inventory of the Historical Monuments in the City of Cambridge* (H.M.S.O., 1959), the Royal Commission on Historical Monuments (England) has been engaged on a survey of thirty-seven parishes in the west of the county. These lie in an area defined to the south-east by the river Rhee, to the west by the county boundary and to the north-east by the so-called *via Devana* (the modern A604). The corresponding *Inventory* is at the time of writing in the press.

In the course of fieldwork in this area it became apparent that the smaller houses investigated, nearly all timber-framed, were susceptible of grouping according to their design. The investigators concerned, at first simply for discussion, found themselves using a rough classification based mostly on ground plans, with nicknames for reference; e.g. one group was labelled *King Alfreds* simply because the best-preserved example happened to have been called by its occupiers 'King Alfred's Cottage'. In the outcome, to avoid repetitive descriptions of these small houses of which there were about 900, it was decided to publish the classification, and this was done in the form of a table (Fig. 1) in which diagrammatic ground plans illustrate twelve classes designated, rather more austerely, by letters of the alphabet. The classes were arranged in chronological sequence, Classes A, B, C and D being medieval or sub-medieval; Classes H, I, J, K and L broadly seventeenth century; and Classes S, T and U predominantly eighteenth century.

The object of this essay is to discuss the applicability of this classification within a region, here called Eastern England, north of the Thames from the Jurassic belt to the North Sea [1].

The renewal of interest in small houses during the last twenty-five years, to a great extent channelled through the Vernacular

Architecture Group, has been marked. Hitherto such structures had excited attention in proportion to an indefinable element of architectural quality; they were subjected, more or less whole-heartedly, to survey techniques devised to evaluate 'important' monuments such as country houses or religious buildings of equivalent status. Today the needs of economic and social historians play as large a part in the direction of above-ground archaeology as those of art historians, and there is corresponding emphasis on wholesale techniques of survey and on the classifying and quantifying of results. It hardly needs to be said that there is a place both for the older, intensive, and for the newer, extensive, approach.

Classification has its pitfalls. A body of material, such as the small houses of West Cambridgeshire, is in fact a continuum, any classification of which entails arbitrary division. Its validity is semantic. The realities are the houses themselves; these are usually the product of more than one building operation and rarely without the sort of peculiarities which encourage us to think of them as deviations from their type. The temptation to regiment material for statistical convenience is irresistible, with consequent distortion. I have tried to resist it, but am aware that I cannot have been entirely successful.

This essay takes the form of an introductory summary of the West Cambridgeshire results, laying special stress on the Class-J house; secondly of remarks on the regional distribution of the Class-J house and of two related classes, not represented in West Cambridgeshire, to which I have attached the vacant letters F and G; lastly of a tailpiece on the Class-T house and on certain hybrid forms of which it appears to be one parent. The word 'essay' has been used to underline the tentative character of a hypothesis which at best leans heavily on the work of other scholars and which at some points rests on the author's impressions eked out by occasional field notes.

West Cambridgeshire, an area of about 100 square miles, comprises a chalk upland covered with Boulder Clay. It is bi-sected by the Bourn Brook which flows east to join the Rhee or Cam at Cambridge. This part of the county has always been something of a corridor; a number of early trackways cross it from east to west, but the importance of these has gradually diminished

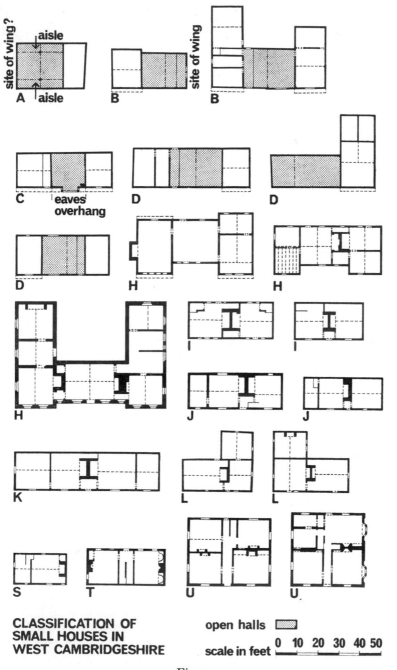

CLASSIFICATION OF SMALL HOUSES IN WEST CAMBRIDGESHIRE

open halls

scale in feet 0 10 20 30 40 50

Fig. 1

as the Ermine Street, later the Old North Road and now the A14, became a main route to and from London.

Place-name and Domesday evidence combine to suggest a picture of a naturally well-wooded area coming rather slowly under cultivation. The impression left by surviving structures is that adequate if not prodigal supplies of timber for building, within immediate or easy reach, were maintained until the latter half of the seventeenth century. By then, even in cases where timber is manifestly being used for display, reductions in scantling and in the quality of construction are evident. The pace of depletion no doubt varied; allowances should probably be made for light re-forestation on marginal land in the later Middle Ages and for releases in the sixteenth century of timber reserves expropriated from religious foundations.

Brick, the most favoured alternative to timber, was probably being made in Cambridgeshire by the fourteenth century, but its employment at vernacular level was later than is sometimes supposed. Ornate chimney stacks need to be evaluated in the light of dated examples, mostly of the second half of the seventeenth century. Studwork chimneys, evolved in the context of the open hearth, are likely to have been quite common prior to the Civil War; a few may survive, although none was found in the area covered by the impending *Inventory*.

The vogue for brick, as far as the walls of small houses are concerned, was most pronounced in the towns and trading settlements on the fen edge. A local example at Trumpington (Cambridge) was attributed by the Commission to the late sixteenth century. A comparable house at Fen Drayton, with stepped gable parapet as at Trumpington but framed side walls, may be a little later; the mixed construction is characteristic of the transition from timber and is echoed in West Cambridgeshire by such houses as Comberton 16 and Toft 6, neither likely to be before the Civil War.

The timber buildings of West Cambridgeshire are all of box-frame construction and close studding is general. They thus belong to 'lowland' traditions of carpentry [2].

By the fifteenth century the commonest house type had an aisleless hall with cross wings at either end (Class B). The wings were usually jettied, at least to the front, and their gabled ends flanking the side of the hall produced an elevation which was to be a recurrent theme in house design for a good 300 years. Croxton 6 is representative of such houses; it is a small manor house in which the essential features have been little altered, although, as is usual, a first floor and chimney have been intruded into the hall, in this instance during the seventeenth century. Like most classifiable houses the manor house at Croxton has its peculiarities; each member of such a group is individual, in accordance with caprice or with departures from the basic function.

By the end of the Middle Ages other designs with open halls are to be found in the area alongside that of Class B. The Wealden house (Class C), common in the south-east and with a wide distribution which includes the midlands and East Anglia, is exemplified by Barrington 20. Bird's Farm, Barton 9, is roofed in one like a Wealden, but without the jetties on the long sides, and there are south-eastern parallels for this also. Kingston 5 had two or three units roofed separately but in line—an arrangement which occurs in south-west Norfolk. Some of the late medieval West Cambridgeshire houses were evidently designed with a single cross wing; such houses form a heterogeneous group which might have had to be split if there had been a bigger sample.

In the course of the sixteenth century the Class-B house became obsolete in the area covered by the Commission. Open halls, save perhaps for the specialised purposes of communities, were no longer being built, and one by one those surviving were divided up. The period 1540-1620 was an inventive one and classification is correspondingly unfruitful. But some generalisations may be hazarded. The new houses tend to be smaller than their precursors, with 'miniaturisation' or fragmentation of the medieval forms; and there is an increase in side jettying, perhaps in association with the influence of urban carpentry.

But although the settled house types which were to be so characteristic of the two generations after 1620 are not clearly discernible, what may be thought of as prototypes can be identified during the sixteenth-century transition. The downward extension of the datum line of permanent housing, allied to conservatism, issues in a syndrome in which designs evolved in a creative spirit for patrons who could apparently well afford them, are extended to ever lower social levels. The largest examples within each type and the most refined in terms of elaboration and architectural extras are commonly among the earliest (or among the prototypes), while the smaller and derivative specimens tend to be late, ending with a trail of dwellings which are little better than shacks, depressingly mean from all but the most austere scientific standpoint.

Two sixteenth-century houses from the area, neither unique and both significant from the standpoint of typological evolution, serve to exemplify the point. Both give the impression of being built for people, who, if not opulent, were at least well-to-do.

Great Eversden 3 is a two-storeyed house with a side jetty, of three-roomed plan. The layout is sub-medieval with a cross passage at the lower end of the hall and an original chimney in a separate chimey bay at the upper end, providing for hearths both in the hall and in the room beyond (parlour?). The location of the hearth looks like a medieval tradition—an important point in view of the tenacity with which the contrary arrangement (fireplace at the lower end) is adhered to in the highland and intermediate zones.

Elsworth 16, known as 'Low Farm', is dated 1595, a generation or so later than the foregoing. It is likewise two-storeyed and three-part including a cross wing at one end. There is a chimney between the two rooms which form the main range. The entrance, protected by a two-storey porch, is on to the chimney, beyond which there is an original stair turret balancing the porch. In contrast to the Great Eversden house there is no cross passage; instead we have the baffle or lobby entry which was to become almost invariable in some districts during the next century. Though more advanced in this and certain other respects, the handling of the wing, which evidently contained the services, still defers to the medieval order of things.

At the head of the house forms current in Cambridgeshire and beyond during the seventeenth century (Classes H-K) is the Class-H house. It is evidently the hall-and-cross-wings (Class B) house but with a main range in two storeys, and in practice is not always easily distinguishable from its medieval forerunner, since the insertion of a chimney and first floor are usually masked by later plaster and decoration. Class H is, in principle, a group of medium-sized houses. Some indeed, for example Bourn 2, are so large as to be in no sense vernacular. But there are humbler versions as well, notably a variant with continuous jettying across the front, Barton 2, University Farm, being one such. The

Class-H tradition is thus only of limited relevance to this essay, but its evident medievalism exemplifies a conservative approach to design which requires to be appreciated to the full if the smaller contemporary houses are to be successfully evaluated.

The four remaining, internal-chimney, groups (I, J, K, and L) are more distinctly vernacular, although their social incidence may not be confined to those below the gentry. Class I consists of houses, two-roomed on plan, with central chimney and baffle entry; those of Class J are similar but three-roomed, the internal chimney being necessarily off-centre. Class L is also three-roomed, but in two ranges at right angles, with the chimney at the junction of the ranges, and most characteristically a third, 'heel', gable at the angle. Class K, four-roomed on plan, though apparently distinct, is rare.

In the West Cambridgeshire area Class J is numerically the most important of the four, such houses possibly outnumbering all the other seventeenth-century houses combined. In Haslingfield fifteen Class-J houses, most if not all seventeenth-century, make up about half the secular monuments in the village. The resemblance of the more self-conscious examples (e.g. Comberton 28) to transitional houses like Low Farm, Elsworth, is obvious: the porch and stair turrets of the latter are mere extras, and but for the fact that the service room with its buttery or similar adjunct is placed at right-angles to, instead of in line with, the rest of the house, Low Farm would have qualified for inclusion within the group. If the resemblance is meaningful a continuous descent for the Class-J design from the Class-B design is to be inferred. However the ancestry of the Class-J house may prove to be more complex; in particular the influence of smaller and less permanent one-roomed houses, medieval or sub-medieval, should be envisaged. Although the gap is likely to be gradually filled by excavation, too little is at present known about these for judgements on the subject to be other than provisional. It would not be surprising if such one-roomed houses, or some of them, were divided internally by light partitions, comparatively movable, or by such installations as dressers and settles, on some sort of three-roomed plan. The facts will emerge, if at all, only by a combination of skill and good luck over a long period. In this connexion the traditions associated with squatter and similar housing on waste-ground, which crystallised during the eighteenth century in the Class-S house, probably need to be more carefully scrutinised than they have been, since these also may well prove, typologically, to have a lengthy descent.

Taken as a whole, the evidence of probate inventories in relevant areas, many of which must refer to Class-J houses, speaks for a process of miniaturisation. Three-room combinations such as *hall*, *parlour* and *kitchen* are fairly common, and these clearly imply a central living space with upper and lower adjuncts like those of a medieval house. In localities where a preference for a hearth at the upper end of the hall is to be inferred, from the positioning of inserted chimneys in older houses for example, it would appear that the 'kitchen' was unheated and was used for the preparation and storage of food, with cooking either in the hall or in an out-house, perhaps of relatively perfunctory construction. The semantics are discussed in *Culture and Environment* [ed. I. L. Foster and Leslie Alcock, 1963, xx: 'A Glossary of Names for Rooms of Houses in the Sixteenth and Seventeenth Centuries', by Maurice Barley, p. 492 s.v. 'Kitchen']. It is unsafe, though, to assume that the various functions of small houses, seemingly identical in design, are necessarily assigned to constituent rooms in a standardised way. It was indeed precisely in this particular that the sub-medieval house, in external appearance relatively conservative, seems to have been most variable. The 'kitchen' may on occasion have been the heated room beyond the hall chimney. A variant of the Class-J house, which should perhaps have been separately classified ('King Alfred's Cottage', Bourn 6, dated 1616, is the best example), has the three-room plan and baffle entry, but the heated end room was lower than the rest and originally open to the roof; it can hardly have been other than a cook- or brew-house. Houses in Class J proper may have differed in functional disposition as a result of contamination by this and other related types.

Documentary evidence makes it clear that many seventeenth-century houses were originally single-storeyed and open, like the end room described above. Archaeological evidence seems to support this, but evaluation of the field data in specific instances is apt to bog down in ambiguities. Modifications in a medieval frame can be inferred with almost complete safety, from incorrectly fitted components (tacked on, or notched in, to a structure otherwise technically orthodox), or from the survival of peg holes or mortices, the members corresponding to which have been removed. There are a few definable exceptions to this generalisation, mostly of early date. The same inferences, where seventeenth-century construction is concerned, need to be more tentative. By this time structures of a single build can include elements which resemble alterations, and re-use of timber is common. Joists, which in some cases seem to have been tenants' fixtures, were often so incorporated as to permit removal if required. Again, structures technically of more than one build seem sometimes to have been erected in several phases over a short period. Such a phenomenon can be explained in terms of crude financing—the absence, in modern parlance, of overdraft facilities, even for the comparatively wealthy—or of piecemeal but systematic replacement, for convenience's sake, of a pre-existing fabric. Such reservations make it difficult to be certain exactly what a particular house must have looked like when first built.

Chimneys are likewise problematical. Some are replacements of probably timber-framed originals; only a few stand in purpose-built chimney bays delimited by tie or cross beams. Baffle entries may be rearrangements and certainty is impossible unless the original door, or a porch, survives; the blocking entailed in such a rearrangement can easily be masked by plaster inside and out.

Nevertheless, from the relatively large sample examined, it is certain that the Class-J house was the dominant design in permanent housing at the lower levels in West Cambridgeshire during the seventeenth century, to much the same extent as the Class-B house had been dominant in the late Middle Ages, and allowing for the different social strata affected, in much the same way. Unpublished fieldwork by the Commission shows that this is likely to be true of most if not all of the rest of the county, with reservations about the Isle of Ely.

The region between the Humber and the Thames, east of the Jurassic belt, comprises eleven counties: Lincolnshire, Rutland and Northamptonshire; Cambridgeshire, Huntingdonshire and Bedfordshire; Norfolk and Suffolk; Essex, Hertfordshire and Buckinghamshire. Of these, Northamptonshire and Rutland are now almost entirely stone country with few timber-framed buildings surviving, whilst Lincolnshire, Bedfordshire and Buckinghamshire include areas in which stone building predominates.

Post-medieval Houses in Eastern England

This discrepancy in materials greatly complicates any analysis of the cultural traditions involved and raises some awkward problems. In particular it is not clear to what extent the building of small houses in stone during the seventeenth century, in the west and north of the region under discussion, masks an earlier rebuilding in framing. The same problem arises in the brick country comprised by much of Leicestershire and Nottinghamshire; both these are outside the region, but there are extensions of the brick country into Lincolnshire and Norfolk, with outliers in the Broads and marshland areas further south. That some stone and brick, including brick-and-rubble, houses are remodelled timber structures there can be no doubt. But although certain instances are obvious, upon the whole the difficulties of recognition are formidable. It is impossible to assess even roughly what percentage of small masonry houses have such a history, and what in general is the date and typological significance of timber-framed houses, cased or underbuilt, awaiting identification.

This uncertainty infects a related problem which has exercised workers in the field of post-medieval vernacular architecture since the statement in 1953 of Hoskins's hypothesis of a 'Great Rebuilding' (W. G. Hoskins, 'The Rebuilding of Rural England', *Past and Present*, no. 4, Nov. 1953); indeed it evidently exercised Hoskins himself: the extent, namely, to which the 'Rebuilding' is to be seen, not as a uniform process affecting the country as a whole at one and the same time, but as a series of waves, episodes in a tidal process it may be, impinging on some areas before others. Thus, for whatever reason, the movement in West Cambridgeshire would seem to have got under way a generation or two later than comparable movements in areas to the south and east; and this, if true, may have been crucial for the evolution of relevant house types, at a time when design was evolving rapidly.

In spite of these complications it is clear from the most superficial observation that the Class-J house enjoys a wide distribution over the eleven counties here thought of as Eastern England: some examples are probably to be found in all of them, and for that matter beyond them. The West Cambridgeshire concentration spills over, not only into the east and south of the county, but also into Huntingdonshire, and some apparent Class-J houses, as well as prototypes resembling those found east of the boundary, are included in the Royal Commission's *Inventory* [3].

Post-medieval Houses in Eastern England

Random samples of the investigators' cards for Huntingdonshire, preserved in the Commission's archives, suggest a high concentration in the east of the county, including some useful dated examples such as Little Farm, Broughton, 1642. The position in Bedfordshire is less clear, as very little field work has been undertaken in the county. Dr N. W. Alcock, who is currently engaged in Eaton Socon and Thurleigh, reports that both Class-I and Class-J houses are among the material examined by him. The cover in the National Monuments Record, though thin for vernacular architecture in Bedfordshire, includes apparent examples, e.g. Home Farm, Swineshead. Among the author's field notes are particulars of some houses in and around Sharnbrook, then interpreted as of Class J, originally framed.

To the south and east of Cambridgeshire enough work has been done in Suffolk, Essex and Hertfordshire to be positive about the incidence of the type, although much detail remains to be filled in before its overall frequency and local distribution can be worked out even approximately. In Suffolk Sylvia Colman (correspondence with the author 13 & 31. xii. 66) describes the Class-J house as 'found very frequently in Suffolk; one might call it the typical farmhouse of the post-medieval period'. Bell's Lane Farm, Stanningfield (Fig. 2), is one of many examples. In Essex Harry Forrester, taking four volumes of the Royal Commission's *Inventory* as a starting point, has worked out a classification of small houses which corresponds closely with that invented for West Cambridgeshire; his figs. 13, 19 and 20 approximate to the Class-J house [4]. From Hertfordshire Gordon Moodey likewise reports (correspondence with the author 21 & 25. i. 67) that 'the most easily recognisable plan is the two- or three-cell with internal stack and baffle entrance, such as your Classes I, J and K'; he adds—what one would expect in the prosperous Home Counties—that 'it is not easy to find a seventeenth-century house with the original plan intact or even traceable beyond doubt'. Barbara Hutton's Hertfordshire results and reservations are similar (*Hatfield and its People*, book 10, Feb. 1963, esp. pp. 13-15; amplified in correspondence with the author).

The timber-framed houses of Norfolk are mostly confined to comparatively restricted upland areas west and south of Norwich and to the towns. Elsewhere surviving houses of the late sixteenth and seventeenth centuries are of brick or local rubbles. There is a certain amount of mixed construction. Three-cell houses with an internal chimney are common in the timber-framed areas. They are in general larger and more sophisticated than their Cambridge-shire analogues, and probably somewhat earlier. A common, ostensibly the prevailing, type has the entrance at one end of a cross passage at the lower end of the hall. This group, here called Class G, recalls the medieval layout with screens passage and is presumably descended from it, via transitional examples, almost certainly local, of the earlier sixteenth century, like Great Eversden 3 in West Cambridgeshire, cited above. Manor Farm, Pulham Market (Fig. 3) is a house of this kind [5].

This Class-G house is reported from Suffolk also by Sylvia Colman: 'Its incidence in Suffolk seems to be fairly widespread', she writes, 'though it is difficult . . . to say how it compares quantitatively with lobby entrances . . . my impression is that this cross-passage type has a shorter time span than either of the lobby-entrance variants and does not occur after about the middle of the seventeenth century.' The Suffolk examples are backed up by transitional or prototype houses, such as Foundry House, Stanton, similar to Great Eversden 3. It looks a little as if the popularity of this cross-passage house, which is in a way archaic, could be explicable in terms of the precocity of rebuilding in the areas in which it is found. In West Cambridgeshire, which is distinctly behind Norfolk and Suffolk in this respect, the developed Class-G house, if it existed at all, was rare; a few cases may have been lost through conversion to the lobby-entrance plan form. Forrester's figure 20 [6] seems to suggest that they exist in Essex, and they probably do, although Barley [7] does not apparently recognise their incidence in this county. Neither Gordon Moodey nor Barbara Hutton recalls any from Hertfordshire.

The typology of the relevant houses in Lincolnshire is com-plicated by the absence of a sufficiently representative body of timber-framed examples, with the consequence already alluded to that it is uncertain to what extent the stone and brick houses in the county, many of the later seventeenth century, are attributable to a 'Great Rebuilding' of comparatively late date. Like Bedford-shire, Lincolnshire, which is a large county with a copious and varied body of vernacular dwellings, has been relatively little worked over by archaeologists in the field, although Barley's

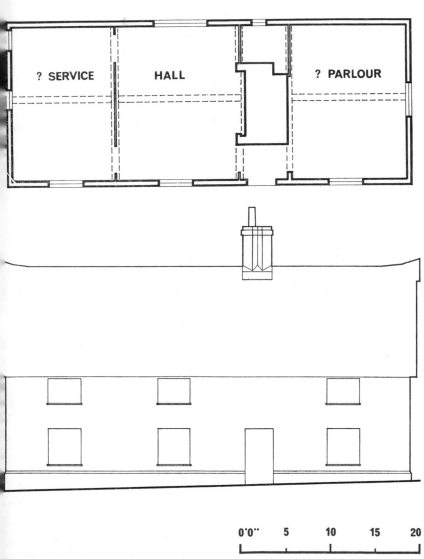

? SERVICE   HALL   ? PARLOUR

0'0"   5   10   15   20

ELLS LANE FARM,STANNINGFIELD,SUFFOLK

Fig. 2

CLASS-G HOUSE

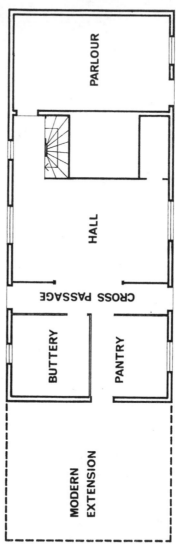
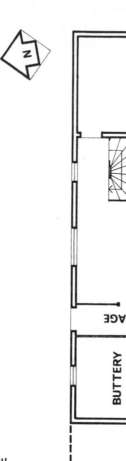

PARLOUR

HALL

CROSS PASSAGE

BUTTERY

PANTRY

MODERN
EXTENSION

0'0'' 5 10 15 20

Fig. 3

MANOR FARM, PULHAM, NORFOLK

researches on the documentary side, especially on the probate inventories, backed up by investigations of a number of surviving houses, is of great value [8]. Observation suggests that there is a tendency, at any rate in Kesteven, towards plan forms with an entrance at one end of the long side of an oblong block; these entrances sometimes give on to a passage, not necessarily a cross passage, at others on to a baffle lobby against an end chimney. *The Priory*, Haydor, discussed by Barley [9], a relatively sophisticated house which may be as early as the late sixteenth century, combines in one range a two-storey block having a single room each side of a central chimney, and a low service annexe of the kind featured in such Cambridgeshire houses as Bourn 6; the entrance is within the main block at the junction. This layout is by no means unique; similar houses, mostly humbler and later, are to be found side by side with other types.

The Priory, Haydor, and its like resemble Classes J and G in having the chimney at the upper end of the hall, thus allowing for a hearth in what would appear to be a parlour. All but the humblest of these lowland three-cell dwellings seem to have such a hearth. The Jurassic belt is differentiated by a quite distinct three-cell design (here called Class F), roughly coeval with Classes G and J, which has a cross passage one side of which is flanked by the back of the hall chimney; the hearth is thus at the lower end. The arrangement has the practical defect that a second ground-floor hearth is precluded. Most houses of this kind are ranged alongside a public way with the passage giving access to a yard which could be easily enclosed. In houses of Classes G and J a siting end on to the thoroughfare is not uncommon.

Detailed work by Raymond Wood-Jones on Class-F houses in an area on the north borders of Oxfordshire has placed discussion of this type in the rural setting on a firm footing (R. B. Wood-Jones, *Traditional Domestic Architecture in the Banbury Region*, 1963; esp. ch. V, 'The Regional House 1550-1640,' pp. 70-106, figs. 18-22 and plate 5b). From his results it is evident that there was a concentrated rebuilding in stone around Banbury in the first half of the seventeenth century, and that a through passage behind the hall fireplace was normal, the three-cell Class-F plan being an important, if not the basic, form. Wood-Jones is of the opinion that this through passage is an upland phenomenon and he is able to show that it is linked with structural techniques associated with the cruck frame, although both the plan forms and the structural techniques are admixed with intrusive lowland elements to produce a hybrid building tradition as adumbrated by Cordingley [10]. The cross-passage theme was evidently cherished, examples of it continuing into the eighteenth century. Manor Farm, Claydon, c. 1720 [11] is in other respects a quite refined small Georgian house, with a front seven windows long, but the front door is awkwardly placed in the third position, evidently for the sake of the old-style arrangement.

These findings are closely paralleled by those of at least one other investigator working in the Jurassic belt. To the north-east, in and around Rockingham Forest, Malcolm Seaborne has described houses of the same stamp as those published by Wood-Jones (M. V. J. Seaborne, 'Small Stone Houses in Northamptonshire', *Northamptonshire Past and Present*, vol. III, no. 4, 1963, pp. 141-50, supplemented by additional material put at the disposal of the writer). All, or nearly all, are stone-built, and a number incorporate raised crucks. The dating of these houses is similar to that of those in the Banbury area. One example from Weldon, with initials believed to be those of Arthur Grumbold, one of a famous family of local masons, may be as late as 1654, but on the other hand one of several houses from Corby bears the date 1609. Another of them, 20 High Street, is here illustrated in Fig. 4.

There can be little doubt that Class-F houses, or houses of similar design with three rooms on plan and a cross passage flanked by the hall chimney, have a wide distribution west and north of the chalk. A number, of stone also, have been discovered in the Pennines by Christopher Stell (C. Stell, 'Pennine Houses: an Introduction,' *Folk Life*, vol. 3, 1965, pp. 5-24), and they are quite usual in Devon [12]. The predominance of the type in stone country immediately to the west of the eleven counties under review is notable, but there are also timber-framed examples, and the possibility of an initial evolution in carpentry is by no means to be excluded. Timber-framed Class-F houses known to the writer include no. 11 Main Street, Great Bowden, Leicestershire, perhaps mid-seventeenth century, and Cottage Farm, Illshaw Heath, some ten miles south-south-east of Birmingham; the latter is related to a quite small holding of a kind which suggests late sixteenth- or early seventeenth-century encroachment on the

CLASS-F HOUSE

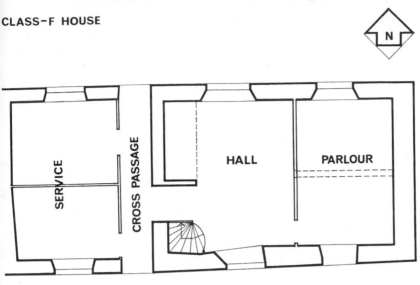

No. 20 HIGH STREET, CORBY, NORTHAMPTONSHIRE

Fig. 4

wastelands of the Forest of Arden. Further south, and perhaps more surprisingly, it is evident from the record cards of the Commission, which include some by the late J. W. Bloe and others, well observed by the standards of the day and carefully illustrated, that both timber-framed and stone houses of Class-F plan are to be found in Buckinghamshire, and that they may indeed be frequent, although they are obviously intermingled at least with baffle-entry forms. Recent work in Hertfordshire tends to show that some technical features to be seen in the western part of the county between the Great North Road and the Buckinghamshire border suggest 'an overlap from the traditions of the north-western highland zone' (Graham Bailey and Barbara Hutton, *Crown Post Roofs in Hertfordshire*, Hertfordshire Local History Council, 1966); so it would not be surprising if Class-F houses or their relatives came to light here, although no convincing instances seem to have been reported. A fifteenth-century house like Bramfieldbury, described by the above, which today has a later chimney against the cross passage, could be a Class-F prototype, since experience suggests that later chimneys are, more often than not, on the site of an original hearth.

It seems, then, that the Class-F house is well represented along much of the western edge of the region comprising the eleven counties; within the region it is largely confined to Buckinghamshire, no unmistakable case having been reported from Hertfordshire, Bedfordshire, Huntingdonshire or Lincolnshire, although it would not be surprising if further search in those counties brought to light at least one or two instances. The Class-F plan, like other now predominantly West-Country manifestations, may well be recessive, and isolated survivals in lowland areas perhaps of relatively early date, can reasonably be anticipated.

The three-cell internal-chimney houses of the late sixteenth and seventeenth centuries, grouped above according to the positions of their entrance and hall fireplace into the three Classes, F, G and J, derive at one or two removes from medieval houses with a single hearth. We are accustomed to think of this hearth as being in the middle of the hall, but it could also be, and with the evolution and spread of chimneys inevitably came to be, located in a variety of positions against the walls, with important results for the evolution of later plan forms. The central position is, arguably, less suited to the small house in any case. The positions adopted are no doubt functional in origin. A side wall was often preferred for the halls of larger houses (and for those of smaller houses in Devon); the lower end wall was the favourite spot in the highland (pastoral) zone, and the indications are that the upper end wall may often have been the location selected in much at least of the lowland (arable) zone [For the antiquity and significance of the highland (lower end wall) position *v.* I. C. Peate, *The Welsh House* (1946), esp. chs. IV & VI.] We are dealing here with the sort of habit which is unlikely to have been liable to sudden change except at levels where purely aesthetic motivation needs to be envisaged.

During the sixteenth and seventeenth centuries the post-medieval house was developed on lines which allowed for more than one hearth, so as to provide additional heated rooms. This was done at first in the lowland zone by building internal chimneys with two or more flues, topped characteristically by shafted and panelled stacks, vulgarly but incorrectly denominated Tudor. Such chimneys made possible a heated parlour and even heated upper rooms. The shafted stack could be elaborated to suggest that the house had more hearths than was actually the case. This sort of luxury was an inviting target for sumptuary legislation and the outcome was the Restoration hearth tax.

The multiplication of flues in a single internal chimney was the most economical way of improving the standard of comfort in a timber-framed Class-J or Class-I house, but the upland house could not be given a second hearth on the ground floor because of the cross passage. Perhaps too the construction of multiple flues in stone proved cumbersome. Even the Class-J layout had the drawback that it was impossible to heat the service end. There was an inevitable trend to forms which included two or more chimneys. The gradual spread of materials alternative to timber for the carcase of the house, brick along the seaboard and navigable rivers, stone within range of limestone quarries or alternative rubbles, was associated with the emergence of house forms in which chimneys were placed in the end walls.

The basic end-chimney house, represented in Cambridgeshire by Class T, was also found to have the advantage of lending itself to symmetry, the solution being the front door in the middle of the long wall set between regularly spaced windows. The medieval screens passage made such an elevation difficult; and the evolution, both of large and small houses, from the mid-sixteenth century to the Restoration is to a great extent expressive of the conflict between a conservatism which clung to the old internal arrangement and the urge to conform to a new aesthetic.

In Norfolk end-chimney houses make their appearance early, not only at manor-house level but also for a humbler clientele whose social composition awaits research. A quite tiny specimen at Field Dalling (Fig. 5), less than thirty feet long internally, which on the grounds of its stylisms is likely to be of the first half of the seventeenth century, is a remarkably early manifestation of architectural taste at the lower end of the social scale. The plan is still sub-medieval. Another somewhat larger house at nearby Hindolveston has chimneys combined with garderobes, in the gable ends, which are of about the same period. Much of the body of the walling in both cases is of flint pebbles (glacial erratics), a normal material in the district, which has very little framing. The vogue for end chimneys early invaded the timber areas of south-west and west Norfolk where houses, originally of mixed construction, have brick gable ends rising to apical chimneys, in combination with framed side walls, as at Dairy Farm, Tacolneston (N. Pevsner, *North-West and South Norfolk*, p. 336 and plate 53*a*); the majority of such houses have had the side walls renewed in brick, but the structural history is clear from straight joints between the original and later brickwork. Small end-chimney houses of the first half of the seventeenth century are to be seen elsewhere in the region, notably in the stone country (e.g. Moor Farm, Humby, Lincolnshire, dated 1631), and it would be difficult to prove where the impulse began.

Thereafter, and persisting into the eighteenth century, three-cell houses which suggest hybridisation between the internal-chimney types—Classes F, G and J, and the end-chimney types—Classes S and (much more) T—became increasingly frequent. These have not only an internal chimney but a second or third at the end or ends. They seem to start in the Jurassic belt, and this centre of diffusion is likely because of the problems there of providing extra hearths by means of grouped flues. In addition to new houses of hybrid form, many older houses were improved by the addition of end chimneys, and it is not always easy to distinguish cases where this has happened from more up-to-date structures of a single build.

These hybrid three-chimney houses did nothing to solve the problems of imposing symmetry on the older plan forms. Further developments designed to cope with this were various. One finds, for example, houses with a fourth chimney (was this fourth chimney sometimes a sham?) and a front door set in the middle of the main elevation. The most popular arrangement was, however, the symmetrical treatment of two-thirds of the elevation, corresponding to hall and parlour, as an end-chimney unit, the remaining one-third—the service end—being subordinated by finishing it to a meaner specification; the division could be emphasised by articulating pilasters at the junction and ends. The logic was often further underlined by approaching the main unit through a walled garden or forecourt, the service end giving direct on to a farmyard or other working area separated from the garden by

CLASS-T HOUSE

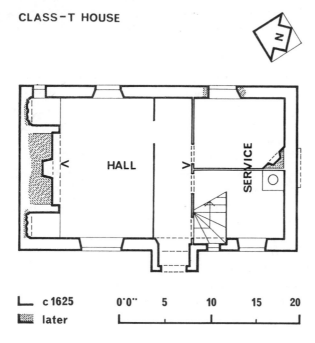

L___ c 1625

▨ later

0'0"   5   10   15   20

No. 32 LANGHAM ROAD, FIELD DALLING, NORFOLK

Fig. 5

its enclosing wall. A similar arrangement, with the parlour in the subordinate one-third, is not unknown. These post-Restoration refinements are outside the scope of this essay, but mention of them serves to recall the protean capacities of the medieval domestic tradition for architectural survival. The relevant houses are spread over much of the region, especially the north end of it; some at least have cross passages.

To sum up: the Class-J house, as identified in West Cambridgeshire, looks to be one of three post-medieval three-cell house forms current in Eastern England during the period of the 'Great Rebuilding'. Its incidence is marked to the west, south and southeast of that area, and examples are probably to be found throughout the eleven counties selected as a testing ground for its wider distribution. In parts of Norfolk and Suffolk Class G, a somewhat archaic lowland cross-passage house with fireplace at the upper end of the hall, may be dominant. An 'upland' cross-passage house, with fireplace at the lower end, Class F, is the equivalent in the stone country immediately to the west of the region; within it, it is represented in Buckinghamshire, and there could be other local survivals on the western confines. By the middle of the seventeenth century end-chimney forms, perhaps originating on or near the east coast, are spreading, and hybrids, having both internal and end chimneys, make their appearance, diffused perhaps from stone areas.

This picture certainly needs to be filled out, and probably to be corrected, as a result of further research throughout the eleven counties, especially in Buckinghamshire, Bedfordshire and Lincolnshire. The attack needs to include both intensive surveys of selected houses and extensive exploration, such as that pioneered by the School of Architecture at Manchester University, based on a simple typology, with quantification of results. The outcome should be important for the study of folk culture in Britain and of the historical processes which have gone to shape it.

REFERENCES

1. The author wishes to thank the Commissioners for allowing access to the proofs of the West Cambridgeshire *Inventory* and for permission to reproduce Fig. 1. References to West Cambridgeshire houses in the text are to the Monument Numbers assigned by the Commission, thus enabling the reader to look up the corresponding description in the forthcoming volume.

   This essay would have been impossible without the help of Nat Alcock, Anthony Baggs, Ronald Brunskill, Sylvia Colman, Barbara Hutton, Gordon Moodey, Malcolm Seaborne, John Smith, Denys Spittle and Margaret Spufford. Jane Holmes helped with survey and drew the figures.

2. S. E. Rigold, 'The Timber-framed Buildings of Steventon (Berks.) and their Regional Significance', in *Trans. Newbury and District Field Club* x, 4 (1958); R. A. Cordingley, 'British Historical Roof Types and their Members—a Classification', in *Trans. A. M. Soc.* n.s. IX (1961); J. T. Smith, 'Timber-framed Buildings in England', in *Arch. J.* CXXII (1966).

3. E.g. R. C. H. M. *Hunts.*, Abbot's Ripton 15 Green Farm, p. 3 and plate 163.

4. Harry Forrester, *The Timber Framed Houses of Essex* (1959); cf. M. W. Barley, *The English Farmhouse and Cottage* (1961), fig. 9, p. 71, Type II.

5. S. E. Glendinning, 'Manor Farm, Pulham Market', in *Norfolk Archaeology* xxx (1952).
6. Op. cit., p. 16.
7. Op. cit., p. 68.
8. M. W. Barley, 'The Lincolnshire Village and its Buildings', in *The Lincolnshire Historian*, no. 7 (Spring 1951); and 'Farmhouses and Cottages 1550-1725', in *E.H.R.* vii, 3, pp. 291-306.
9. *The English Farmhouse and Cottage*, p. 158 and plate XIIIa.
10. Op. cit., esp. fig. 1, p. 75.
11. Wood-Jones, op. cit., p. 189 and plate 12c.
12. *The English Farmhouse and Cottage*, ch. V, and 'The West Country', pp. 108-13 and fig. 18.

Landbeach in 1549:
Ket's Rebellion in miniature

J. R. Ravensdale

Among the archives of Corpus Christi College is a large collection of papers relating to Landbeach in Cambridgeshire. Several of the bundles throw interesting light on the background to Ket's Rebellion of 1549. With the value of rents being eroded by soaring prices, Matthew Parker, then Master of the College, gave close personal attention to reforming the chaotic administration of College properties in this and other villages. I am grateful to the College for allowing me to use and quote from their manuscripts.

THE DISCONTENTS OF 1549

The opening years of the reign of Edward VI had been disturbed and desperate. Religious changes had unleashed fierce controversy. A series of worsening harvests and rising prices brought many people to the edge of disaster. In 1548 unrest, rioting and disorder swept through the Midland shires. Where John Hales's Commission on Enclosure had done its work well there was relative quiet again, but in East Anglia sporadic outbreaks in the spring of 1549 were to blaze in the Norfolk summer into Ket's Rebellion, just when Cranmer's Prayer Book brought the Cornishmen up in revolt across the Tamar. The situation was critical for the government, but until the struggle for power in the King's Council was over firm control could not be re-established. Calvin urged Somerset that the people should be kept in good discipline. Somerset wanted to deal with the causes of the discontents. Northumberland ousted him and crushed the rebellions.

The outbreaks of these years were at once unusually spontaneous and unusually widespread. In almost all the affected places particular local issues seem to have stirred up people already irritated by the general troubles of the times. Organisation

94

and rebellion only came later. Ket's neighbours at Wymondham saw the outward and visible signs of the bad new times in the hedges and ditches of the new enclosures; the Cornishmen in the New Prayer Book which deprived them of their old Mass: their own enclosures were ancient landmarks. Yet the previous year the Cornish complaint to Somerset had been of dearth and shortage of foodstuffs. Cambridge and Cambridgeshire were deeply affected by discontent but remained outside the fringe of the East Anglian rebellion. Landbeach peasants suffered the same troubles as the Norfolk villagers who marched on Mousehold, and yet their only connexion was through the person of their Rector, Matthew Parker, whose sermons failed to bring Ket's men back to obedience. In the controversy about the driving force behind the risings, the problems of Landbeach, a miniature of the greater troubles, may have something to tell us.

The old view of the discontents of 1549 echoed the complaints made by Sir Thomas More a generation before, complaints reiterated at the time by Somerset's friends, the *Commonwealths*, in the biting sermons of Latimer and Crowley, and in the speeches of the official, John Hales: men were enclosing ploughland for pasture, driving husbandmen from the land and putting flocks in their room; silly sheep were eating up men. Moralists saw covetousness behind all. Rack-renting and extortion were blamed as prices and rents stubbornly refused to be frozen. Government and preacher together called for a return to the old virtues, to old ways and manners, to check man's inhumanity to man; they deplored the collapse of social morality and called for a crusade against the degeneracy of the times.

Ket's Rebellion in Norfolk certainly began in riots against enclosures at Wymondham and Hethersett, with the breaking down of hedges, filling in of ditches, with restoration of old arable to the plough, of old commons to the commoners. But in the demands of the rebels there is only one mention of enclosure, a request that the peasants may keep their enclosures for saffron, and that henceforth no man shall enclose more.

By the time that the rebels had reached Mousehold the dominant issue appeared to be that the peasants wished to exclude their landlords from using, not merely from over-using, the commons:

We pray your grace that no lord of no manor shall common upon the commons.

Landbeach in 1549

We pray that all freeholders and copyholders may take the profits of all commons, and there to common, and the lords not to common nor take profits of the same.

We pray your grace to take all liberty of let into your own hands whereby all men may quietly enjoy their commons with all profits.

We pray that no lord, knight, esquire nor gentleman do graze nor feed any bullocks or sheep if he may spend forty pounds a year by his lands, but only for the provision of his house [1].

There was a legend in circulation at the time that the commons were lands that had been set aside for the use of the poor. This was unknown to the law which saw all the wastes as vested in the lord of the manor although his powers over them were very limited.

Scholars have found that there was less enclosure in the mid-sixteenth century than in the fifteenth century, when much enclosure and eviction took place, or than in the last years of Elizabeth and the seventeenth century, when opinion was often a little more favourable and much enclosing was done by agreement. It is common now to regard the outcry against enclosure either as a popularised intellectual inheritance from the days of Sir Thomas More, or as a natural emphasis on the outward and visible sign of the clash of warring property interests. It offers such a clear symbol of issues a great deal more complex, that it may even be read into documents where it is astonishingly absent. Reg Groves in *Rebels' Oak*, a work which keeps very close to documentary sources even if somewhat propagandist in purpose, sums up the 'Request and Demands of the Rebels': 'The Twenty-nine included: the ending of enclosures, and *the return*—with some exceptions—*of enclosed land*' [2]. But neither in the version which he prints as his second appendix nor in any other version is there any demand for the 'return of the enclosed land': their plea is in fact for the mitigation of the working of the statutes against enclosure. Their only positive request on the subject in general, that from henceforth no man should enclose any more, can only imply the acceptance of the past, if a general policy is to be deduced at all. And yet we are still faced with the fact that Ket's Rebellion began with riot against enclosures; that Ket laid open his own enclosures and led the rioters to break down those of his local rival, Serjeant Flowerdew; and that skirmishers and outlying parties from the rebel camp continued to break down hedges and fill in ditches from time to time. The issue is obviously quite complex, and politics within the rebel councils may have made it so, or, alternatively, other resentments might have been deeper but less explosive.

Cambridge rebels do not appear to have made common cause with Ket, although the borough seems to have been much affected by the troubles. The very incomplete evidence which we have suggests quite threatening rioting. On July 10th the crowd that went to Barnwell to break down Bailiff Smith's enclosures marched to a drum. The Mayor and Vice-Chancellor who had some difficulty in calming the mob reported to Somerset. His reply urged that they try to cure 'the disorder of certain light persons there attempting disclosures and remedies of their own griefs' first by the example of their own behaviour, and further by a declaration of 'the pleasure of the King's Majesty, now signified by His Majesty's Commission for the redress of unlawful enclosures and such enormities'. If such measures failed they should go on to threats, and finally to the execution of justice. William Cecil, the future Lord Burghley, once married to a Cambridge wine-merchant's daughter, sent an appeal for clemency. Three days later Somerset wrote a reply to this appeal and acceded to the request since His Majesty had perceived 'amendment upon this admonition' [3]. In spite of the speed of the reply, Cambridge authorities do not seem to have waited. Payment for the carrying out of the gallows and a new rope suggests that the Sheriff had tempered mercy with discretion.

The complaints made at Cambridge are in part similar to those made elsewhere in the Midlands and East Anglia in these years. There had been several small enclosures from the commons; men who had held town office, Bailiff Smith and Bailiff Jennings, were involved. Mr Hynde, the ex-Mayor, had overstocked both commons and fallows with sheep and cattle. There were a few decayed houses reported and some cases of the separation of grazing rights from the houses to which they properly belonged. But the bulk of the complaints show that Cambridge had its special problems: the expansion of population in both University and town was pressing hard against the limits of fields and commons. The hunger for land was for arable and for building as well as for pasture. Old field ways were being shut off and put under the plough. Other ways, especially those associated with former monastic foundations, were being quietly appropriated. The Colleges were reclaiming the Backs and taking in old pieces of common in so doing. King's, Queens' and Trinity were specifically accused. Trinity not only enclosed and blocked access to a common green by the river and took it to themselves, but were undertaking development of the Backs rather different from our present delightful picture: 'The said College doth commonly use to lay their muck and manure on their backside upon the aforesaid common green, where they will suffer no man else to do the like, and have builded a common jakes upon part of the same' [4]. The town seems to have regarded this as not in accordance with the planning intentions of local custom. Because the official enquiries were investigating enclosure, and looking for the conversion of arable to pasture, increase in sheep flocks and the decay of men's houses, these are the things which they often found, and in fact these seem to have been the immediate cause of riotous assembly. Dearth, high prices and shortage of food, which one would imagine to have been felt as more urgent and pressing, appear not to have attracted the attention in this year that they did later.

Recent opinion as to the root causes of the troubles has tended to discount the attacks of the *Commonwealths* on enclosure and the commercialisation of the countryside, and to veer to the more sophisticated explanation of the author of *The Discourse of the Commonweal* who places the emphasis on inflation. Indeed he provides us with our best analysis of the process before Keynes's work at the beginning of the Second World War. But there has been some neglect of the economic problems of the 1540s since Tawney provoked the great flurry of controversy over the 'Rise of the Gentry'. Scholarly opinion has begun to take less notice of the price rise, and interest has been focused a generation or so later. The year 1549 was, however, important for the making and testing of English country gentlemen. In Landbeach we find one such gentleman, Richard Kirby; his activities nearly provoked a miniature Ket's Rebellion. It was Matthew Parker's intervention which restored order. To do so the old common rights had to be redefined and this is why the Field Book was produced.

Landbeach in 1549

Landbeach is a small village five or six miles from Cambridge. To this day its landscape speaks eloquently of its history. The larger of its two manors, Chamberlains, was acquired in the fourteenth century by Bene't College (Corpus Christi). Its extensive moated site and the earthworks marking the foundations of its medieval hall tell of something quite grand in the life of the old village. Although this manor was owned by an immortal corporation, even after its lands had been leased out to tenants Corpus Christi was never an absentee landlord in the way that many such bodies were to become. The College held the advowson of the church, and it became the regular practice for a senior Fellow, often the Master himself, to hold the living. Even by medieval roads Landbeach was within easy riding distance of Cambridge, and in spite of the provision of curates, it is clear that the Rectory and the souls of the village received more personal care from successive Masters than might be found elsewhere. William Sowode, who was Rector from 1528 to 1544, rebuilt the Rectory House at great personal expense, upwards of £400, and did this work so well that most of the present house, in spite of outward appearances, dates from this time. In its day this new house must have been in the van of fashion, with its Great Hall ceiled over, with chambers above, and a large brick crow-stepped chimney above a massive fireplace. This bore Sowode's initials, until a fire in the last century destroyed the old oak beam. When Thomas Cosyn leased the parsonage during Henry VIII's reign, he made provision for a three days' stay at each of the Three Great Festivals and kept chambers reserved for him and his assistants. When Matthew Parker leased Parsonage and Rectory together in 1553 he reserved rooms for himself and his curate and undertook to serve the cure either by himself or some other [5]. The Rector never appears to have played the rôle of resident squire, but he was far from unknown, and on his frequent incursions into village life he came as a great man.

The nearest to a squire that Landbeach knew at this time was Richard Kirby, the Lord of the Manor of Brays, resident but without a continuous family connexion or the personal dignity which could rival the Master of Corpus Christi College, particularly a future Archbishop of Canterbury. All the lands of the village in the Field Book of 1549 are carefully distinguished as belonging to the College or to the Armiger, the Gentleman, Richard Kirby. His roots in this village were not deep, his father having come there from London in the previous reign, but gentility is formally accorded to any member of his family entered in the Parish Registers. The term is very limited and formal in the Articles drawn up against him which describe his behaviour in 1549: only an Ibsen could have made him a 'Pillar of Society':

He will do no pains for the King's Majesty in keeping of the Common Watch nor bear any other charges belonging unto him for those grounds.

He will pay neither scot nor lot, nor be contributor to the watching of the beacons, but all these charges resteth in the poor men's necks, for none of all the grounds that he so unjustly taketh profit of.

Where out of mind of man certain willows set and cherished by the Town to help bear the common charges of the town and of the church, with other lots of grass and hay, have always been so used with whole assent, yet he of late for covetous defiance hath converted the half to his private use, and will be contributor to charges, as of wages to the clerk, at twopence but as other poor inhabitants there do, and for all his decayed houses, nothing [6].

Landbeach is still a small agricultural parish; on the map (Fig. 1) its pattern appears to be in the main an inheritance from the Middle Ages. Its house and garden plots are of three types, much the same as those of Wharram Percy, a village deserted in about 1500. North and south between the houses runs the King's High Way of the medieval documents, and the old lanes, now grown into a metalled road, cross this from east to west at the village centre. Around the crossroads the village is blazoned in heraldic counterpoint: to the north, the old fen; to the south, the old arable of the open fields; to the east, gravel; to the west, gault clay; in the south-west quadrant, the deserted moats of the old Manor of Brays, with Friesian cattle grazing peacefully on soft green sward; in the north-east, the bigger moats of the Manor of Chamberlains, where a donkey struggles to keep the grass from growing too lank; in the northern parts, the church and Rectory that Matthew Parker used; the wooden village hall on old glebe-land below the garden plots of the old Green to the west. In the centre, the village cross, 'the little piece called "Tree at the Cross" ', and 'Nuttree Yard', are all gone [7]. No longer common but more kempt, the Common hides behind

Landbeach in 1549

a transformer station, and its old unloading places for the watermen, Shawes Weights and Coxes Bridge, are shadows on the turf. Pasture has encroached on the village centre from the west, where shallow hollows of old ditches tell a little of the story that was fresh in 1549.

Villages on the margins of the fens were particularly suited to mixed farming. In the sixteenth century Landbeach still had much rough dry grazing in its 'mores', for use when the fen was too wet or was down to hay. On its boundary with Waterbeach it had meadowland that could in case of need be turned to arable (Fig. 2). Winter keep was relatively plentiful, and after the hay harvest the fens provided abundant lush pasture, producing cheeses as fine as anywhere in the country. In the mid-eighteenth century Landbeach still had 250 acres of common pasture open from Old May Day to Candlemas, and 220 open from Lammas to Lady Day. In 1549 Richard Kirby claimed that the commons exceeded 2,000 acres; his opponents that they were less than 1,000; they must indeed have been a great deal less. But pasture and feed there were in plenty for all the normal seasonal needs of a moderate sized village. The taking in of other men's beasts from less favoured towns was tempting and profitable. In moderation this had become normal and aroused no outcry, and the Commons were not usually stinted (limited as to the number of beasts that could be fed for each common right). But when the state of demand was such that men wanted to concentrate the business of their farming upon stock and the agistment of foreigners' cattle, the limit was reached and trouble arose from the competition for the now scarce feed. The College tenants claimed that overstocking by Kirby was so serious that their cattle would not have had half their full feeding unless the honest care of other townships adjoining to them had relieved them. Compared with the fens of Cottenham and Waterbeach on either side, those of Landbeach were much less; they lay in the main in a long acute angle between the Roman road and the Beach Ditch. It was likely to be expensive to have to turn to these better endowed neighbours. The College tenants added another complaint very special to the fens and gave it a twist calculated to appeal to the official mind of the day: 'Whereas the said poor people are pinched in their white meat as is commonly poor man's food they have not therefore their full feed and so the less strength, and consequently

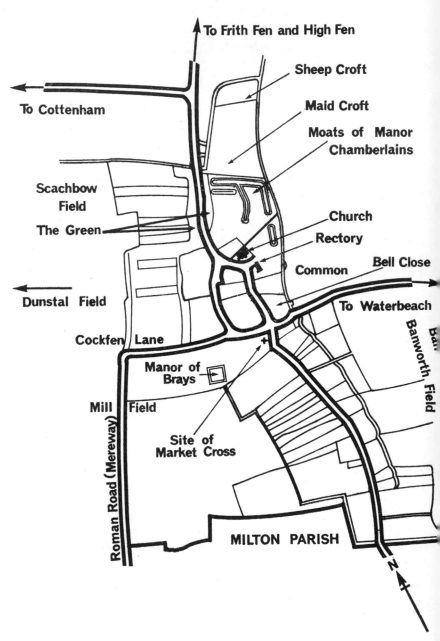

Fig. 1. The village of Old Landbeach

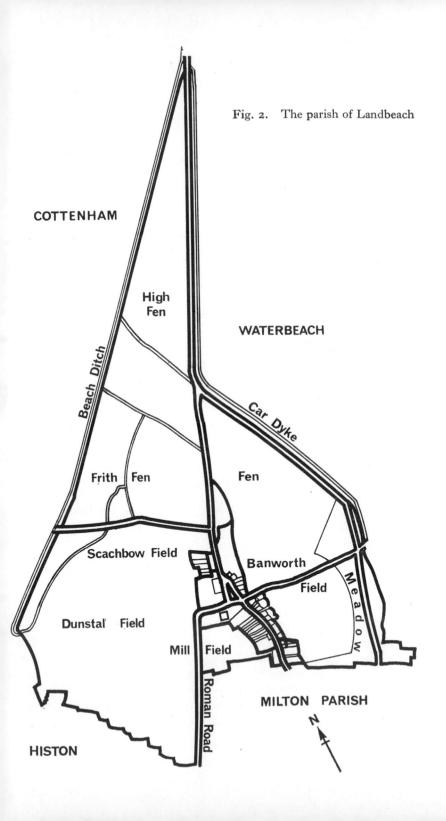

Fig. 2.   The parish of Landbeach

COTTENHAM

High
Fen

WATERBEACH

Beach Ditch

Car Dyke

Frith   Fen

Fen

Scachbow Field

Banworth

Field

Meadow

Dunstal   Field

Mill   Field

Roman Road

MILTON   PARISH

N

HISTON

is [*sic*] less able to do the King's service' [8]. Although this is clearly worded to impress the King's justices looking into the case, the substance is a foretaste of what the later drainers of the fens were to meet from the Fen Tigers of their day, violent resistance to any threat to wildfowling rights.

The effective management of a holding in an open-field village where stock-raising was on the increase made pasture near the homestead not only highly desirable but the means of a great saving in labour and expense. It was almost a prerequisite for the building up of flocks on a scale sufficient to overstock the parish commons of the villages on the edge of the fen, but could only be secured by taking in lands from the arable fields that backed on to the crofts, or by amalgamation with adjacent empty tofts and crofts. The first process was used in the south-west of the village the most densely developed housing area (Fig. 1). Unfortunately we cannot yet date the change. The other had begun in the north near the Rectory by the mid-fifteenth century. In a Rental of 1459 in the College archives, for the Manor of Chamberlains, Master Adam the Rector had acquired the lease of one of the Prior of Barnwell's closes. This close, then the Parsonage cowyard, corresponds to the part of the Rectory's present garden which lies to the south of the house. Across the road a little further to the north and beyond the green, but still conveniently near, the Rector had another close. He held the site of the old manor, Berye Acre, adjoining his rectory ground, and Mayde Crofte following on to the north, with Hall Yard and Sheep Croft. Opposite the Rectory across the main street lay the Rector's garden and the parish glebe, made up of a long oblong plot and a triangular one joined together many years before. To these had been added the parson's pynfold, the old pound. Altogether this made a very useful set of grass fields and closes handy to his house and barns. There is not much sign of others in the village having acquired anything comparable, although at the north end of the town John King had one large enclosure made from a messuage and a croft. In the southern part were a few double holdings, one at least of which had been made up by the addition of a close made from a former bondage tenement. It appears that the College had completed its enclosure and consolidation of a central block of pasture for its Manor and Rectory a century before anything similar was attempted for the Manor of Brays [9].

The College had stocked its lands with sheep before the beginning of the fifteenth century, and when they had been swept away by rot in Sowode's time, the flocks were swiftly restored under his successor [10].

Among the College papers relating to the lawsuit against Kirby is an undated copy of a grant by Kirby to the College when Sowode was Master. Sowode died in 1544. The deed conveys to the College six messuages without houses on them, and one with a house, Copt Hall. This transaction may never have been completed as Copt Hall and other identifiable tenements remain firmly in the Manor of Brays in 1549. But it is quite clear that Kirby held decayed tenements, and not unlikely that an exchange was being negotiated, as the holdings of the two manors were for the most part very intermixed. Had such a transfer taken place the College would have had a consolidated block in the north-east quarter of the town with a good deal of the north-west as well.

Kirby's progress in ridding his manor of houses and tenants is shown still more clearly in the second set of Articles against him:

1. He and all his predecessors hath letten all his tenements fall down to the number of fourteen of which divers were standing within the mind of man and some of very late days decayed.

2. Likely he intendeth the destruction of the rest of the town for he wishes that there were no more houses in the town but his own and no more.

With the reply of the College and tenants to Kirby's original charges the picture of his property in houses is completed: witness their description of his holding, the Manor of Brays:

Whereupon there is at this present time no habitation or dwelling house remaining but only the chief mansion house wherein the said Richard Kirby inhabiteth himself; which Richard Kirby hath not within the township of Landbeach in all above four tenants freeholders (to their certain knowledge) and which hath but small parcel and quantity of land in the fields and town of Landbeach holden of him [11].

The evidence of the Field Book, which lists all the tenements and houses in the village, confirms that there were current tenants for only four of Kirby's properties; it would seem that the charge against him was not exaggerated. The picture of decay of houses as due to the deliberate policy of Kirby, and the fear of eviction shown by his opponents, may not be simple fabrication. He begins to look very much like the stereotype of the social villain of the period, the enclosing sheep-farmer, newly grown gentleman, destroying his poor tenants' houses and livings, gathering all to himself.

Trouble was already brewing in Sowode's time. There is in the College archives a fair copy of what appears to be a letter of instructions to Counsel about to come to Landbeach. There is a set of notes from this in the Parish Fen Book, but unfortunately both are undated. The original, however, cannot be before 1542 or after 1544. They show that the Town House or Gild Hall was built at the common charge of the Township in 1527. It was apparently built upon common land as quit rents of 1d. per annum were due, though often in arrears, to both Maister Kirby and Maister Parson. Presumably the Rector received his share as Master of the College on account of the lordship. This rent the Churchwardens paid and accounted for, taking the money from the receipts for the renting out of the Church Lott. Kirby several times took the Church Lott himself, paying the rent. At the time these instructions were written he was claiming part of the rent of the house, but the Town was not inclined to pay since he had enclosed, together with a yard of his land lying next to Bell Close, a lane containing a rood or more. This lane had been planted with timber which was always felled and sold to the use of the town. Kirby was now taking the whole profit as if he were sole lord of the waste, and the profit of this was worth much more than the rent he claimed. He was also claiming a road in the fens to his ground called Bitts, but the old men of the village were prepared to swear that there had never been any such road until the last few years, six at the most.

One of the few common general complaints made at this time which was not levelled at Kirby was that of rack-renting. He scarcely had any tenants who might come into conflict with him over this. How he rid himself of so many is not known in detail. The College tenants felt that 'they were not able to stand against him, being a gentleman so well allied and friended' [12]: perhaps his own tenants felt still less able. Rack-renting or the improvement of rents (according to whether one was paying or receiving) was certainly known in Landbeach about this time, but our evidence for it all comes from the College estate. Among the

Landbeach in 1549

College's Miscellaneous Papers of the time is an explanation written in Mary's reign of the complicated position with regard to the 'whole rent of the farm in Landbeach' [13]. The old rent had been £8 9s. 4d. In Matthew Parker's time (1545–53) it had been leased at that rent to Mr Baker of Cambridge, Parker's half brother, who had resold the lease to Mrs Parker, the Master's wife. From the lease she had reserved the crop of two closes called Maydecroft, the ancient site of the Manor House, from the Feast of the Annunciation to the Feast of All Saints, together with the feed for fifty sheep, and certain other pastures. These reservations were worth £6 15s. 4d. a year. The rest she leased to Henry Gotobed for £22 17s. 4d. This may seem a considerable improvement in rent, but when the next Master leased the farm on these improved terms he was able to charge an entry fine of £80. About the same time he used increased entry fines to raise the yield of both copyhold and demesne leases. It is fascinating to speculate on Mrs Parker's part in the transaction; was this an attempt to provide a marriage allowance against the still very novel and insecure position of a wife of an important Clerk in Holy Orders? If so it failed, as the new Master's lease shows. The Lease of the Rectory and Parsonage to John Gotobed which Parker made in the very early days of Mary's reign was on the contrary confirmed by his successor, Whalley. Parker's intention was that the improvement in rent should eventually go to provide 13s. 4d. a year for the Master and each of twenty scholars. Baker gave up his part in the transaction to enable this scheme to be put into operation before his lease had half run out. John Parker as his father's executor finally surrendered all interests in the lease some ten years later. By this time it had become appropriated to the use of the Master and Fellows. When a later Master held the lease himself it was said to be worth £266 13s. 4d. All those who shared in these arrangements, including Gotobed the farmer, seem to have been pleased. It is a pity that we have no knowledge of the opinions of the College tenants except through the cases where they were joined in the common battle with Kirby. If the improvement of rents was resented, we hear nothing of this. But we do know that such improvement was going on. Parker is remembered for his successful administration, especially in raising the income from several of the College properties, Landbeach among them. There is a complex analysis of the rents, which is said to be in Parker's writing, at the end of the Parish Field Book, a fair copy in the College which might perhaps more easily claim his authorship, and a complete analysis of the tenancies which he has signed and dated. Masters says that he wrote out all the Terriers and Rentals in his own hand [14]. But whether he was his own scribe or no, he certainly directed the project to raise the rents. Of all the common issues of the time, rack-renting may well be the one where the literate are least likely to be thick among the accusers, and where more cases remain unheard because they adversely affected only the mute and inglorious. In Landbeach the question of rents created a division of interests within the forces united against Kirby. The micropolitics of the village had a pattern not unlike its topography, all the lines of cleavage cutting across each other.

VIOLENCE IN THE SUMMER OF 1549

In July 1549, when Ket's rebels marched around Norwich and set up their camp on Mousehold Heath, Matthew Parker was in the City visiting his admiring brother, the future Mayor. On several occasions he denounced rebellion from City pulpits. The rebels were keen to have sermons from the 'new preachers', and on his second visit to the camp he managed to deliver a good part of his sermon from the platform made in the 'Oak of Reformation'. But when he began to inveigh against the evils of rebellion and urged the rebels to go home, hecklers began to threaten his feet with pikes and spears, and he had to run for his life while the chaplain covered his retreat by singing the 'Te Deum' in the new English style. Nevertheless he returned to the attack the next morning with a sermon in St Clements in the City, and was afterwards again molested by supporters of Ket who threatened to commandeer his very fine horses. Parker had the horses doctored so that they appeared lame and were left. On the following morning he took a walk, ostensibly for exercise outside the City, but made rendezvous with his horses, mounted, and rode off for Cambridge and Landbeach. Nevylle [15], Parker's secretary, in his account of these events, made great play with his fear and his flight, while never losing an opportunity for adulation. It is difficult to imagine Nevylle writing in this way if it did not suit his Master, who paid him £100 for writing the book; it may have been intended to place Parker's appearance at Mousehold beyond all shadow of suspicion, the suspicion of sympathy which was already falling on some of his earlier friends. He could in any case scarcely afford to be away too long from Cambridge and Landbeach whose troubles pressed him more directly.

If Matthew Parker was at Landbeach more than usual that year he did not waste his time there. Violence was being threatened and used in the village. The villagers called in the Justices of the Peace who charged Kirby 'to use himself in sober manner towards God's and the King's his people; and that he should leave off his sword and weapon and walk like a man of peace; and also that he should command them of his house and divers of other servants that he had hired for the maintaining and fostering of his quarrel, that they should lie no more in wait with ironed staves and other unlawful weapons for other men of the town that should chance in to the fen about their business'. This seems to have had no effect, as the following day his hired men went unlawfully weaponed into the fen, one of them having a crabtree staff with two 5 inch iron tines set into it. This party were out to fetch in the peasants' cattle from the fen to impound them. Kirby himself meanwhile sat at the cross, armed with his sword and dagger, 'meaning to maintain his said hired men in their unhonest acts' [16]. Serious violence had happened before in such disputes in the village. At the taking in of a common plot Master Beach's constable (presumably Kirby's chief servant) had stabbed a poor man with a dagger. The troubles of 1549 could easily have blazed into something on a much larger scale from this running battle for the commons.

Kirby himself appears to have first called in the law in May 1549. He accused twelve named men with two or three others 'in riotous manner arrayed, having upon them divers and sundry weapons, arrayed after the fashions and manner of war, that is to say, with bills, bows, arrows, swords, daggers and other kinds of weapons'. They were alleged to have gone into the fens on the first three days of May, and to have unlawfully impounded all his beasts and those of his tenants and to have kept them in the pound for three or four days. He claimed that he and his tenants were unable to resist 'for fear of manslaughter, murder, breach of His Highness's Peace, or some other enormity which riotous persons daily use themselves in riotous fashion'. The accused answered that they were only six in number, either acting on instructions from the College, or freeholders in their own right, and that they carried only the usual small rods or wands used for driving cattle. Kirby did not say how many cattle had been impounded, but claimed that his tenants, time out of mind, both free and copy, had been used to common in the waste grounds of Landbeach in all times and seasons of the year at their will and pleasure, without let or hindrance. The defendants' version of the custom did not directly contradict this. 'Richard Kirby and his ancestors, for them and all their tenants there, had going in and upon the said waste ground or common never above the number of six or seven hundred sheep and their cattle besides, as common appurtenant to the said manor'. While not denying complete freedom of common, they alleged that Kirby had put in 1,200 sheep belonging to strangers, and had taken sixty cattle in agistment besides his own eighty. Some of the inhabitants had 'made moans to divers men of worship in the county there to move the said Richard to remove the said overcharge, and be contented that his poor neighbours should live by him as they had done in time past. But he remained unmoved by any gentle motion or request'. As to the charge of unlawful impounding, they had come upon the strangers' cattle in the fen, had taken them 'damage fesant', and lawfully impounded them until they were freed by a writ sued out by Kirby [17]. This was turning Kirby's favourite weapon, seizure and impounding of cattle, against him.

Rival bands seizing each other's cattle is the very stuff of melodramatic violence and could quickly build up dangerously into local civil war. Not far away Ket's men were eating silly sheep during that summer. The Justices had told Kirby, who appears to have been using systematic impounding as a source of additional income, not to take more than a penny for four or five cattle when justly impounded. His opponents alleged that he was not only demanding whatever seemed good to him as poundage, but also sending to have beasts seized on ground that was not his. Where cattle had in fact trespassed, the damage had been grossly over-assessed. The College tenants singled out a case particularly likely to appeal to royal officials: 'Where a poor man named Thomas Mytton, lately coming out of the King's Majesty's wars, having no cattle of his own hired a poor nag for his meat, the said poor nag grazing upon the common, the said Kirby seized him to his pound treyce in two years, and at one time he took for

the harm that the said nag had done (which indeed was none) 4d.,
and at another time 4d' [18]. Practically all the poor men in the
town had suffered in the same way. Matters were getting out of
hand. Kirby's sons-in-law and other relations with their servants
had taken to lying in wait for townsmen going into the fens and
pastures. Certain poor women had been assaulted at the Town's
End, being cruelly beaten with a tined staff, and one of them big
with child at the time. The Town Constable had paid Kirby an
official visit, but had been answered opprobriously: Kirby had
said that he would take no notice of any of the Constable's words.
On the other hand sauce for the gander was not to be sauce for
the goose. It was in Landbeach an ancient custom that after
harvest all men turned out their hogs to the shack. But if any of
the town hogs came into the shack in the common field near
Kirby's house they were promptly impounded and their owners
fined 4d. or 8d. a man. Should any man's cattle happen to harm
his corn or hay in harvest or hay time, he not only demanded
unreasonable recompense, but sent the spoiled hay or trodden
corn as his tithe. If the commons seem to have been the main
battleground his sharp practice did not stop there. He was
accused of altering the common fields by ploughing in the lands
next his to enlarge his own, and of interfering with the ways.
'He blindeth in their bounds meres and doles by his covetous
dealing' [19].

Kirby's violence alarmed the inhabitants, who feared that he
intended to provoke an uproar and perhaps murder, because,
when they and their wives had tried to withstand his fury as he
attempted to drive all their beasts from the common to his pound,
he threatened to bring in a force of outsiders to outnumber and
overpower the townsfolk. Here for one moment one can see how
such disturbances spread. The villages of East Anglia, under the
pressure of violent economic forces, split socially. As the opposition
polarised, like the City States of classical Greece, each faction
could call on its neighbours and find support from outside. This
was how the disorders at Wymondham and Hethersett began
first to spread in July. The sanctions of custom were breaking
down: the successful use of force was replacing the old accepted
ways with violence.

It was the old ways that Matthew Parker sought to clarify and
restore. In Landbeach he arrived in time to succeed, whereas in

Norfolk, by the time the rebels were encamped on Mousehold, matters had gone too far. It is difficult to believe that Parker's gallop from Norwich to Landbeach was entirely due to fear. We have no official record of the outcome of the lawsuits, but we can see things for which he was clearly responsible and which bear the marks of his close personal direction, in the restoration of stability to the village. First there was the College's support and union with its own tenants in the actions against Kirby. This was practical and effective, where vague if sincere sympathy with the oppressed peasantry from some other churchmen served only to inflame feelings. Then there was the construction of the new Field Book in the autumn. This was made under Matthew Parker's supervision on October 1st, 1549, by an extraordinarily thorough perambulation of all the lands in the Parish. Every house-plot, close and balk in the village was set out topographically, as well as every selion in the field. Everywhere the acreage, and past as well as present tenancy and ownership, were recorded. From then on dispute and friction over land ownership could be quickly solved. It became the little Domesday of the open field village of Landbeach as long as such a village lasted: all later terriers were based on it until the enclosure of the nineteenth century. The results of the perambulations were carefully collated and compared with all the old and recent records, and at least four copies of the book as well as these raw materials for it still survive [20].

There had been an attempt to define the rights of grazing sheep on the commons a year earlier. A set of new 'Ordinances and Pains' was made at the Autumn Court Leet in 1548. These clearly had a special importance, and there is a paper copy of those intended to be of general significance written in a law hand in the bundle with the Court Roll. They deal with stinting of the commons, scouring ditches, and repair of decaying houses. Had they been in operation in 1549 it is difficult to see how the troubles of that year could have arisen. Tenants and inhabitants including the College Farmer were to be allowed three sheep of their own on the commons for every acre, and in addition they might take a maximum of two sheep for an acre from strangers [21]. Yet there is no mention of these regulations in the lawsuits of 1549, nor any claim that common was stinted. Since they are recorded on the Court Roll, we can only look to one source for their becoming a dead letter, failure to agree by the lord of the other manor, Richard Kirby. He seemed to have wanted more than a fair share. His opponents felt that he deserved less than this. One of the articles against him in the summer of 1549 says: 'That notwithstanding the decaying of the tenements, he claimeth all manner of profits there of the common and otherwise in an ampler manner as if they were still standing' [22].

What Parker's practical remedy was at this time we do not know. The inhabitants had abandoned the hope that Kirby might be reformed by persuasion from the other gentry, or 'by his own conscience calling to mind the grevious plagues and strokes of God falling from time to time upon himself in his own person, upon his corn and cattle, upon his children perishing by the stern hand of God as may be feared'. In face of these Egyptian plagues he retired next year, reserving to himself only a third of the fruit of the orchard, and Copt Hall across the road to live in: the rest of the Manor he leased to his sons-in-law. Even then he does not seem to have found peace. Twelve years later we find him at law again against these lessees too, his own family [23].

We next hear of the problem of Landbeach sheep in the middle of the seventeenth century. There we find that the commons have been divided into four separate sheep-walks, one for the College, two for the lord of Brays, and one for the College copyholders. The process of disentangling, as distinct from clarifying, the skein of property-rights has begun. But there is still trouble. Neither the date of the division nor the ownership of the waste, where the sheep-walks were, was known. The difficulty was that the shepherd of the Brays flock had taken to driving his sheep out on to the stubbles across the College walks. Short of the final solution of complete enclosure and division of the parish lands, such disputes involving most of the village could only too easily arise. But all the orthodox and governmental opinion of 1549 made the solution of enclosure quite out of the question.

One can also see in operation in Landbeach something of the system of inbuilt resistances to enclosure by agreement, the number of different ways in which the village could split according to different interests: one manor against the other; lords against tenants over rents and fines; freeholders against copyholders; arable interests against pastoral; wildfowling and fishing against flocks and herds in the fen; both against the improvement of navigation; the home herds against cattle of agistment; sheep against cattle. At every point while rights were still intermingled there was always the possibility that one of the affected parties might be able to get more than it would if the rights were divided and shared. If we examine the enclosure that had taken place by 1549 in Landbeach, it is clear that it was done not for sharing and division, but for acquisition. The old and accepted enclosures of the College in the north for home paddocks, and the recent enclosures of Kirby, were to improve the facilities of the home farms of the manors as a base for overstocking the commons. Some of Kirby's enclosures seem to have been simple occupation of the common property of the township. The attempt to share rights of the common pasture by stinting seems to have failed. The only possible safeguard against sectional advantage when internal competition was fierce seems to have been clarification of the old law, and this is exactly what Matthew Parker's great Field Book did.

The College was not as a landlord pure white against Kirby's black in the sense that it was the disinterested champion of the poor. Its own enclosures had been created when there was no general opposition to them, and it was soon raising rents and fines to recoup something of the values that rising prices had passed to its tenants at the College's expense. There is also the mysterious business of Mrs Parker's lease. But there is no sign that the College attempted to exploit its own interests oppressively at the expense of the peasants of the village, and this seems almost the constant preoccupation of Kirby. The contrast here between what many contemporaries thought of as the old and the new, the landlord who tried to do right by his tenants and the new ungentle gentleman with an eye to the main chance, could scarcely be greater. Perhaps 1549 was really a much better year for Matthew Parker than the accounts of the happenings at Norwich have led us to believe.

There seems little doubt that the great issue in Landbeach was the overstocking of the commons by one of the lords. This also seems to have been the chief concern of the rebels by the time their camp had settled on Mousehold. There was a connexion between Kirby's enclosures and his overstocking, but it was clearly the latter which most nearly began civil war in the village. Ket was a landlord and a grazier. It would be most interesting to know if he overstocked the commons at Wymondham. Perhaps he suffered from too sudden a conversion; perhaps the rebel emphasis on enclosure was in part diversionary. However once Ket was on the move he would in any case have swept up all sorts of the discontented in his path; indeed the demands of the rebels can only be explained in this way. It is because it suggests what was the most serious cause of the East Anglian discontents of 1549 that the story of events in Landbeach has general value.

It cannot be a coincidence that conflicts about overstocking developed independently and simultaneously came to breaking-point over a wide area. It is necessary to look for some general explanation. Overstocking may well have been becoming wide-spread over the past few seasons as the great boom in the export of woollen cloth was building up. East Anglia was the most developed area of the woollen industry, and probably its villages were most affected by the short-term sudden expansion. The villages in East Anglia in 1549 were like agitated droplets: when two began to run a whole mass coalesced and a torrent swept down on Norwich. Drops produced by other storms than over-stocking were swept along in the current. One of the forces which may well have helped to rouse peasant resistance was the feeling that the government was on their side, and this had been spread through the countryside by the work of the Commission on Enclosures in 1548. After hay harvest, when the beasts were turned out to graze, would be the great moment for the battle for the commons, and in 1549 this would have found the peasants in a mood to resist.

But why did not Cambridge and Landbeach join with the other rebels? They were agitated, but outside the path of the torrent. And in Landbeach a bitter struggle was resolved without the intervention of Ket. If Matthew Parker had not intervened, might not Landbeach have started a local torrent which could have swept up Cambridge's discontents? The speedy action in Cambridge and Parker's swift journey from Norwich were so successful that they are almost forgotten. Had they failed in that year of troubles to deal with these minor outbreaks when rebellion was in full flood in the next county, the cost of such failure might indeed have been memorable.

I

Landbeach in 1549

REFERENCES

ABBREVIATIONS: CCC, Corpus Christi College Archives.
LPC, Landbeach Parish Chest.

1. Bland, Brown, and Tawney, *English Economic History* (1914), pp. 247–50.
2. R. Groves, *Rebels' Oak* (n.d.), pp. 34, 103–5.
3. C. H. Cooper, *Annals of Cambridge*, vol. II, p. 37.
4. Ibid., p. 39.
5. CCC, xxxv, 117.
6. CCC, xxxv, Bundle 194.
7. CCC, xxxv, 170, and LPC, Field Book.
8. CCC, xxxv, Bundle 194.
9. CCC, xxxv, 150.
10. R. Masters, *The History of the College of Corpus Christi and the Blessed Virgin Mary, commonly called Bene't, in the University of Cambridge* (1753), p. 36.
11. CCC, xxxv, Bundle 194.
12. Ibid.
13. CCC, Miscellaneous Documents, 1430–1700.
14. Masters, op. cit., 78.
15. Alexandri Nevylli Angli, *De Furoribus Norfolciensum Ketto Duce* (1573), p. 43: 'Enimvero tum viro optimo pavor iniectus, et ad hunc pavorem, insuper alterius mali suspecti et occulti terror adiunctus . . . magnoque in timore fuit'.
16. CCC, xxxv, Bundle 194.
17. Ibid.
18. Ibid.
19. Ibid.
20. LPC, Field Book and Dukman Book; CCC, xxxv, 170 and xxxv, 206.
21. CCC, xxxv, 133.
22. CCC, xxxv, Bundle 194.
23. William Bendlowes, *Les Reports de G.B., des divers pleadings et cases en le Court del Comon-banc, &c.* (1689), p. 126.

Politics and Religion in Hertfordshire, 1660-1740

L. M. Munby

The history of English politics, of parliamentary representation, has been written from two very different points or view. G. M. Trevelyan argued, in his *England under Queen Anne*, that 'the Protestant nonconformists and the Whig aristocrats, combined to form the irreducible minimum of the Whig party. . . . The Whig alliance and tradition answered to something persistent in the national mind and character, just as the union of the Church clergy and the squires in the equally long-lived Tory party expressed the other aspect of England's needs and ideals' [1]. In the Hertford County election of 1727 the majority of squires and identifiable dissenters (Quakers) voted with freeholders, London merchants and local tradesmen for a Jacobite candidate, who was elected. Opposing him, in support of the sitting members who were Hanoverian Tories, were the majority of the local peerage and of the Anglican clergy [2]. These strange alliances cannot be explained by Trevelyan's dictum. Behind this election lay at least half a century of complex manoeuvrings. They can be studied in some detail in the political history of the County Borough which was closely linked with County politics and which Charles Caesar, the Jacobite victor in 1727, had represented on six occasions between 1700 and 1713.

The traditionalist view of the two-party system, to which Trevelyan adhered, has long been replaced by a new orthodoxy, stemming from Sir Lewis Namier. His 'greatest achievement', it has been claimed, was 'to exhibit the personal and local nature of political issues and political power', to interpret 'British politics in terms of local or personal connexions and family prestige' [3]. It is quite possible to interpret the representation of the Borough of Hertford, at least for certain periods, in this way, but to do so would be misleading.

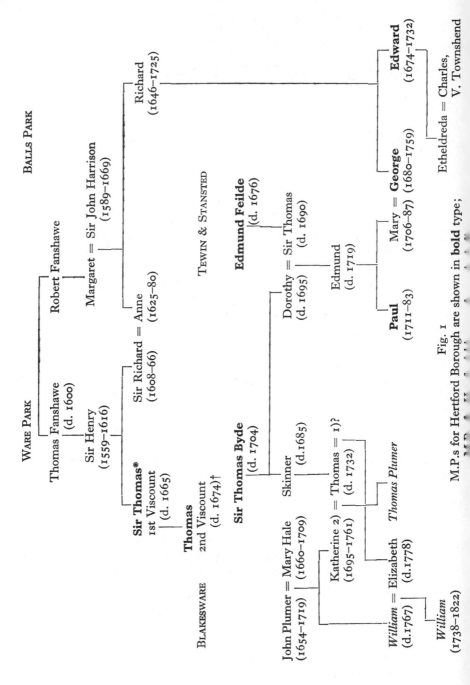

Fig. 1

M.P.s for Hertford Borough are shown in **bold type**;

Politics and Religion in Hertfordshire

In the 150 years between 1624, when the borough reacquired the right to elect two M.P.s, and 1774, there were thirty-three general elections and ten by-elections in the borough; this excludes the elections for Cromwellian parliaments, but includes the Conventions of 1660 and 1689. In seventeen general elections and four by-elections, one of the elected members belonged to the family nexus which united the estates of Balls Park, just outside the borough, and Ware Park, only a few miles away (see family tree, Fig. 1). But there was a long break in this local influence, between 1689 and 1721, which can only be explained in *political* terms. In nineteen general elections and one by-election one of the members was connected with the owners of Hertford Castle. From 1624 until the Civil War the main influence in the borough's politics was that of the Earl of Salisbury, who agreed to share the representation with Sir Thomas Fanshawe of Ware Park. Hertford's first two members, in 1624, were Thomas Fanshawe and William Ashton, Salisbury's servant. In 1640 Viscount Cranborne and Fanshawe represented the borough. The Salisbury interest was strengthened by the purchase of Hertford Manor and Castle from the Duchy of Lancaster in 1630. The Salisburys let this property on a long lease and during the Restoration it provided a base from which the Cowpers acquired control of the borough's politics. From 1679 to 1689 Ware Park and Hertford Castle shared the representation again. In 1690 Sir Thomas Byde of Ware Park was defeated; the Cowpers monopolized the borough representation in 1695 and 1698. Then came a sudden reversal of fortune; from 1700 to 1721, the Ware Park–Balls Park and the Cowper–Hertford Castle interest were both ousted. It is true that the Cowpers seem to have supported Sir Thomas Clarke of Brickendon who represented the borough in 1705 and 1708 and from 1715 until 1734, but they were not able to put up any member of their own family or a relative. In the period between the 'Glorious Revolution' of 1688 and the Hanoverian Succession of 1714 there was a break in the 'traditional' political alignments of the borough. This break cannot be explained by a Namierite approach.

It is even more ironic that Trevelyan, in his Romanes lecture on *The Two-Party System*, referred to the aftermath of the sensational 1699 trial of Spencer Cowper for murder, which led to the ousting of the Cowper political influence, as evidence for the continuity of English politics [4]. In fact it produced an

119

Politics and Religion in Hertfordshire

important discontinuity: Cowpers had represented Hertford from 1679 to 1699, but no Cowper was M.P. again until 1759; and the Quakers who had been supporters of the 'Whig' Cowpers turned away from Whig politics for at least a generation.

To understand the dramatic local politics of the first two decades of the eighteenth century it is necessary first to look at changes which began before the Civil War and later to look forward to the County politics of the 1720s. The control of Hertford politics by the Castle and Ware Park was frequently challenged. The opposition seems to have come from Puritans and dissenters. Local electioneering was complicated for the franchise was in dispute from about 1660 to the 1720s.

THE POLITICAL REPRESENTATION OF THE BOROUGH OF HERTFORD, 1624–98

At the very first election in 1624 there were four candidates and separate voting for each seat. Ashton, Salisbury's nominee, was elected with 103 votes, to 58 for a local tradesman, Mr Wyllowes, and 42 for Sir William Harrington, nominee of the Prince of Wales' Council who owned Hertford Castle before 1630. Fanshawe won the second seat with 101 votes to Wyllowes' 86 and Harrington's 48. 'It may well have been to secure his electoral control that Salisbury' bought Hertford Castle [5]. Opposition within the borough was a continuing reality and soon it obtained a powerful head. Gabriel Barbour ran Fanshawe very close for the second seat in 1628: Sir Thomas Fanshawe had 83 votes to Barbour's 68. Now Barbour was 'a member of the Providence Island Company' and 'one of the largest contributors' to the funds of the Feoffees for Impropriations whose aim was to buy up impropriations and instal their own preachers [6]. All Saints, Hertford, was one of the first purchased. Barbour emerged in 1642 as one of the most important local parliamentary leaders [7]. When Fanshawe was 'disabled' as M.P., because of his support for Charles I, William Leman of Northaw, London woollen draper and member of the Fishmongers' Company, replaced him in the by-election of 1645. This 'recruiter' M.P. had been one of the two Clerks to the Feoffees. Barbour and Leman appear side by side on most of the local committees through which the Parliament organised its military efforts. They were both members of the Central Committee of the Eastern Counties Association.

Politics and Religion in Hertfordshire

In spite of Archbishop Laud's attacks, the Feoffees had lasting success in building local support for Puritanism. The Presbyterian, Thomas Edwards, was curate of All Saints about 1636, and remarked in passing in his *Gangraena* (1646): 'at Hartford about ten years ago, when Independency and the Church began to be fallen to by some men of note and some people to look after it, I preached against it early, and by all means laboured to preserve the people' [8]. During the Commonwealth and Protectorate Hertford's parishes were well staffed with sectaries. Christopher Feake, a leading Anabaptist, was in charge of All Saints between 1651 and 1654; Edwards suggests that he was preaching in the town as early as 1646. Hertfordshire produced its quota of women and 'mechanick' preachers, according to Edwards, who mentions one of the latter, 'Field, the bodies-maker of Hartford'. This was the situation when George Fox came to the town in 1655: 'and so to Hartford, where there are some convinced also, and are become a fine meeting' [9]. James Naylor was said to have been 'the first Publick friend that came into Hertford' [10].

The conversions of these years survived the Restoration and the persecutions of the Clarendon Code. In 1669 it was reported:

In the towne of Hertford there are public conventicles held every Sunday at the time of divine service. There is one meeting of Anabaptists to the number of four hundred and upward, to whom one Capt. Spencer is the preacher. Another there is of Quakers of as great a number, to whom Capt. Crooke is preacher [11].

These were almost certainly regional congregations, but that Hertford was full of dissenters cannot be doubted. According to the Compton Return of 1676 one third of the adult population of the two parishes of St Andrews and All Saints were dissenters. Returns made towards the end of the first quarter of the eighteenth century suggest that dissenters were an even higher proportion of the population [12]. And Quakers were to be important and influential in the town for half a century at least.

This dissenting influence among the inhabitants must have acted like yeast in the political conflicts which arose between the inhabitants and the Corporation and which centred on voting rights. Hertford had had borough status and elected M.P.s in the Middle Ages, but this practice had lapsed; the borough's first

Charter was granted by Mary I. The third Charter of 1605 had given the mayor and chief burgesses the right to 'choose inhabitants living without the borough within the parishes of the borough' as burgesses [13]. The borough boundaries were most complicated: many parts of the town and its constituent parishes were not in the borough. When the borough's claim to elect two M.P.s was accepted in 1624, 'the Speaker refused to define the franchise' [14]. The Corporation made Freemen, normally these were inhabitants; whether the Corporation had the right to make non-residents Freemen was never made clear. If an unlimited number of non-resident Freemen were made and allowed to vote in parliamentary elections the Corporation could swamp a hostile majority of inhabitants with hand-picked non-resident voters. It must be remembered that the Corporation was non-elective, a self-perpetuating body of men named in the Charter.

The 'tory' view of the borough franchise was put by Sir Henry Chauncy, Hertfordshire's first historian, Steward of the Borough Court from 1675–80 and Recorder under the new Charter from 1680–1700; he claimed that until the election for the Short Parliament of 1640 'all the Elections of Burgesses of Parliament for this Borough were made only by the Freemen of the Borough'. In 1640 'the Inhabitants, who were Housekeepers, were introduced by an High Hand, to over-vote the Freemen . . . and since that time, the Inhabitants that have been Housekeepers, and contributed to the Charges of the Church and Poor within this Borough, have given their Voices at all such Seasons, without any opposition' [15]. The 'whigs' argued that 'all the Inhabitants (which did not receive Alms) whether Free or not Free, have voted in the Choice of Parliament Men. . . . This continued to be the constant Practice of Hertford . . . till Richard Cromwell's Convention. And then in a Dispute that happened between Mr James Cooper and Major Packer (who stood for Burgesses for that Town), one of these Gentlemen brought in and polled about thirty out-lying Freemen, who began the Abuse by this colourable pretence, That they had formerly traded and lived in the Town' [16].

County families wishing to control the parliamentary seats needed either the support of an overwhelming majority of the inhabitants, and this needed organising and paying for, or of the Corporation and a substantial body of residents. The Earl of

Salisbury had won the borough in the election to the Long Parliament (autumn 1640) by sending to 'acquaint Mr Keeling (the Steward) and such other of the better sort at Hartford of my desire of their continuance of their respects to me and my son', 'but only at the cost of £47 for diet for 237 persons, two hogsheads of French and canary wine and three hogsheads of beer' [17].

One of the 'whig' broadsheets claims that the Corporation 'had not transgressed their Charter as to Freemen, in more than about ten Persons' until 1668 [18]. In this year Viscount Fanshawe sold Ware Park to a London brewer, Sir Thomas Byde, whose 'politics' were very different from those of the Royalist Fanshawes. Another 'whig' broadsheet states that 'about the year 1681, and afterwards, some arbitrary Magistrates . . . that the Interest of the Corporation might be able to out-weigh that of the Burrough (i.e. the inhabitants), . . . took occasion from the Abuse of suffering a few Out-lyers (as they were termed) to vote . . . to improve it to a very enormous and plainly illegal Practice, by making great numbers of Clergy-men, Gentry, and others, free of their Corporation, inhabiting far distant from the Town' [16]. And these new freemen were 'afterwards admitted to poll at the Elections in order to the said Parliament in the first years of James the Second and in the first of the now King and late Queen' (William III and Mary) [19].

Several developments may explain the conflict which began in the later years of the Cavalier Parliament and the general elections of 1679–80. Ware Park under a new owner took control of the borough's representation: Byde was elected in a by-election in 1673 and his daughter-in-law's father in 1675. This may have irritated the Corporation. In the first general election since 1661, that of February 1679, the borough elected Sir Charles Caesar of Benington alongside Sir Thomas Byde. In the second election of 1679 the Hertford Castle interest was revived in the person of Sir William Cowper. There was a contest between him, Byde and Henry Dunstar, which Byde and Cowper won. Byde and Cowper were re-elected in 1681, possibly unopposed. There may have been incipient conflict between Ware Park and Hertford Castle.

Caesar's election in 1679 introduced a new element. His father, Sir Henry, had twice been Knight of the Shire, representing local dissenters and moderate opponents of the Court. In the second election of 1679 Sir Charles Caesar became Knight of the Shire by the choice of 'the gentlemen of the countrey' and in opposition to the recommendation of 'the Earls of Essex and Salisbury and Master of the Rolls' (Sir Harbottle Grimston of Gorhambury) [20]. In 1690 Sir Charles was to have his election for the county reversed by the Commons 'as his majority consisted of Quakers' [21].

In November 1680 Charles II granted the borough a new Charter. Later Whig critics of the Corporation's actions were to imply that this change was aimed at local liberties, but in fact the officials, the Aldermen, and the Assistants named in the new Charter did not much differ from those holding office before. The new Charter did not produce a shift of power; no doubt it encouraged the Corporation members in their political stance. Perhaps as a result of Corporation actions Cowper does not seem to have stood for Parliament in 1685. Sir Francis Boteler of Watton Woodhall and Byde defeated Sir John Gore of Sacombe. Cowper returned, with Byde, in the election for the Convention parliament of February 1689. A year later, in March 1690, William and Mary's first parliament was elected and Sir Thomas Byde was defeated after seventeen years' representation of the borough through six elections. Sir William Leman, son of the 'recruiter' member of 1645, and Sir William Cowper were chosen. After this victory Cowper was able, apparently, to stop the Corporation admitting unlimited numbers of outliers to vote.

Hertford Castle had effectively ousted Ware Park and tamed the Corporation. By 1695 Sir William Cowper was strong enough to carry both seats, with his son as his fellow-member. Byde's vote in this election was derisory, 80 or 88, as compared with Leman's 223, William Cowper's 244 and Sir William's 308. The Cowpers carried the following election equally successfully, but this was their last triumph. The Cowper victory was based on the support of local dissenters, in particular the Quakers. Henry Stout, a leading Hertford Quaker imprisoned on many occasions, seems to have been Sir William Cowper's man of business and political agent in Hertford. It was claimed that 'at all elections (he) promoted the interests of the Cowpers, to the utmost of his power'. After Stout's death his son John 'continued his respects to that family, and spared no pains to espouse and carry on their interest, in order to their being chosen parliament men for the town' [22].

This was the situation when in 1697 John Dimsdale became mayor and set out to end the Cowper political control of the

borough. He revived the practice of creating non-resident Freemen as potential voters. 'Contrary to the Charter and usage of
the Town (he) suffered himself to be continued four years
successively in the said Mayoralty the better to perfect the destruction of the Petitioners' rights' [19]. The Dimsdales, like the
Stouts, were new rich local tradesmen; the Stouts were brewers,
the Dimsdales 'barber-surgeons'. The Dimsdale family was in
1697 at the beginning of a remarkable rise to wealth and titles
through its involvement with an advancing profession: there
were fourteen Dimsdale doctors in five generations between the
Restoration and the Napoleonic War, and one of these was the
Thomas Dimsdale who inoculated Catherine the Great against
smallpox; she made him a Baron of the Russian Empire (see
family tree, Fig. 2). John Dimsdale and his family were to be at
the centre of the Corporation's struggle with the Cowpers for a
quarter of a century. There is no evidence that any of them were
Quakers, but John's brother, Robert, and his descendants were;
two of them, incidentally, Baron Thomas and Baron Nathaniel,
were to represent Hertford in Parliament at the end of the eighteenth century.

It is probable that Henry Stout was serving one of his gaol
sentences in 1661, when Robert Dimsdale found himself imprisoned for Contempt of Court in not attending Church. Two
years later, in 1663, Dimsdale was excommunicated and sent to
prison again for practising physic without the Bishop's licence.
Robert's brother, John, became a Chief Burgess in 1672 and
Mayor for the first time in 1675. John Dimsdale, then, had many
close relatives who were Quakers and this link may have been
useful in breaking the Cowper–Quaker alliance. In the election of
1698 John Stout voted for the two Cowpers and John Dimsdale's
two sons voted for Leman and Ca(esar). A week before the poll
Sir William Cowper wrote triumphantly to his elder son: 'the
Election goes so well on for us, that they all (I mean our adver-
saries) yield it to me; and I am assured by our most knowing
friends that you will carry it by at least forty votes. Besides Sir
William Leman is down with the gout and will hardly appear
himself but one of the Dimsdale's must (ride/preside?) for him'
[23]. The Cowpers won the election but almost exactly a year
later disaster overtook them. Sir William's younger son, Spencer
Cowper, had to stand trial for his life.

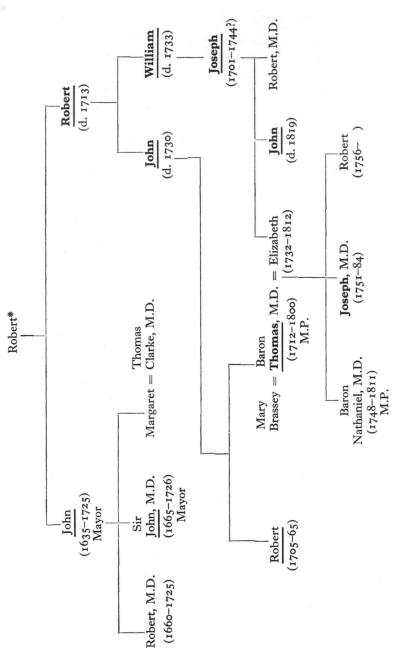

Fig. 2. The Dimsdale Family

Names of Surgeons or Surgeons-Apothecary are underlined; names in **bold** type are those known to have been practising Quakers (others may have been).

Politics and Religion in Hertfordshire

The trial which opened on 16th July 1699 at Hertford Assizes was dramatic and rich with historically significant incidents. A detailed report is unfortunately impossible here. The accused Spencer Cowper was to become Lord Chief Justice of Chester; his unofficial legal adviser, and a key witness, was his elder brother, William, later Lord Chancellor. Cowper was tried along with three other persons for the murder of Sarah Stout, daughter and heiress of Henry Stout, who had died only a few years earlier. On the morning of Tuesday, 14th March 1699, Sarah Stout's body had been pulled out of the mill dam. The coroner's inquest sat the same day and found that the deceased had drowned herself, being *non compos mentis*. Two surgeons and a midwife viewed the body and gave evidence. The surgeons were John Dimsdale junior, whose father was Mayor, and Sir William Cowper's surgeon, Mr Camlin. Their evidence at this time appears to have been consistent with suicide. The Quakers did not relish the idea that one of their number had taken her own life. Spencer Cowper argued in his defence: 'it seems they fancy the reputation of their sect is concerned in it: for they think it a wonderful thing, nay, absolutely impossible . . . that one who was by her education entitled to the "light within her", should run headlong into the water, as if she had been possessed with the devil' [24]. In saying this, as by the whole character of his defence, Cowper opened a breach between his family and the Quakers.

On 28th April Sarah Stout's body was privately exhumed in view of scandalous suggestions that she had been pregnant. Six doctors then examined the body; Mr Camlin was one of them and there were three Dimsdales, the Mayor and both his sons. All the doctors signed a statement that 'the uterus (was) perfectly free and empty', but they added the statement: 'we found no water in the stomach, intestines, abdomen, lungs or cavity of the thorax' [25]. This statement and others submitted to the Lord Chief Justice led him to commit Cowper and the other three to trial. Cowper, in his defence, argued that these actions by inhabitants of the borough were motivated by 'prejudice against me, upon feuds that have risen at the elections of my father and brother in this town; . . . to destroy, or break at least, the interest of my family in this place' [26].

The trial centred around two kinds of evidence, medical arguments as to whether the condition of Sarah Stout's body proved that she had died before or after entering the water, and attempts to show that the movements of the prisoners on trial on the evening of Sarah Stout's death were, to say the least, highly suspicious. Both prosecution and defence produced rows of 'expert' witnesses on the first point.

Mr Jones, the prosecutor, created quite a sinister picture of Spencer Cowper's and his acquaintances' actions on the evening of 13th March, but the defence was able to disprove much of the evidence given and to explain other actions quite plausibly. In the process Spencer Cowper revealed himself as at least mean and boorish in his behaviour towards the widowed Mrs Stout and her daughter. Then with William's help he exploded his bombshell, producing letters from Sarah Stout which clearly suggest that she was in love with him and pursuing him passionately, although he was a married man. Spencer Cowper's rejection of Sarah's improper advances, it was implied, was the reason for her committing suicide. Mrs Stout and Sarah's half-brother, John Stout, when shown the letters, bravely but rather evasively tried to suggest that they could not be Sarah's because 'she was no such person' [27]. They did not give evidence, because as Quakers they would not take the oath. The jury found the prisoners not guilty. A flood of pamphlets followed the trial and a vain attempt was made to initiate another, private prosecution for murder. In pamphlets attacking Spencer Cowper a motive for the murder was suggested, that £1,000 had been loaned by Sarah Stout to Spencer Cowper and misappropriated. This could not be established in the trial, it was argued, 'because their evidence that could speak materially to that point were Quakers, whose affirmation will not be taken in criminal cases' [28]. Cowper's defenders replied: 'You say there are a thousand pounds wanting of her original fortune: I wish you had told us whether you had set aside the charge of the prosecution: . . . I suppose there was nothing spared to carry it on' [29]. All this only added fuel to the fire. The damage was done: the Cowpers and the Quakers were irretrievably divided. The way was free for the Corporation led by the Dimsdales to deploy their forces to end the political domination of Hertford Castle and the 'Whig' Cowpers.

The next general election took place on 3rd January 1701.

Sir William Cowper wrote to his wife on 31st December 1700 from Hertford. He was despondent: 'I find a great change here for the worse, insomuch that I think our enemies need not poll honorary Freemen to carry their Election, and I wish myself at home again' [30]. Sir William's gloom was justified. His son did not stand; William Monson of Broxbourne replaced him. Charles Caesar, son of the Member elected in 1679, and Thomas Filmer of Great Amwell, were returned by the Mayor as duly elected. Caesar received 445 votes, Filmer 344; and only 186 votes each were cast for Cowper and Monson. John Stout voted for Caesar and Filmer. Caesar's voters included Robert Dimsdale, Henry Chauncy and Thomas Clarke, presumably the Mayor's son-in-law and not Sir Thomas Clarke of Brickendon, who was to oppose Caesar in 1705.

Filmer died almost before the dust had settled and a by-election followed on 21st February 1701, at which Richard Goulston of Wyddial was declared elected; Monson was the defeated candidate. There was a second general election on 24th November 1701: Caesar and Goulston were elected with 482 and 303 votes respectively; Monson stood against them, by himself, and received 220 votes. Two Dimsdales voted for Caesar and Goulston; John Stout for Caesar only. William III's death in March 1702 made a third general election necessary and this took place in July 1702. Caesar and Goulston were again elected, defeating Monson. Mr Justice Dimsdale, Dr Robert and John Dimsdale junior voted for Caesar and Goulston; John Stout once again for Caesar only.

The defeat of the Cowper interest was decisive: the votes cast, the repetition of the same result in four elections in less than two years, but above all the withdrawal of members of the Cowper family from the contests all underline the extent of this reversal of fortune. The Cowpers had lost their local influence, but the Tory members and the Corporation had not acquired an automatic majority among the inhabitants. What the trial seems to have achieved was a sufficient switch of local votes to make practicable the mobilisation of non-resident Freeholders. It was this vote which gave Caesar and his fellow Tory members their clear majorities in the years after 1699.

It was left to Monson to protest at the behaviour of the Corporation. One large volume of Hertford Corporation Records is filled with documents which arose from disputes following the contests in which Charles Caesar was a candidate. He stood in every one of the nine general elections between 1701 and 1722 and in one by-election, was defeated twice and elected eight times, but unseated twice. The first protest at the Tory victory came after the by-election in which Goulston replaced Filmer. Monson backed up a petition from the inhabitants with a personal petition in which he claimed that 'before the said Election and during the same Severall Gifts, Promises, and Menaces and other undue Practises were used by the Friends and Agents of Mr. Goulston. . . . The Mayor refused to poll some who offered and polled many illegitimately who were not inhabitants' [31].

Following the general election of November, Monson renewed his protests. He argued that he had had a majority of eighteen over Goulston even among those allowed to poll, if the votes of honorary freemen were excluded. In addition he claimed that some of his supporters had been refused the right to vote though entitled, and others admitted to vote for Goulston as inhabitants who did not in fact have a proper residence. In one set of notes occurs the comment that Dimsdale the Mayor 'never lived in the Burrough' and the following items: 'William Harding. A Single-man went into a little House just before the Election, that none ever polled out of. Benjamin Manning. English Schoolmaster lives in Blewcoat School, no dwelling house, a single man.' [32]. The distinction between lodger and householder, and uncertainty as to whether a particular property was within the bounds of the parliamentary borough or not, were important causes of dispute in the contested elections of 1715 and 1722 [33]. The former was still causing trouble in 1826–32. But the major dispute, as to whether any, and if so how many, outlying Freemen could vote, was to be finally decided by a Commons Resolution of 1705, although the Corporation attempted to neglect this decision in 1715 and 1722.

The disputed election of November 1701 went to the Committee of Privileges in January 1702. The Committee examined the Charters and took evidence from Sir Henry Chauncy among others. They ordered the Town Clerk of Hertford to allow William Monson or his agents to examine any books of town by-laws and to bring such books before the Committee. On 17th January the Committee, reflecting the views of the parliamentary majority, 'Resolved That the Right of electing Members to serve in Parliament for the Borough of Hertford is in all the Freemen, and also in all the Inhabitants, being Householders, and not receiving Alms' [34]. Monson had lost his case, but in 1705, in a different political climate, this decision was reversed and the decision then taken lasted.

At the election which took place on 7th May 1705, Thomas Clarke of Brickendon stood against Caesar and Goulston. The Mayor returned Caesar and Goulston as elected with 348 and 319 votes; Clarke with 256 votes petitioned against Goulston's election. Parliament met on 25th October and Clarke's petition was received on 2nd November. The investigation by the Committee of Privileges which followed led to another accumulation of voting calculations, petitions, counterpetitions and claims by frustrated electors.

On 6th December 1705 the Committee of Privileges reported in the sense opposite to that of their 1702 decision: 'Resolved That the Right of Electing Burgesses, . . . is in the Inhabitants not receiving Alms, and in such Freemen only, as, at the Time of their being made free, were Inhabitants of the said Borough, . . . the number of the Freemen, living out of the Borough, not exceeding three Persons' [35]. The Report was carried by a narrow majority in a large House. The vote was significant of the growing decline in High Tory strength.

Charles Caesar's parliamentary politics had made him enemies. He was utterly intransigent in his opposition to Godolphin. On 29th October 1704 he had voted for 'Tacking' the Bill to end Occasional Conformity on to the Land Tax. This vote distinguishes the High Tories from the moderates. During a debate on the Act of Succession in 1705, 'Charles Caesar . . . standing up in his Place, saying the words following . . . "There is a noble Lord, without whose advice the Queen does nothing, who, in the late reign, was known to keep a constant correspondence with the Court at St. Germains. . . ." '. The lord was Godolphin and the House sent Caesar to the Tower for these remarks [36]. Caesar and Ralph Freeman, his brother-in-law and a County Member, were Tellers for the opposition in the vote on the Bill of Succession. Robert Harley, who was to become a great friend of Caesar, describes how Caesar offended Queen Anne. Mr Caesar was amongst the Commons who had participated in a procession to St Pauls, 'but before that he had endeavoured to present an address from the borough of Hertford to her Majestie. But the Queen sent him word she would receive nothing from his hands'. In spite of this he tried to press the address upon Secretary Hedges. 'The Queen has ordered him to be put out of the commission of the peace and lieutenancy, for he had before refused the County address because, he said, it applauded the administration' [37]. It is not surprising that Caesar and John Dimsdale were defeated in the general election on 4th May 1708; Clarke (now Sir Thomas) and Monson were elected.

But Caesar remained the favourite candidate of Hertford Tories and on 4th October 1710 was re-elected along with Goulston, to represent the borough; Clarke and Monson were defeated. Harley had formed a Tory administration and was in correspondence with Caesar, offering him a governmental post. After some manoeuvring Caesar became Under Treasurer of the Navy. A letter written to Harley on 28th September, just before the general election, is revealing of electoral pressures: 'Though I do not in the least doubt being put into some place, I can't help begging that what what is intended may be done before my election, which will be on Wednesday, 4th October. Mr Goulston and I are both sure of being chosen by a great majority' [38]. Office in those days meant resignation and facing a by-election. Caesar was re-elected at a by-election in 1711 and again, with Goulston, at the general election of August 1713.

The general election of 25th January 1715, the first of George I's reign, saw a full-scale clash between the two parties. The *Flying Post* described Caesar's supporters in hostile vein: 'There came the morning of the election about 600 persons from Mr Cesar's of Bennington . . . who had maintained them with victuals, drink, and gave them more than the Common wages for labouring men for more than two months. They spent it in playing at hatfarthing, carding, ringing the bells, and going a-shooting, when sometimes they killed the fowls and sheep of the neighbourhood. This noble crew made their entry by beat of drums, and streamers flying . . .; their usual cry was, No Presbyterians, High Church and Sacheverell, Low Church and the Devil; and some of the gang were heard to cry in the night, No Presbyterians, No King George' [39]. Joseph Calton, the Mayor, returned Caesar and Goulston as elected. Clarke and John Boteler appealed to the Committee of Privileges.

Clarke and Boteler received massive financial support from the Cowpers. The Panshanger papers contain an account of £1,122 13s. 'expended for Sir Thomas Clarke and John Boteler' and a further account for £122 16s. 4d. 'lent and expended on account of the last election that was not charged in the last account but was promised to several persons'; this includes expenses of witnesses in London, presumably when the Committee of Privileges was investigating the dispute [40]. There is a significant item in these accounts. £83 2s. 6d. was 'laid out and gave away by me and my sons on several occasions: viz. to the men several weeks before, we drew beer expenses on Freemen abroad, for horse hire and expenses in getting them in'. The Cowpers were mobilising outliers, in spite of the Commons' decision of 1705.

The Committee of Privileges heard the dispute in May 1715 and unseated Caesar and Goulston. After which the Committee 'resolved that Joseph Calton, Mayor of the Borough of Hertford, is guilty of acting in an illegal and arbitrary Manner in the late Election . . . (and) Ordered that the said Joseph Calton be, for the said Breach of Privilege, taken into the custody of the Serjeant at Arms attending this House' [41]. It is all the more remarkable that Joseph Calton, who was once again Mayor, repeated his offence at the following general election of 20th March 1722, although Clarke's supporters had read the House's judgement of 1715 to him during the polling. Calton declared Charles Caesar and Edward Harrison of Balls Park elected. The defeated candidates were Sir Thomas Clarke and John Dimsdale. The voting for Caesar and Clarke was 291 and 254 respectively. Sir Thomas Clarke petitioned and by 190 to 126 votes Caesar was unseated.

This election marked the end of Caesar's electioneering in Hertford Borough, a final defeat for the Corporation led by Dimsdale and Calton and the restoration of the local influence of Balls Park. But it was not the end of Caesar's electioneering nor was it the end of Caesar's alliance with the Quakers.

It is interesting that in all the disputes over the borough elections no mention was made of the Quaker votes. The refusal to take an oath stood in the way of the Quaker voters, since the voter had to take a whole series of oaths of loyalty. In 1695 an Affirmation Act allowed Quakers to affirm in civil cases. The form of words was not to the liking of most Quakers and the application of the Act was not uniform. Quakers were still refused parliamentary votes in some places. The polling-lists in Hertford Corporation Records contain no indication as to whether voters took the oath or affirmed, although an alternative form of Affirmation in place of the oath taken by Freemen exists for 1700. John Stout, who was a Quaker, voted and for Caesar, at least in 1701–2; whether he changed sides again later we do not know. The Hertfordshire Quarterly Meeting of 1719 thought it 'reasonable to move for greater ease in the matter' of Affirmation [42], and in 1721 a revised form of Affirmation was authorised. The poll-books for County Elections in 1722 and 1727 reveal the Quaker vote, quite clearly: there is a column headed 'Jurat vel affirmat'. From these we find that the Quakers in Hertfordshire were still solidly behind Caesar. Their influence, it is reasonable to assume, was an important factor in the support which Caesar had within the borough.

CHARLES CAESAR OF BENINGTON

Who was this Charles Caesar who dominated the borough's politics for a quarter of a century? For more than a decade after 1714 he was one of the leading Jacobite conspirators. Keith Feiling, in this connexion, described him as 'the very quarrelsome member for Hertfordshire . . . hardly fit to manage a wine club' [43]. Dr J. H. Plumb, referring to his part in a parliamentary debate in 1730, called him 'a rabid old Jacobite' [44]. His friends and neighbours had quite a different idea of the man; and it is this other Caesar whose considerable electoral support in Hertfordshire outlasted the outlawing of his ideas.

There is no doubt about the surprising breadth of local support which Caesar enjoyed. It is revealed in his correspondence and in the polling in the County elections of 1722 and 1727, in both of which he was a candidate. The full significance of this support can only be appreciated when it is seen what kind of Jacobite Caesar was. Feiling and Plumb's comments are misleading. Caesar was arrested in January 1717 and sent to the Tower for his suspected part in the conspiracy centred on Gyllenborg, the Swedish ambassador. While Gyllenborg was compromised by papers he had kept, Caesar was not, although he was 'the only person of all our friends, who dealt immediately with Gyllenborg' [45]. In February Caesar was released; 'nothing material is found amongst Mr Caesar's papers, and he is out on bail' [46]. As little daunted by this stay in the Tower as by his first, he resumed his correspondence with St Germains in April. In May he was acting as an intermediary between the two quarrelling Jacobite leaders, the Earl of Oxford (Robert Harley) and Atterbury, Bishop of Rochester, being seized of the 'necessity there was for the good of all the relations to keep peace among them'. Anne Oglethorpe, who reported this to the Old Pretender's Secretary of State, the Duke of Mar, described Charles and Mary Caesar as 'honest without any of the common alloy' [47]. Lord Oxford wrote to Mar in June: 'there are few in England so useful in the King's affairs' [48]. In August Caesar wrote to Mar that 'the narrative you sent has dissipated the groundless jealousy Flint (the Bishop of Rochester) had got in his head that affairs were kept here as a secret from him' [49]. In February 1718 Mar wrote of Caesar: 'He is a particular friend of Lord Oxford, and not ill with the Bishop of Rochester and his set'. In November it was suggested to Mar: 'if you will call away Menzies, you may put all the affairs he is entrusted with into Mr Caesar's hands, who is entirely a man of honour trusted by everybody and will obey punctually the King's commands and yours and will never go into any little villainous contrivance with any whatsoever' [50]. The Jacobite papers are full of evidence suggesting that Caesar was the least quarrelsome of plotters. His only 'falling out' was with James Murray because of the latter's bad habit of spreading political gossip, 'which Mr Caesar would have brought a greater length, had it not been that he has too good discretion to make any great noise with anybody that pretended to belong to the King' [51].

Caesar not only kept the peace among the Jacobites, he got on well with ordinary people. Mrs Caesar records a revealing incident in her diary: 'the other day chancing into a common boat, the man looked earnest upon him, and though more than twenty years has passed, he said "Sir I'me shure I was your servant when Treasurer of the Navy", and whilst he was expressing his joy for seeing him, the Crew of the Treasurer's Barge came by in a Shallop, and he was as soon huzza'd as the grateful Waterman cried out, "My Boat is honoured with our old Master Treasurer Caesar" ' [52]. To judge from their letter-books the Caesars had many aristocratic and episcopal friends; their neighbours respected them and even the Cowpers became friendly in the 1720s, perhaps because of the attempt to involve Lord Cowper as a guilty party in the Layer conspiracy. It is only when Caesar's genuine popularity with different classes is appreciated that his electoral support can be properly judged.

Hertfordshire was not a County in which a few great men could swing a majority of votes. Throughout the eighteenth century the freeholder electorate preserved a genuine independence; there was a real element of popular influence alongside the conflicting 'interests' of individuals and social groups. In 1722 and 1727 Caesar, standing in the County elections, received widespread support in spite of the opposition of most of the local Peerage. In 1727 he headed the poll, 'Lord Salisbury being against him . . . Lord Essex was also against Mr Caesar'. In 1736 Caesar was elected at a by-election. He had been defeated at the general election of 1734, but in the by-election 'the general voice of the freeholders had called upon him to be one of their representatives in parliament' [52]. In the County poll of 1722 Caesar received 1,340 votes as against 1,614 and 1,464 for the two sitting members, his brother-in-law Ralph Freeman, who had been member since 1697, and Sir Thomas Sebright of Beechwood, who had been member since 1715. Sebright and Freeman were Hanoverian Tories. In 1727 Caesar headed the poll with 2,021 votes to Sebright's 1,424 and Freeman's 1,012.

Caesar's candidature in 1722 and in 1727 was clearly backed by local supporters of Walpole's government, as a means of ousting the sitting members and winning a new influence in the County. Dr Plumb comments: 'There was no chance of a Whig, and Walpole always preferred an avowed Jacobite to a Hanoverian Tory' [53]. The Whig front runner was William Plumer of Blakesware (see Fig. 1) who approached Caesar on 15th January 1722 in a most circuitous manner: 'Sir, I have ordered my servant to carry home one of your hounds . . . I was a few days since carried by a hare very near your seat and had a great inclination to have paid my respects to you, but as the approaching elections make people very jealous of one another I did not know but my waiting on you might have been some disservice to you. . . . I shall always be ready and proud to do you any service I can be capable of, consistent with the obligations I owe to my particular Friends . . . I have no regard to my own particular interest . . ., having determined not to attempt being in the next parliament. . . . Sir, I beg pardon for thy trouble which if what I have said be improper,

I desire may be taken as a letter about hounds'. A postscript followed: 'if now I am at home or any time hereafter you will please to honour me with your commands, you may depend upon my inclination to serve you' [54].

This circuitous proffer of an alliance was accepted: both in 1722 and 1727 Plumer acted as Caesar's chief 'election agent'. His 'particular friends' included, in 1722, Sir Robert Raymond of King's Langley, Walpole's Attorney-General, John Boteler of Watton Woodhall, and Edward Harrison of Balls Park. Boteler had been Sir Thomas Clarke's fellow-candidate at Hertford in 1715, defeating Caesar and Goulston. On 10th October 1714 he had written to Lord Cowper about the possibilities of exploiting divisions among the Tories to win the County seats. In 1722 he had pressed Plumer to stand for the County but 'assured me (Plumer) he would come into any opposition' [55]. In 1727 he was working for Caesar's election. Edward Harrison had been elected M.P. for Hertford Borough in 1722. In 1726 he became Walpole's Postmaster-General. Sir Robert Raymond had become Lord Chief Justice in 1725. It is clear from Caesar's correspondence that all these governmental Whigs supported Caesar actively in the elections of 1722 and 1727. Their real intentions were revealed in 1734 when Plumer stood himself and defeated Caesar.

That Whig support played a part in Caesar's triumph in 1727 is obvious, but why was it necessary for the Whigs to ally with Caesar? Harrison's support for Caesar had a warmth which went beyond party tactics. When Sir Thomas Sebright died in 1736, 'Mr Caesar's opposers had set Mr Halsey up, to have been chosen, as they thought, on the Thursday, but the Saturday before at the Hertford Club, Mr Caesar's friends without his knowledge . . . resolved to publish that for him they would demand a Poll, which they carried'. It was Harrison who led the demand for a Poll, though Plumer was 'against him' [56].

Analysis of the poll-book of 1727 reveals the broad basis of Caesar's support, to which Whig tactical support gave added strength; but the fact is that Caesar was a strong candidate anyway. In 1727 he had the votes of 156 of those described as gentleman or esquire, as against Sebright's 126 and Freeman's 95. Nine-and-a-half per cent of Caesar's total vote came from the inhabitants of Hertford and Ware; the eighteen most populous places in the County gave him nearly half his votes, twice as many as Freeman and sixty-two per cent more than Sebright. London residents, with a Hertfordshire vote, used it predominantly for Caesar: here the Whig support may have counted for a good deal, for this vote was organised by Edward Harrison and the Radcliffe brothers of Hitchin Priory, Levant Company merchants, a member of whose family had stood in 1715 against Freeman and Sebright. Eighty-one of the ninety-one local Quakers who affirmed when voting polled for Caesar, thirty-seven for Freeman and only five for Sebright. The importance of this vote is suggested by the efforts made to turn it against Caesar. Plumer wrote to him, in the middle of the election, of a story that 'you should order a man to be discharged from your Work, under one Rayment if I mistake not, because he was a Quaker with the further circumstance that you should say you not only would have nothing to do with such but that you hoped that they and Dissenters of all sorts would everywhere be rooted out' [57]. The Anglican clergy alone voted firmly against Caesar: he had thirty-nine clerical votes in 1727, as against sixteen in 1722, but Freeman had fifty-nine in 1727 and Sebright seventy.

The local Peers and the Anglican Church opposed Caesar overwhelmingly: freeholders and country gentry, the merchants and artisans of local market-towns, the dissenters, and London voters all supported him. This was not the result of a tactical manoeuvre. It suggests a deep-seated and popular opposition to the Hanoverian establishment.

CONCLUSIONS

How can one explain these apparently confusing events? If there was any 'enduring element' in the political life of seventeenth- and eighteenth-century Hertfordshire, it was not Trevelyan's 'Whig alliance and tradition' with its symbiotic 'union of the Church clergy and the squires in the . . . Tory party'; nor was it merely the 'personal connexions and family prestige' of the Namierites. What seems to have occurred was the creation of a continuing popular opposition, an opposition to government, to the establishment, to all Governments. This 'Country Party' attitude of mind has been recognised as influencing the parliamentary legislation of the early eighteenth century and as predominant among the Knights of the Shire, but its local roots and its influence on local elections in the boroughs as well as in the shires have not been sufficiently explored. Because it was essentially anti-establish-mentarian it could express itself in different political ways at different times. It was a political factor which individuals, families and 'parties' could harness to different ends.

In the fifteen years before the Civil War Hertford Puritans formed an opposition to landlord control of local politics. The fact that the local families took opposite sides, Salisbury for Parliament, Fanshawe and Harrison for the King, no doubt helped the opposition. For the two decades, 1640–60, the 'opposition' controlled Hertford. With the Restoration of Charles II there was a restoration of Fanshawe influence in the politics of the borough and County. But as early as 1666, two years before Fanshawe had to sell out his local estate through impoverishment, he was defeated in a by-election for the County seat which fell vacant on his father's death. Sir Henry Caesar, who had been a County member in the Convention of 1660, was elected by an alliance of local dissenters and Anglican conformists who had been Parlia-mentary supporters two decades previously [58]. In the stormy years 1678–81 the opposition again triumphed in Hertford. Sir Charles Caesar's election, early in 1679 for the borough and later in the year for the shire, by the choice of 'the gentleman of the countrey' and in opposition to the local Peerage, becomes all the more significant when one remembers that there is evidence, for 1690, that he had strong Quaker support.

The swelling of 'Country Party' feeling against Charles II's government, of which Sir Charles Caesar's elections are local expressions, was used by the Whig leaders to form a Whig party and Whig governments. It seems that the Cowper family capture of Hertford Borough seats was a local example of the same process. But by its very nature the ground-swell of opposition was likely to turn against those in office and power. All that was required for a reversal of fortune was an occasion, and this was sensationally provided by the death of Sarah Stout and the subsequent trial of Spencer Cowper. But was this accident really the cause of the political *volte-face* in Hertford? Or were there deeper and more universal currents of change upon which events in Hertford were carried?

It is arguable that the 'Good Old Cause' element in the late seventeenth-century opposition was disgruntled with the Whigs after 1685 and reacted against the closing of the ranks of the establishment in 1688. Some turned to Jacobitism; how wide-spread was this reaction? The origins and extent of popular Jacobitism have been singularly neglected by social and political historians in modern times, their study left to ultra-Tory senti-mentalists. But surely there is more than casual significance in the transfer of loyalties by several of the more expert plotters of the years 1683–8. Robert Ferguson and Major John Wildman sailed with William to Torbay; yet Ferguson certainly and Wildman possibly became active Jacobites [59]. A Hitchin Quaker, William Bromfield, became Mary of Modena's doctor and was involved in a host of Jacobite conspiracies [60]. Seen in this light it is not so surprising that Charles Caesar, the heir of a Country Party 'Whiggish' family, should have become a High Tory and a Jacobite; nor that the Quakers in the borough and County should have so consistently supported him. The apparent alliance between the Corporation and the Quakers after 1699 may not have been unprincipled but rather rooted in a joint dislike of the consequences of 1688, the Revolution Settlement.

The conventional picture which we have of the England of Queen Anne and George I, a picture of growing prosperity and tolerance, makes insufficient allowance for the deep unease which also existed. There was an undercurrent of disgust with the self-satisfaction and the small-mindedness of the time, which is not unlike that of our own day. It is present in Swift and in a different way in Pope; both were intimate friends and corres-pondents of Charles Caesar. This dissatisfaction began to take political form in the 1720s; it crystallised around the opposition to Walpole's control of government. Its literary expression is found in John Gay's *Beggar's Opera* (1728) and in Henry Fielding's political plays; it is immortalised in Fielding's *Jonathan Wild* (1743).

Caesar's correspondents in the 1720s reveal a common dislike of the contemporary structure of political power. Dan Dodson of Waltham wrote in support of Caesar's electioneering in 1722: 'I have a just sense of your capacity and ability to serve your Country at a time when it never more wanted the assistance of true Englishmen'. In a postscript he added 'let the odious names of whig and tory, high church and low church perish—now not them but England'. The Earl of Essex, seeking Caesar's support for Sir William Stanhope's candidature in the Hertford by-election of 1726, wrote: 'I will give him, I think, one of the greatest Caracters, when I say he is independant of a—Ministry, and scorns those little mean arts that are now the fashion'. Sarah Churchill, Duchess of Marlborough, wrote to Caesar during the 1727 election: 'And I beg you not to believe that 'tis anything of Party that is the Occasion of it. For I have long since been weary of everything of that nature, having seen by woful experience that the names of Whig and Tory have been made use of only to gratify the ambitious in both parties, without any regard to the true interest of the public'. In a moment of depression towards the end of the election campaign, W. R. Lytton of Knebworth wrote to Mrs Caesar: 'I am very sorry to see disaffection appear in the latter end of the day . . . I fear we shall distinguish a great many of that sort these few days to come, for I find several equivocating in relation to their promise, which makes me apt to think the Court is for the courtiers and that no luck attends, not theirs, but your Ladyship's friends'. After his electoral defeat in the 1734 general election, Caesar wrote to Shippen, the Tory leader in the Commons, arguing significantly that his defeat had been achieved by 'all manner of vile and infamous practices, one of which was making many well meaning Freeholders believe that if I was chosen I would now widely differ from my former behaviour in the House of Commons and be ready to prostitute my vote upon any occasion' [61].

It was not the mere tactics of local family alliances which drove the Walpole Whigs to support Caesar in 1727. Caesar represented a political force, upon which parliamentary careers could be made or broken. The independence and opposition-mindedness of Hertfordshire electors, which expressed itself in support for Caesar in the first part of the eighteenth century, lasted until the Reform Act of 1832. In the general election of 1754 Edward Gardiner, 'a Tory . . . enjoyed considerable support among the smaller freeholders and polled more than 1,000 plumpers: the independent element rallied strongly to his side', although the Peers and most of the country gentlemen were against him [62]. In 1761 T. P. Byde topped the poll, although 'much fewer of the gentry' voted for him than for the other two candidates: he 'had the support of the Dissenters and there seems to have been an element of popular support on his side' [63]. Oldfield commented on the County's politics in 1792: 'This County has the singular advantage of maintaining its independence, which it has neglected no opportunity of exerting' [64]. All the six M.P.s from Hertfordshire voted for the no-confidence motion which ended Lord North's government in 1782, for the censure motion which broke the younger Pitt in 1806, and for the Reform Bill in 1832. William Plumer of Blakesware, son of Caesar's Judas-like 'election agent', represented the County for thirty-nine years from 1768 to 1807. He was one of the small band of Whigs who remained faithful to Charles James Fox as national hysteria mounted during the war against revolutionary France. In his regular rôle as Teller for the Opposition motions against the war or wartime repression and for parliamentary and other reforms, he was a more consistent heir to Charles Caesar the Jacobite than might appear at first sight.

When Thomas Slingsby Duncombe captured one seat in the Borough of Hertford in 1826, and held it until the first election after the passing of the Reform Act, he was in fact repeating Caesar's successes. Duncombe, a wealthy Yorkshire manufacturer and an extreme Radical, first stood at a by-election in 1823 challenging the Salisbury family nominee. 'In 1824, there were forty-eight young men that raised an independent club, in order to get an independent member against the Marquis of Salisbury; we continued that club for a year and a half at our expense' [65]. This was the basis of Duncombe's local support. The campaign in 1826 was openly directed against 'an attempt on the parts of the County Gentry and the Old Family Interests, to prevent us from exercising our Freedom of Choice, and reduce us to the situation of Slaves to the capricious dictation of the surrounding Squirearchy' [66]. 'What are the Electors to think, when they see the most violent Tories, united with Whigs of high and Independent Principles, for the sole purpose of Enslaving this Borough?' [67].

> The M(arqui)s of H(atfiel)d, that quizzical prig,
> Sends us Byron, the wise; from E(ar)l C(owpe)r, the Whig,
> Comes Bulwer, with Helmets, and Autumns in Greece;
> He *flatters* and *weeps*, and SOLICITS FOR PEACE . . . [68].

In his speech at the poll Duncombe declared his intention was 'to ensure the independence of Hertford, and to rescue it from the fangs of the aristocracy' [69]. Charles Caesar would have found himself at home in this electoral contest and, after a moment's puzzlement no doubt, he might well have taken the Radical's side.

REFERENCES

1. G. M. Trevelyan, *England Under Queen Anne: Blenheim* (1930), p. 189.
2. Lionel M. Munby, 'The County Election of 1727', in *Hertfordshire Past and Present* no. 1 (1960).
3. Richard Pares, *King George III and the Politicians* (1953), p. 2.
4. G. M. Trevelyan, 'The Two-Party System in English Political History', reprinted in *An Autobiography and other Essays* (1949), especially pp. 185–6.
5. Lawrence Stone, 'The Electoral Influence of the Second Earl of Salisbury, 1614–68', in *English Historical Review* LXXI (1956), pp. 384 et seq.
6. Christopher Hill, *Economic Problems of the Church* (1956), p. 255.
7. Alfred Kingston, *Hertfordshire during the Great Civil War* (1894), pp. 16, 28, and Lewis Turnor, *History of the Ancient Town and Borough of Hertford* (1830), pp. 181, 284.
8. Thomas Edwards, *Gangraena* (1646).
9. *The Journal of George Fox*, ed. J. L. Nickalls (1952), p. 219.
10. *The Victoria History of the County of Hertford*, ed. William Page, vol. IV (1914), p. 356.
11. Lambeth MSS. Miscellanies, 639, quoted in W. Urwick, *Non-conformity in Hertfordshire* (1884), p. 537.
12. Lionel M. Munby, *Hertfordshire Population Statistics 1563–1801* (1964), pp. 24, 34.
13. Turnor, op. cit., p. 151.
14. *V.C.H.*, op. cit., vol. III (1912), p. 498.
15. Sir Henry Chauncy, *The Historical Antiquities of Hertfordshire* (1700), vol. I of 1826 edition, p. 496.
16. *The Case of the Antient Burrough of Hertford in Relation to their Electing of Burgesses to serve in Parliament*, p. 2—printed broadsheet, unsigned, of c. 1689 in Hertford County Record Office, Panshanger Papers, Box 30.
17. Stone, op. cit., p. 394.
18. *The Case of Sir Thomas Clarke, Petitioner against Charles Caesar, Esq.; for the Borough of Hertford*, p. 1—printed broadsheet of 1721 in H.C.R.O., Panshanger Papers, Box 46.
19. 'The humble Peticion of divers Inhabitants . . .', in Hertford Corporation Records, vol. 23, no. 149 and summarised in *The Journals of the House of Commons*, vol. XIII, p. 382, 7th March 1701.
20. Letter of James Wittewronge to his father, Sir John Wittewronge of Rothamsted, Harpenden, Herts., in Calendar of Wittewronge Papers, vol. I, pp. 92–3. (Copies in H.C.R.O. and in the Library of the Rothamsted Experimental Station.)
21. *V.C.H.*, op. cit., vol. II (1908), p. 40.
22. 'Some Observations . . .', reprinted in *The Harleian Miscellany* II (1809), p. 250. In his defence argument, when on trial, Spencer Cowper tried to suggest that he did not know Mrs Stout. This may

have been true. But Henry Stout's dealings with the Cowpers are confirmed by entries in the Hertford Friends Minute Book for 1692, in which occur scribbled accounts—'Received of Henry Stout for the A/C of William Cooper'.

23. Panshanger Papers, op. cit., Box 51.
24. *State Trials*, vol. XIII (1812), p. 1149; the trial is covered on pp. 1106–1249; a large number of pamphlets were published at the time arguing the case of the Stouts or the Cowpers.
25. 'Some Observations . . .', op. cit., pp. 255–6.
26. *State Trials*, op. cit., p. 1149.
27. Ibid., p. 1175.
28. 'The Hertford Letter', in *State Trials*, op. cit., p. 1214.
29. 'A Reply to the Hertford Letter', in ibid., p. 1235.
30. Panshanger Papers, op. cit., Box. 51.
31. Hertford Corporation Records, op. cit., vol. XXIII, no. 154, and see note 19.
32. Ibid., no. 222.
33. Ibid., nos. 247–50, 278.
34. Ibid., nos. 225, 228, 229, 243, and *The Journals of the House of Commons*, vol. XIII, p. 709.
35. *The Journals of the House of Commons*, vol. 15, pp. 54–5.
36. *The Parliamentary History of England*, vol. 6, 1702–14 (1810), pp. 509–10.
37. Historical Manuscripts Commission 13th Report, Appendix part II—*MSS. of the Duke of Portland*, vol. II, p. 194.
38. Ibid., 15th Report, Appendix part IV—*MSS. of the Duke of Portland*, vol. IV, p. 602.
39. Quoted by W. T. Morgan, 'Some Sidelights upon the General Election of 1715', in *Essays in Modern English History* in Honor of Wilbur Cortez Abbott (1941), p. 157.
40. Panshanger Papers, op. cit., Box 30.
41. *The Journals of the House of Commons*, vol. XVIII, pp. 136–7.
42. Arnold Lloyd, *Quaker Social History 1669–1738* (1950), p. 142.
43. K. G. Feiling, *The Second Tory Party 1714–1832* (1938), p. 19.
44. J. H. Plumb, *Sir Robert Walpole—the King's Minister* (1960), p. 214.
45. Historical Manuscripts Commission *Calendar of Stuart Papers*, vol. VI, p. 293.
46. Ibid., vol. III, pp. 530, 538.
47. Ibid., vol. IV, p. 301.
48. Ibid., vol. V, p. 556.
49. Ibid., vol. IV, p. 414.
50. Ibid., vol. VII, pp. 467, 518.
51. Ibid., vol. VII, pp. 13/14–173.
52. Manuscript Diary in the possession of J. K. Busby, Esq., who kindly allowed me to make extracts.
53. Op. cit., p. 98. But Plumb is quite wrong in attributing the Quaker vote in this election to Walpole's bidding. It is embarrassing that he

quotes as evidence an 'unpublished article' of my own, which in
fact argued the opposite case, developed in the present essay.

54. Cottrell Dormer Manuscripts at Rousham, Oxon. Caesar Letter-book, A 23.
55. Ibid., B 24.
56. Mrs Caesar's diary, op. cit.
57. C. D. Caesar Letter-book, B 16.
58. The resulting quarrel is revealed in Historical Manuscripts Commission *Report on the Manuscripts of the Earl of Verulam* (1906), pp. 61–72.
59. James Ferguson, *Robert Ferguson the Plotter* (1887), chaps. 13–19, and Maurice Ashley, *John Wildman* (1947), chap. 21.
60. R. L. Hine, *Hitchin Worthies* (1932), pp. 97–127.
61. C. D. Caesar Letter-books, A 24, B 5, B 14, E 20 and C 32.
62. *The History of Parliament: The House of Commons 1754–90*, ed. Sir Lewis Namier and John Brooke, vol. I, p. 306.
63. Ibid., vol. II, p. 166.
64. T. M. B. Oldfield, *History of the Boroughs of Great Britain* (1792), vol. II, p. 123.
65. *Report from the Select Committee on Hertford Borough* (1833), Parliamentary Papers IX (1833), p. 473.
66. Poster dated 2nd May 1826 and signed 'Glenarvon' in Old Election Papers 1790–1914 in Hertford Museum.
67. Poster dated 4th May 1826 and signed 'An Elector' in Hancock Papers in Hertford Museum.
68. Song 'Duncombe the True' in ibid.
69. *Hertfordshire Mercury*, 17th June 1826. For the politics of this period see F. A. Taunton, *Hertfordshire Politics from 1826–1832*, dissertation (1957) in H.C.R.O.–H.C.C. Records, 204/102/B.

Colchester in the Eighteenth Century

A. F. J. Brown

In 1700 Colchester was an industrial town, largely dependent on its cloth industry; apprenticeships to clothmaking were twice as many as those to all other trades put together. Defoe admired its businesslike atmosphere and found adjacent villages full of women spinning yarn for its weavers. A petition of 1699 foretold distress for twenty miles around if Colchester clothmaking collapsed, because spinners were always unemployed when looms were idle. North Essex farmers, too, enjoyed a major advantage in the 'quick consumption' of their produce by cloth-workers. Town and country were thus interdependent, with the cloth industry as the source of their moderate prosperity and large population.

Colchester made the New Draperies, bays and says, introduced to the town in 1571 by Dutch Protestants, who received powers to inspect at their Bay Hall all cloth of this kind and, by imposing exacting standards, gained for Colchester cloth an international reputation. Bays had a worsted warp and woollen weft, and says were similar except that they had a twill-weave. By 1700 the production of says was localised at Halstead and Sudbury, while Colchester specialised in bays, almost all of which went to Spain, Portugal and Latin America to be made into uniforms for monks, nuns, clergy and soldiers. The town probably produced more bays than the rest of Essex put together.

The clothiers organised the whole process of production from their offices, but without employing workers on their premises. They obtained the wool, some of it by sea from Boston, Rye and London, some by road from London and elsewhere. They sent it first to be cleaned by the beaters, a trade which in 1734 included twenty borough freemen. Next they passed it to the woolcombers, another large group who styled themselves 'gentlemen wool-combers' and held an annual public procession. The combed wool was then taken from the clothiers' warehouses to the spinners, who in 1700 numbered perhaps 10,000 and, apart from some 2,000 in Colchester, consisted of women and girls in the villages. The yarn, when collected, was given out to the weavers. Their total number was about 1,600, two-thirds living in Colchester and the rest in Dedham, Langham, Boxted, Ardleigh and other villages. Those in Colchester mostly lived in St Peter's, St Martin's and St Botolph's. They too held annual processions to honour their mythical Bishop Blaize, had 'club houses' at favourite inns like the Weavers' Arms, Bishop Blaize and Woolpack, elected their wardens under Borough supervision and constituted a powerful force in municipal affairs and town life generally. They included some women. The cloth, when woven, was fulled in water-mills; Chapman and André's Essex map of 1777 shows two such mills on Roman River, two on the Colne at Lexden and Cook's Hall, and three on the stream between Ardleigh and the Hythe. Next the bays were stretched on tenterhooks in tenterfields near Magdalen Green, below the Castle, east of Butt Road, west of Balkerne Lane and elsewhere. Finally they were roughed by teazles and their surface cut smooth by shearmen. The clothiers then sent the bales to London, usually undyed, sometimes by their own or public waggons, sometimes by sea; two hoys took cloth weekly from Wivenhoe and in 1725 some 20,000 pieces travelled this way, representing over a third of the annual output. The clothiers now waited for payment from their distant customers; they had financed the whole complicated process and therefore needed to possess more capital than any weaver could hope to acquire.

Almost no first-hand records of clothmaking businesses survive. One exception is the letter-book of a Colchester clothier which, though referring to transactions of a much later date, reveals a system of operation which had scarcely changed since 1700, and so may be used to illustrate standard eighteenth-century practice. The clothier, Isaac Boggis, operated from his house near the Castle, now called The Minories, and made at least a dozen different types of baize almost entirely for export. Employing a leading Colchester carrier, he sent regular consignments to his London factors, usually in response to their orders but partly to keep up stocks in their warehouses so as to meet unexpected demands. In one year he sent up some 1,700 pieces, perhaps comprising 70,000 yards and worth about £9,000. From the

L

proceeds he paid for wool by draughts on his factors and for labour with cash sent down weekly by waggon from his factors. His organisation for production was the standard one. He ordered wool from suppliers whom he met annually at Stourbridge Fair, near Cambridge, and obtained additional supplies as best he could. Much of it came from beyond London and was often deposited at the Bull, Leadenhall Street, for collection by his carrier. He sent it, when cleaned and combed, to his 'Spinning Houses', groups of spinners in certain villages who did regular work for him; doubtless with a view to low transport costs, these lay chiefly in one direction, westward from Colchester, in Belchamp Walter, Helions Bumpstead and Ashdon in Essex, and Hinxton and Abington in Cambridgeshire; he may also have employed spinners in the Kersey–Hadleigh district of Suffolk. He apparently used only Colchester weavers and had his cloth fulled at local mills.

Throughout the eighteenth century the industry declined and by 1815 was nearly extinct. Decline began with a crisis that arose in 1715 when the Spanish market had become glutted. Poor rates rose, unemployment increased and a hundred weavers left the town, while employers restricted production and attempted wage economies. Already in 1707 a by-law of the Dutch Bay Hall had made it illegal for anyone who had not served an apprenticeship to an existing baymaker to run a baymaking business; this helped to reduce the number of employers from about one hundred in 1707 to fifty-seven in 1715. In 1711 baymakers had to accept severe restrictions on their output of bays and consequently some of them seem to have introduced a lighter and cheaper type of cloth, perhaps intended for the home market. However the weavers complained that piece-rates were lower for this new product and that employers were trying to increase the proportion of apprentices in the industry and even to introduce non-apprenticed labour. They also alleged cases of truck and excessive fines at the Dutch Bay Hall for deficient work. This exploitation, they maintained, was facilitated by the decrease in the number of businesses and a general trend towards monopolistic control. In 1715 they petitioned for redress and then surrounded the Bay Hall demanding abolition of truck and of the compulsory unpaid August holiday, restrictions on new types of cloth, restoration of former piece-rates and cancellation of the 1707 by-law. Conceded the first three points, they struck work to gain the last two and forcibly released some arrested comrades. Their resolution impressed the Mayor who persuaded the Bay Hall governors to give in, whereupon the workers dispersed. Even the arrival of dragoons was not used to suppress the rebels, but the issue was taken to the Privy Council which upheld the new piece-rates and the Bay Hall's right to make the by-laws of 1707 and 1711. So the weavers turned to Parliament, which decided that 'the poor weavers had been most greviously oppressed' through the 1707 by-law and therefore annulled that decision [1].

The discouraging economic circumstances, in which the 1715 struggle took place, dominated the industry with more or less intensity throughout the century. The only alleviation occurred in the months following the end of each war, when communications with the Spanish market were re-opened. Thus in 1729, with the prospect of peace with Spain, the Corporation clerk reported that 'abundance of looms are standing still for want of hands'. After the Seven Years War prosperity returned briefly and the Rev. Philip Morant, in the second edition of his *History of Colchester*, expressed guarded optimism about the prospects. Again, when the American War ended, joyful weavers paraded the streets and were soon so busy that there was no unemployed man in the town. Yet these booms were short-lived in comparison with the slumps. Prolonged hostilities against Spain early in the century shattered economic confidence. Baymakers failed to pay their rates, went bankrupt or left the industry. Weavers migrated and many sons entered other trades. The Dutch community, already disintegrating, was formally disbanded in 1728. A petition asked Parliament for assistance 'before it is too late'. In the 1740s Morant wrote of the previous period as one of economic breakdown which had left the town shattered and impotent. In the next major collapse of the early 1760s several bankruptcies occurred, which re-emphasised that a general decline was afflicting the industry; for some of the bankrupts were not men of small resources, such as had failed in the 1715–40 period, but substantial manufacturers and eminent citizens, including several ex-Mayors. From then onwards deterioration proceeded almost without interruption. In one month of 1772 three firms suspended payments. Apprenticeships to cloth fell sharply and weavers migrated in even larger numbers. Fulling-mills turned exclusively to corn-milling; an advertisement for Cook's Hall mill at West Bergholt stressed that, though recently re-equipped for fulling, it could now advantageously be used for full-time flour-milling. In 1782–3 the American War caused the cessation of all cloth-carrying traffic to London. The Baptist Meeting's records noted 'many nearly starving for want of employment to earn bread . . . the times are awful beyond expression'. The short boom of 1784–5 was followed by a new depression, which, ominously, was not caused by any loss of contact with the Spanish market. One leading clothier was left with 1,173 bays in his Colchester warehouse and a further 392 unsold in a London warehouse and, as these remained on his hands for many months, he reduced his labour force to a mere eighteen weavers. There was now manifestly no truth in the assertion, made in a Directory of 1793, that 'the town chiefly subsists by the trade of making bays'. The Napoleonic Wars virtually extinguished the industry, almost halting production and closing several businesses. The short peace of 1802 brought the surviving weavers out in a procession with banners proclaiming 'May The Bay Trade Flourish', but the resumption of war reduced the number of firms to four in 1811 and to two in 1815. One of the latter continued into the 1830s and, on its cessation, the industry was completely at an end.

The decline is reflected in Borough poll-books which record the voting of freemen at Parliamentary elections:

	Clothiers	Roughers	Weavers	Woolcombers
1768	24	36	224	47
1790	10	5	115	31
1797	4	4	39	4
1820	2	—	34	3
1830	1	—	11	3

Of the resident freemen, clothworkers comprised about a half in 1768, a quarter in 1790 and a ninth in 1797.

Estimates of the total number of weavers in the Colchester district show a similar decline:

1707	1,600
1715	1,500
1784	500
1807	150

Colchester in the Eighteenth Century

Of the 150 reported in 1807 some were certainly unemployed, as the poor law accounts of St. Botolph's and other parishes show.

The number of businesses also declined, but their size increased, as the following estimates show:

	Clothiers	Weavers	Average number of weavers per firm
1707	100	1,600	16
1715	57	1,500	26
1768	25	700	28
1790	10	400	40

The number of woolcombers and spinners employed by each clothier also rose, since the fly-shuttle, despite the alleged opposition of Colchester weavers to its introduction, was apparently soon in use and causing an increase in the amount of yarn required by each weaver. Thus in a declining industry the individual clothier operated on a larger scale. Some acquired considerable property. Michael Hills, besides his own house, owned land and buildings in Colchester and several parts of Essex. Thomas Wilshire in 1772 owned six houses at Colchester, farms at Marks Tey, West Mersea, Abberton, Peldon and Aldham, as well as property at Stebbing, while James Robjent owned land within Colchester and a large house at the foot of North Hill with fifteen adjacent cottages, besides other house property. M. R. Hills created Colne Park in Colne Engaine and several others moved into genteel county society. Surviving clothiers were thus men of substance and social ambition, who remained influential even when their industry was visibly failing.

The cause of the industry's decline needs longer discussion than can be undertaken here. What was not the cause is easier to discover than what was. Lack of coal did not prevent Colchester clothiers from using steam-driven machinery, because, as the preceding pages make clear, decline was far advanced before the first power looms were used to weave wool anywhere in Britain. The immediate cause of decline was undoubtedly the frequent interruption of trade with Spain and Portugal which prevented the marketing of the bays which were the town's only type of product. This specialisation, while giving pre-eminence in this branch of the industry, also made Colchester dangerously vulnerable. Why did Colchester clothiers fail to make other kinds of cloth? That it was partly due to the weavers' opposition is suggested by their attitude in the troubled year of 1715. But why thereafter did clothiers apparently abandon further attempts to escape from fatal dependence on a single product? Why did they not seek a share of the expanding home market? Instead, some abandoned baymaking altogether or saw their own businesses fail in the general collapse. Presumably the clothiers' attitudes and aspirations were such as to discourage experiment, innovation or enterprise. The industry compared badly in security and reputation with farming, land-ownership, commerce or moneyed gentility, and in Colchester society of 1750–1800 such considerations as these were not light ones.

THE TOWN IN 1700–50

In 1700 the town was dominated by the cloth industry, not only economically but in public affairs generally. In the Borough Corporation clothiers constituted a powerful group who used their power to protect their interests. Exact figures for 1700 are unobtainable, but in 1740 at least a dozen of them belonged to the so-called Select Body which governed town affairs. Though clothiers usually spoke for themselves on matters affecting their industry, on at least three important occasions at this time the Corporation itself took the lead in asking Parliament for measures of relief. As in Braintree's Select Vestry, so in Colchester Corporation the businesslike methods of the clothiers were reproduced in its administrative work. Its Court dealt with the community's daily problems, the Justices going out in person to inspect the town for cleanliness and once fining surveyors of five parishes for neglected roads. They licensed approved alehouses and suppressed illegal ones, protected apprentices from harsh masters and masters from misbehaviour by apprentices, condemned unwholesome meat, protected footpaths, punished drunkenness, profanity and sabbath-breaking, and generally controlled daily life. Such was the Corporation's vigour that in 1698 it virtually centralised poor relief, when it obtained an Act to establish a Workhouse Corporation. This body built and administered a municipal workhouse, drawing considerable income from the inmates' spinning, and distributed outdoor relief competently and with some humanity. Another sphere of municipal initiative was the improvement of the Colne. In 1698, the year which saw the centralisation of poor relief, the Corporation obtained power to tax certain goods passing through the Hythe and to spend the proceeds on river facilities. It proceeded to clear and deepen the channel below Colchester so thoroughly that it had to borrow a large sum to supplement the river duties. In 1719 it petitioned successfully for the Act's renewal, though Parliament reconstituted the river authority to include, in addition to the Corporation representatives, interested individuals like Sir Isaac Rebow, two of the Martin family which owned property on the Doniland side of the river, and several clothiers from the town. The new commissioners paid off the debt, built up a large reserve and yet could afford to construct a large lock about half a mile below Hythe Bridge, which facilitated navigation and kept the channel clean by periodic releases of water.

For all its workaday atmosphere the town impressed visitors. Defoe saw 'the streets fair and beautiful . . . abundance of very good and well-built houses in it'. Celia Fiennes also liked the streets and the broad pavements protected from traffic by rows of posts, though she thought the houses old-fashioned. Private benefactors added to the amenities. Joseph Thurston and Sir Isaac Rebow helped rebuild St Mary's-at-the-Wall and the latter presented to the town, as a promenade, the lane which still bears his name. In 1707 Alderman John Potter constructed a public water supply. In 1709 some churchmen started the Blue-coats School for poor boys and girls, acquired a schoolhouse and within a year were receiving sufficient subscriptions to give 150 pupils a free education. Arthur Winsley's bequest of almshouses in 1726 was outstanding among a number of other benefactions. With these and with its Grammar School, churches and Noncon-formist chapels, Colchester seemed to Defoe, who knew it quite well, to be a well-provided and self-sufficient town. Yet it was not an isolated community. There was continuous movement of rich and poor in and out of the town, a process facilitated by a system of communications already well used by the cloth trade, commerce and agriculture. Defoe noted the volume of agricultural traffic from East Anglia passing through the town. Regular carriers travelled to London and a few stage-coaches ran through to Harwich or London along a road which Parliament took special measures to maintain. Two or three hoys sailed weekly to London with cloth, farm produce and fish, while coal came in from the

North-east and chalk from Kent. On the average two ships monthly came in from abroad, with timber from Norway, iron from Sweden, cork from Portugal, and toys, paper and 'Spaw water' from Holland. Oysters were exported to Dieppe and Dunkirk, wheat to Stockholm and cloth to Rotterdam. Other international connexions were the town's Dutch and French Protestant communities. The most important link with Europe was the indirect one provided by the cloth trade with Lisbon, and Parliamentary petitions from Colchester show acute awareness of how international affairs were affecting the town's chief industry.

The slump of the early decades shattered not only the cloth trade but the town's confidence in itself and its future. The Exchange, centrally situated at the top of North Hill and once the focus of the industry's daily business, was described by Morant in the 1740s as silent and deserted. The Dutch community had been disbanded, houses were being demolished or left empty, and population seemed to be falling, an impression which contemporary parish registers fully confirm. In the prevailing despondency the town offered little resistance when in 1742 its Borough Charter was withdrawn because of electoral corruption, the Corporation disbanded and the centralised Poor Law administration ended. In the absence of effective authority householders withheld rates and let the road outside their frontages deteriorate. The borough's oyster fisheries were freely plundered. The work of the River Commission stopped, its income accumulated and maintenance ceased. By 1749 the lock was inoperative, the river was choked and shallow, banks were slipping into the waterway, shoals and obstructive points were forming. Traders thus found an excuse to withhold their dues and there was no Borough Court to compel them. It was fortunate that the River authority of 1719 had included non-Corporation members. For in 1749 these remained as the nucleus of a new governing body, which, with additional revenue, succeeded in repairing the channel and other facilities sufficiently to permit the carriage of farm produce and coal, from the distribution of which Colchester was soon to draw an increasing part of its livelihood. The only other bodies to display the vigour now needed were the sixteen parish vestries, which replaced the disbanded Workhouse Corporation as poor law authorities. Manned by wider circles of the ratepaying public than the Select Body of the former Corporation, they resumed an active existence not terminated until the New Poor Law of 1834. Otherwise civic leaders showed apathy and negligence. John Potter's water supply was allowed to decay, the Grammar School entered one of its least glorious periods, and the town's newspaper, *Pilborough's Journal*, ceased publication. The chief townsmen did little to recover Borough status, the eventual restoration of which was due more to the persistence of a Charter Club of humbler freemen. Weavers implied that employers preferred the continued absence of an authority which, through its Court, might have helped to maintain wage-rates. When Morant wrote in the 1740s, his pessimism aptly reflected the town's loss of confidence and initiative.

RECOVERY, 1750–75

Even as Morant wrote, the first indications appeared of one new trend that was to give the town reason for continued existence. The subscribers to his *History of Colchester* included men whose patronage of literature was one facet of a widening gentility. Morant noted not only Sir Isaac Rebow's gift to the town of Sir Isaac's Walk, but also St Mary's churchyard footpaths, which 'being the best walks about the whole town, are much resorted to by people of the best fashion'. Another glimpse of this new trend is provided by two Prospects of Colchester, panoramic views which gave prominence to features of the town's landscape considered elegant or creditable. In a Prospect of 1724 there was depicted a single couple, fashionably dressed but inconspicuous against the background of civic buildings, windmills and, in two places, sturdy tenterhooks for stretching woollen cloth. The Prospect of 1741, though in several ways similar, ignores the town's great industry and gives prominence to a party of gentlefolk promenading against a background of churches and other antique buildings. The bay trade is only mentioned in a footnote and economic life is represented by ships and warehouses at the Hythe and windmills stretching away towards Mersea. Here is foreshadowed the Colchester of the future, a fashionable centre made eligible by its antiquities and a market-town serving the adjacent countryside and distributing farm produce by sea, but with its disagreeable textile industry offering nothing that its new gentility was proud to display. Morant, describing the decline of cloth, wrote that 'some inconsiderate persons have been wishing that it was entirely out of the place' and he warned that Colchester would gain more from its continuation than from retail shops, ministering to 'luxury and pride'.

In 1750–75 economic prospects brightened. Cloth, though declining generally, remained the greatest source of employment, giving work to some 3,000 weavers, spinners and others. More important was the progress in Essex farming which was to bring prosperity to landowners and farmers, provide employment for the fast-growing rural population and so create more custom for Colchester's market-town services. Market-days became more important to the town, which twice in mid-century advertised in the press during smallpox epidemics to assure country people that it was safe to attend them. Borough poll-books show that weavers remained quite the largest group among the freemen, but other trades were becoming prominent, like millers, maltsters, wigmakers, clockmakers, cutlers, bookbinders, booksellers, clerks, gardeners and coachmen. Tailoring, leatherwork and metalwork were also well represented, but forty-one building workers and forty-two shoemakers were the largest non-textile groups. Though population was stagnant, the building trade was active, extending, rebuilding or replacing private and commercial premises, farm-houses and farm buildings; in 1765 no less than seventeen master carpenters signed an advertisement offering steady work to three or four pairs of sawyers. The expansion of shoemaking, which was presumably due to increased demand from the countryside, proceeded so fast that shoemakers were soon to be the first Colchester trade outside textiles to form a union. Prospects were encouraging enough to attract newcomers to the town, such as the London tinplate worker who set up near the Castle and the leather-stay maker from Diss who took a workshop in Bear Lane.

No new industry adequately replaced that of cloth, but minor market-town industries now grew in importance. Milling expanded as cereal output increased and, though village mills, so far from disappearing, claimed their share of the increasing work, at Colchester new windmills were built and watermills increased their capacity. Malting became an important minor occupation, as demand increased from the growing rural population and from London breweries. In all parts of Colchester substantial concerns were now at work, some attached to breweries, others run as separate undertakings; one adjoining a Crouch Street distillery had a particularly large capacity. However the industry was moving to the Hythe, where in 1756 one large malting was advertised as 'convenient for shipping to London, Holland and elsewhere'. In the years following, the Hythe maltings were enlarged. One could handle 100 quarters of barley weekly in its three kilns and send malt from its own wharf, 'whence the freight of malt (to London) is only 10d a quarter'; with its adjoining brick-kiln, two houses and three acres of land, it formed a comfortable business. Another comprised a four-storey building, 90 by 18 ft., and, besides its main London trade, sold 700 quarters a year locally. Brewing also grew from the small concerns referred to in Borough records around 1700 to fewer but larger businesses, like that in St Botolph Street which, besides its large brewery, owned two maltings and seven inns; two of its proprietors rose to prominent positions in municipal and public life. From a Priory Street brewery one lady acquired a fortune which financed the building of Greyfriars, one of the most pleasant buildings of this time. Other industrial concerns included three or four distilleries, a ropery, a soapworks, a pottery, two extensive tanneries and so large a candle factory in the High Street that, when damaged by fire, it sustained a loss of £1,000.

The most striking evidence of Colchester's new importance as a market-town was the increase of shops along her main streets. These included the luxury shops which Morant deplored, and their dependence on the patronage of affluent rural customers was increasingly emphasised by their frequent advertisements in the Essex and Suffolk papers. Some concerns were quite large, such as Esther Courtney's at Headgate, where she employed women making and selling muffs, trimmings and artificial flowers. Other shopkeepers sold not only their own manufactures but goods obtained from travelling salesmen or London wholesalers. Artisans were now opening their own retail shops on the main streets in which to sell both their own products and goods made elsewhere, such as the carpenter who in 1756 sold bureaux, chairs and tables from his workshop and also glassware and china, and the saddler near The Cups who sold whips, bridles, portmanteaux, silk caps, coaches and chaises. A Colchester tailor in 1766 was selling, besides his own products, the 'latest clothes' from London. London fashion was influencing local taste and Londoners moved to Colchester to sell goods allegedly better than 'those of the same sort made by ignorant workmen in the country', while local shops countered with offers of articles 'as neat and as cheap as in London'. Some Colchester businesses employed London craftsmen and advertised this in the press and increasingly shops obtained large supplies regularly from London wholesalers. It was also possible to buy Staffordshire pottery or Spa water from Germany, Bath, Hotwells and Scarborough.

Aware of the importance of rural customers, some enterprising shopkeepers and artisans were not content with the trade that came on market-day, but sought out new custom by travelling around the country districts. Once every three weeks a staymaker left his shop at Scheregate to measure customers at the Ipswich Admiral's Head and the Chelmsford Ship and he soon added a rural circuit which took him to inns at Long Melford, Sudbury, Bures, Boxford, Hadleigh, Manningtree, Harwich, Tolleshunt Darcy, Tollesbury and Maldon. He would fit ladies in their own homes within twenty miles and supply rural shops with stays which were 'better goods and as cheap as in London'. A rival staymaker, also from a shop at Scheregate, travelled the Tendring Hundred, calling on customers and hiring fitting-rooms at inns in Brightlingsea, St Osyth and Great Bentley. He also visited Wood-bridge and, on the death of a staymaker at Wivenhoe, established a branch of his business there. A tailor waited on gentlemen within seven miles to fit them with clothes 'as fashionable and compleat as in London'. Other Colchester businesses supplied village shops, one cheesemonger advertising that 'country shopkeepers may be served with butter, cheese and sope, wholesale or retail'. A mercer opposite the Moot Hall also supplied village shopkeepers, as well as sending patterns to individual rural customers.

Professional services expanded less rapidly than did shop-keeping. However the developing North Essex countryside required the aid of more lawyers, and this profession now became very prominent, occupying some of the best of the new houses and playing a considerable part in public life. Some became in effect estate agents, a lucrative occupation in these years of rural change and progress, and others sold insurance. Newspaper advertisements show several auctioneers at work in the town. A surveyor and a cartographer joined forces in 1766 to map farms and estates. Private schools for both boys and girls, often of a pretentious character, sought the patronage of the well-to-do of town and country. Doctors also prospered. There were at least ten of them in 1753 and, with an expanding rural population and more parishes ready to pay a yearly sum for the care of their paupers, these found their practices growing quite lucrative. Some improved their incomes by offering inoculation against smallpox, at first in face of local anxiety and opposition. One charged three guineas for gentlefolk and two guineas for their servants at his Milend hospital and later claimed to have inoculated 3,000 patients without killing one of them; another advertised that he had a hundred patients currently under treatment in their own homes.

Another important development was the increase in road traffic through the town. Before 1750 a few stage-coaches served Colchester. The earliest had been the one linking London with the Harwich packet-boats, which in 1711 was running twice weekly and stopped overnight at Witham. In 1732 a coach ran from Colchester White Hart to London and by 1748 this had become a daily service. Since the Harwich coach was also running daily and another came through from Ipswich, Colchester in 1750 had the beginnings of a passenger service. Steady expansion followed, as roads improved, population grew, rural affluence increased and ever more Londoners moved into Essex and Suffolk. A second coach ran from Colchester and a fast Machine was also provided. From Harwich a Fly was running and other vehicles ran daily from Ipswich and Norwich. Vehicles could also be hired privately. From about 1750 post-chaise travel was promoted by Colchester innkeepers in co-operation with other inns along the route to London, where fresh horses were kept available for the next stage of the journey. Thus the King's Head operated a joint service with Witham Blue Posts, Ingatestone Red Lion and Romford Dolphin. Fares were high, however. In the 1760s the Colchester stagecoach charged 8s. inside and 5s. outside for a single to London, while the Post-Coach cost 12s. 6d. Post-chaise hire was as much as 9d. a mile in 1759 and fell only to 6d. a mile as competition developed. Poorer people therefore used the stage-waggons and other carriers' vehicles, which had plied between the town and London since the late seventeenth century but which from about 1750 so increased the frequency of their service that at least six vehicles made the journey weekly. The Red Lion, for instance, operated a weekly cart which took new horses at stages along the route. A vehicle from the Three Black Nags carried passengers to London for 5s. 'commodiously and dry'. By 1767 Colchester stage-waggons took only eighteen hours for the journey and the Ipswich Caravan only thirteen hours from the Colchester George to Aldgate. Meanwhile private transport by horse or vehicle was increasing, and so was the amount of agricultural produce sent to London from Suffolk, Norfolk and Essex. As Colchester grew into a large market-town, its local communications with nearby villages expanded also. The whole of this increasing traffic had most important social consequences, but its economic advantages were considerable too. When Thomas Stevens offered his waggon business for sale in 1766, he could claim to have made his fortune, as well as educating his children 'handsomely'. Blacksmiths, wheelwrights, saddlers and suppliers of fodder were among other trades to benefit and the greatest beneficiaries of all were the town's innkeepers.

Colchester's inns, once the resort of clothmakers, now changed their style to suit new customers. Their first concern was with farmers, their wives and other country people who in growing numbers and with more to spend used the inns for refreshment, entertainment or business on market-days, at fairs and whenever occasion brought them into town. Travellers by public coach or private vehicle now provided additional revenue. The fashionable inns benefited most; the King's Head on the West side of Head Street, with its 'Great Room' used for meetings of the Charter Club or the Turnpike Trustees, with its regular Assemblies and its fresh venison for sale every Tuesday; the White Hart at the south-west end of the High Street, 'new, elegant, large, . . . in the great road to Harwich', with over thirty beds and stabling for sixty horses, with Harwich and London coaches calling daily; the Three Crowns near the corn market, which specialised in letting horses and vehicles to private travellers; the Three Cups, which had yet to carry out the elegant extensions that gave it prominence towards 1800 but which already worked profitably in public and private transport and catered for the three-day race-meeting on Milend Heath. Inns were greatly improved. Thus in 1756 the White Hart was brickfronted, its windows sashed, its chief rooms 'genteelly fitted up with wainscott', its sleeping and stable accommodation enlarged. Other inns meanwhile were serving humbler customers. At the Maid's Head at Headgate waggoners could use the steelyard at 1s. a time, while enjoying a free quart of beer, and the Castle on North Hill offered pasture for animals on their way to Smithfield or Colchester market.

The economic developments of the preceding half-century had meanwhile widened social divisions. In 1700 the gentry of the town and neighbouring countryside had constituted a select class, to which the richer clothiers had been admitted. Many smaller clothiers, however, were little removed economically and socially from the mass of weavers, while in other trades businesses were even smaller and movements from journeyman to master not difficult, so that among nine-tenths of the population there was little rigid class division. By 1750–75 the emergence of a few large clothiers, the elimination of small clothmaking concerns, the growth of market-town industries, of commerce and of luxury trades, the increasing number of prosperous farmers, the movement of well-to-do London families into the district, and the development of the professions, all helped to enlarge a middle social group, aspiring to the society of their superiors and sharply distinguishing themselves from the working population. Theirs were many of the new brick or newly brickfronted houses that now and for the rest of the century made their appearance in almost every part of the town and in nearby villages. Rate-books and newspaper advertisements reveal the identity of their occupants. The surviving clothiers were prominent among them: Michael Hills, for instance, who took the chair at meetings of the trade, and Thomas Boggis who in 1776 built the house now called the Minories at the top of East Hill. They also included lawyers, doctors, clergymen in rebuilt parsonages, leisured people of wealth, merchants, builders and, later, small industrialists and some shopkeepers. Fashions in domestic architecture and decoration, as well as in garden layout, reached Colchester quite quickly and Colchester builders in their turn are found moving up to London. Characteristic of the new houses of this period was one next to the Three Cups on the north of the High Street, built shortly before 1769, possibly by a surgeon. Brickfronted, with sash windows, it had a handsome frontispiece, a hall with wainscotted parlours on either side, a dining room 'wainscotted in the newest taste . . . with an elegant chimney piece', and six other rooms on the ground floor. Attached were a brewhouse, stable and coachhouse. A large walled garden contained fruit trees, a summer house and a grotto with 'a curious piece of old pavement', and there was 'a pretty prospect from the backside'. These features, and others in the latest fashion, were to be found, and are often still to be seen, in dozens of houses and farmhouses in the town and rural district.

In Colchester the elegance of the new houses was set amid dismal poverty and mean cottages. A few yards from some of the finest houses were noisome courts, surrounded by overcrowded dwellings, often sharing a single wash-house and privy. Disease was prevalent and burials exceeded baptisms, especially in poorer parishes, as the Registers make clear. Yet the well-to-do did not move away to secluded suburbs and there was little expansion beyond the old area of the town. In the nearest part of Crouch Street there was some development, but Lexden Road was still praised for its rural seclusion. Clothiers and other men of business lived next to their place of work. When in the 1760s a baymaker brickfronted his St John Street house and put in sash windows, he retained at the back his wool chambers and warehouses, which, as was normal, were approached by a carriageway from the road. As late as the 1790s the workshops and warehouses of William Argent's cloth business adjoined his North Hill 'mansion', as did those of Benjamin Hall on East Hill. Clothiers lived next to their businesses possibly because to move might invite even more burglaries than they suffered already. Gentlemen not gainfully employed may well have decided not to move out of town because here they enjoyed the amenities of urban life as well as the spaciousness of the large gardens and pleasant prospects which were quite attainable in eighteenth-century Colchester. Below Greyfriars the Rector of Easthorpe made good use of the ample room available, while across the road at East Hill House George Wegg demolished nine cottages to secure the scope he wanted. In several other parts within the Roman walls there were areas without housing, such as that between Head Street and Balkerne Lane, where lay St Mary's churchyard with its promenade, a flower nursery, two bowling-greens and a garden.

Pleasant houses, elegant shops and smarter inns facilitated Colchester's growth into a social centre of some liveliness and gentility. Better transport kept it in closer contact with London influences and fashions. Already in 1762 a Colchester house was put on sale in London with the following recommendation: 'Colchester is a fine market town and a post goes and comes every day; a stage coach and machine the same; a waggon and packet every week'. A new gaiety was observable among the well-to-do. The focus of social life were the Assembly Balls, now held more frequently and on a grander scale than in the 1730s when only the King's Head had held them quarterly at 2s. 6d. In the 1750s the same inn held one a month at 5s., usually at full moon so that rural patrons could attend. In 1758 it was holding additional balls and concerts, while the White Hart also advertised monthly concerts, followed by a ball. Another amenity was the new theatre. From the 1740s the Norwich Company of Comedians had visited Colchester, but, lacking their own building, they performed at the Moot Hall, offering frequent changes of programme to secure the attendance of their then limited audience on as many nights as possible; patrons included on one occasion the gentlefolk of Wivenhoe Hall and on another the local Hunt. In 1764 the Norwich Company ventured to build a permanent theatre behind the Moot Hall, the simple elegance of which impressed the local newspaper, though to a French visitor it was 'one of the most pitiable places I have ever seen', with rough seating, indifferent decoration and poor performances [2]. It held 200 and took about £18 from a full attendance. Support came from gentry and farmers, from Colchester groups like the Freemasons and the Blue Coat School trustees, and from the King's Head Club which united gentlemen from town and country. Shakespeare and Sheridan were performed, and other plays included Farquhar's *The Beaux' Stratagem* with which the new theatre opened, *Love in a Sack*, and *Woman is a Riddle*. The theatre season usually coincided with the fashionable St Dennis' Fair in October, when there were also public breakfasts with up to 200 guests, balls and similar diversions. Other genteel entertainments included Scholars' Balls, where young people practised steps learnt from local dancing instructors before attending the adult Assemblies. Interest in music was growing, with frequent concerts at two of the inns and a performance at St Peter's of the *Messiah* by leading artists from London and Cambridge and the boys of St Paul's choir. There were shows of auriculas at the Castle Inn on North Hill and at the Angel, while Lexden Mill held displays of hyacinths, polyanthi and tulips, which were open 'not to all the meaner sort of people, but only to such of them as love flowers, can behave civilly and come without dogs'. This interest in flowers was fostered by the opening on the west of Head Street of a 'New Flower Garden', while from a nursery on East Hill peach, apricot and nectarine trees, mulberries and evergreens could be bought. There was a wider interest in polite learning, shown by the issue of a second edition of Morant's *History*, a course of nine lectures on Electricity and Astronomy at a fee of 10s. 6d., some interest in the discovery of Roman mosaics, the foundation of the Castle Book-club and the success of two, possibly three, circulating libraries which included much first-class literature alongside romantic novels. Colchester had its men of learning and taste. Besides Morant there was his successor at St Mary's, Thomas Twining, translator of Aristotle's *Poetics*; the historian, Benjamin Strutt; the Rev. Nathaniel Forster, a man of benevolence and scholarship who nevertheless pamphleteered with vigour on politics, economics and education; William Cole, well-informed master of the Nonconformist Greencoats School in Priory Street; James Deane, the talented architect who also supplied Morant's illustrations; and Dr Samuel Parr, master of the Grammar School for two most successful years.

Organised sport was gaining popularity. Well-to-do supporters gave the £50 Town Plate for the annual races on Milend Heath. Cricket, increasingly popular from 1750, was played not by all classes, but apparently by young men of the middle classes and the farming community. There was a shortlived Colchester club, but mostly matches were promoted by inns like the Fencers in Maidenburgh Street or the Cock and Pye on North Hill and played on East Donyland, Abberton and Lexden heaths, in King's Meadow below the Castle, or in Hythe Meadow. At first players' stakes were low, sufficient to give the winners a pair of gloves each or 'a fashionable hat', but forty-four guineas were involved by 1777. The poor rarely played, but thronged to watch and bet, so that matches were often abruptly ended amid recriminations which might not cease when teams parted. Colchester players were denounced in the press both by Nayland and Harwich opponents. Organised hunting, not yet the popular sport that it was to become later, was chiefly provided by the Lexden 'subscription pack of hounds'.

A FASHIONABLE MARKET-TOWN, 1775–1815

The economic developments, which had helped to rescue the town after 1750, gathered pace in 1775–1815. The cloth trade pursued its fluctuating, yet ever downward, course, but agricultural output was increasing fast and bringing new trade to Colchester's mills, maltings, shops and workshops. The growing volume of business was reflected in the advertisement columns of the press and in the establishment of two banks which attracted deposits from gentry, farmers and tradesmen. A 1784 trade directory showed eight clothiers still in business, but these were outnumbered by thirteen lawyers, ten drapers and thirty shopkeepers; also represented were industries using agricultural products, brewing, distilling, milling and malting, while cornmerchants, a fellmonger and a woolstapler further emphasised Colchester's increasing dependence on her market-town functions. A new directory of 1791 still recorded a few baymakers, but showed an even greater preponderance of non-textile occupations in the sixty-five shops, some of them of a specialist nature, two banks, twenty-one non-textile industrial establishments and 133 artisan workshops. Lawyers had increased to seventeen and there were twelve merchants, a majority of them at the Hythe. A directory of 1811 showed the cloth-trade as almost extinct and Colchester as a market-town serving the surrounding countryside.

The increasingly commercial character of Colchester's economy was reflected in the development of the Hythe. Wheat shipments had risen from some 10,000 quarters in 1700 to 80,000 by 1810 and coal imports from 4,500 tons in 1725 to 9,000 in 1749 and 23,000 in the early nineteenth century. Commercial and industrial establishments of all kinds at the Hythe increased from nine in 1761 to twenty-nine in 1805 and forty in 1809. These included eight granaries, nine large coalyards, enlarged and modernised maltings, a foundry, a shipyard building fishing-boats and colliers for local purchasers, and a lime-kiln. One man held the salt-works situated opposite Hythe Hill, with its three boiling-pans, cinder and liquor houses, salt-bins and store-houses, and he also kept a retail shop in Colchester, ran a coalyard and granary, and owned three vessels in the coastal trade. Several other merchants plied more than one trade. The lime-manufacturer was also a coal-merchant. The shipbuilder also imported coal, made coke in his ovens, dealt in corn and timber, owned the Rising Sun and cultivated a four-acre field. This expansion attracted population to the Hythe and led to new building there at a time when Colchester itself remained generally within its existing limits.

The Napoleonic Wars completed the economic transformation, by closing the Spanish market to the expiring cloth industry and bringing thousands of troops to the town and its vicinity. Farmers and market-gardeners prospered, and they, together with the military, provided valuable custom for Colchester's shopkeepers, artisans and professional men, replacing the customers lost by the collapse of cloth. Arthur Young thought that the presence of the troops had averted economic disaster. Population was at last rising, and soldiers and their families occupied every vacant house, causing rents to rise, while new buildings, domestic and commercial, were to be seen all over the town but especially near the barracks.

The town meanwhile was acquiring new amenities consistent with its growing gentility. Schools for Young Ladies and Young Gentlemen, already thriving, after 1775 increased in number, some being of poor standard but a few offering fair value for their not inconsiderable fees; vacancies at Thomas White's Academy were so sought after that he could require from parents evidence of their respectability. A registry for servants opened in 1778. Shops looked more attractive; a German described them as:

the fine shops, which jut out at both sides of the front doors like big, broad oriels, having fine, large window-panes, behind which wares are displayed, . . . far more elegant than those in Paris [3].

Streets became safer and brighter when the Lighting Commission erected 200 lamps on tall oak poles. Another visitor recorded:

As our stay was but short, I shall only remark
That the shops blazed with light, though the evening was dark.
The lamps were so splendid, the street was so wide,
It resembled a taking a peep at Cheapside [4].

The coach service had further improved. On a Monday, for instance, passengers for London could catch either the Norwich or the Yarmouth mail-coach at midnight at the Fleece, the Colchester Stage at the Cups or the New Machine at the George at 7 a.m., the Colchester Coach at the Cups or the Colchester Post-Coach at the King's Arms at 9 a.m., besides two Ipswich, two Harwich or one Woodbridge coach at other times. They could travel to Yarmouth, Woodbridge, Ipswich, Norwich and intermediate places when these coaches made their return journeys. Colchester also became linked by coach with Nayland, Hadleigh,

Braintree, Bury St Edmunds, Newmarket and Cambridge. Consequently Londoners visited friends in north Essex more frequently, while Colchester people attended the theatre and other entertainments in London. London papers and journals were delivered in Colchester by coach. All this enabled middle-class society to follow current fashion, so that in drama, literature, dancing, music, domestic architecture, interior decoration or the planning of gardens Colchester was not much behind the times.

Balls, concerts and the theatre drew increasing attendances. Of St Dennis' Fair in 1783 an observer wrote:

> Our town has not wore such a face of business and pleasure for many years; the assemblies and theatre have been crowded; last night I went to see the *School for Scandal*, when I was enchanted with the splendid appearance of near 200 ladies in full dress, among whom were ladies Smyth and Affleck and many others of the first fashion in the county . . . I never saw a play so well performed or so cordially received in this town [5].

Similar support was given to a music festival at St James' in 1790, at which leading London musicians performed. In 1794 the officers added to the gaiety. Howe's 'Glorious First of June' occasioned an illumination and a dinner at the Three Cups. At the Coronation anniversary huge crowds watched the Surrey Fencibles march to St Peter's for consecration of colours; that evening the officers entertained the north Essex gentry to a ball and the colonel gave the privates 'a plenteous dinner' and £10 to spend 'as a reward for good behaviour'. St Dennis' Fair was the most brilliant ever and official pleas for austerity did not diminish the splendour of the customary White Hart dinner. In November when the Duke of York, returning from Northern Europe, called at the White Hart for fresh horses, crowds dragged his carriage towards Lexden to demonstrate their loyalty. This pace was not maintained, but, with barracks built at Colchester and Tendring, the town remained gay throughout the War. In 1807 the final ball at St Dennis' Fair attracted a 'brilliant assemblage of fashion and beauty; upward of 400 were present'. Theatre seats could only be obtained through advance booking. John Hanson of Great Bromley Hall recorded in his diary:

> Colchester rendered very gay by the military . . . having in their numbers many of the nobility of the first rank with their ladies, under

the gay auspices of Sir William and Lady Howe. . . . Lady Howe was
the general promoter of gaieties of all descriptions, not excepting the
rustic sports of footraces, sack races, gingling and grinning matches.
We gave a ball and supper to the military . . . and, a few days after,
another to the Tendring Troop with the principal respectable yeomanry
and their families. . . . We had regular Assemblies at Colchester and
Dedham; for six weeks in the Autumn the Theatre at Colchester was
well supported by the Norwich Company; amateur concerts, military
entertainments including garrison balls at Weeley, grand reviews,
sham fights. . . .

Parallel with this gaiety more serious causes made some recovery.
The zeal of 1700 had flagged in the economic distress that followed
and had not revived in the pleasure-loving mood after 1750.
Nonconformists maintained their sober societies, but showed
evangelical spirit only in the founding of two Charity Schools.
Wesley found Colchester rather difficult, but, when in 1790 he
paid his last visit, his heart was cheered by lusty singing from a
large, affectionate congregation. By then there were other signs of
recovery. Anglican Sunday Schools, founded in 1785, claimed
500 scholars within a year and Lion Walk Independents were
equally responsive to this new movement. Social reform had
evoked little interest except for a few bequests for apprenticeships,
but in 1774 some doctors formed Colchester Medical Society to
promote medical science and in 1776 benevolent gentlemen
planned a public infirmary. This venture proved unsuccessful
but one doctor did open a free clinic and dispensary. However,
these efforts amounted to very little and only when the French
Revolution, which was not without its sympathisers in Colchester,
disturbed the complacency of respectable society, did a more
general movement develop. Then one by one charitable institu-
tions were founded, or old ones reorganised, to relieve poverty,
promote religion and teach obedience. Prominent among them
were denominational elementary schools, subsidised provident
societies, and the Essex and Colchester Hospital. When Thomas
Cromwell published his *History of Colchester* in 1825, he was able
to give an impressive list of such bodies.

Changes in the town's economic character were followed by some
changes in municipal government. In 1700–42 when cloth-making
supported the town, the Corporation had been controlled largely
by clothiers, a few other tradesmen and some local gentlemen

like Sir Isaac Rebow and Sir Ralph Creffield who possessed the standing and assurance to speak for the borough when such advocacy was needed. Through the Corporation and its associated organs the clothiers had regulated their industry and ensured order among its workers, besides dealing with some of the social problems of a large industrial town. This purposefulness was weakening even before municipal status was lost in 1742, and after the restoration of 1763 it did not revive. No longer did the Corporation send a stream of petitions to Parliament about economic policy and the problems of the cloth trade, even though the latter was even more in need of help, and the industry went down to final extinction with no apparent reaction from official Colchester. Clothiers on the Select Body like John Baker and Thomas Boggis were not without business competence or public spirit, but they did not feel the same resolute responsibility for the town's whole economic and social health as their predecessors had done when the town had, so to speak, belonged to the cloth industry. They seem, in the fashionable Colchester of the later eighteenth century, to have valued municipal eminence for the social distinction which they supposed it to confer, rather than for the opportunity it might give to help save their dying industry.

The town's new economic leaders failed to provide alternative municipal leadership, though they were soon well represented on the Select Body. After the Charter's restoration in 1763 they did not, or perhaps could not, immediately push their claims, but by 1786–94 the Aldermen included three lawyers, a doctor, a tanner, a currier, a builder, a cabinet-maker, an upholsterer and others from the middle class, while the lesser orders of the Select Body were similarly manned. The way was certainly open for them. By now there was a paucity of clothiers, and the local gentry were perhaps finding rural or martial duties more interesting than municipal service. Yet little was done by municipal action to help create the Colchester which its new middle class would have wanted. Order was preserved; weavers were whipped through the streets for embezzling yarn and once thirty-seven unlicensed alehouses were prosecuted. The Corporation's voice was apparently the only one raised in Essex against the widespread smuggling of the 1780s, which it denounced as unfair to law-abiding tradesmen. It made some effort during the War to provide better facilities for the markets, in the efficiency of which many of its members had a strong interest. The provision of new services it left to other bodies. Voluntary societies founded the schools, a subscription library, a reading room and a lying-in charity. Whereas Chelmsford Vestry concerned itself with the water supply, Colchester Corporation had no part in the new waterworks of 1808. The Corporation did some work on the bridges, but the major improvements in the roads, the river and street lighting were carried out by the Improvement Commission, which had grown out of the old river authority, had acquired paving powers and in 1781 was also given responsibility for lighting; its very existence implied incapacity on the Corporation's part. In one matter the Corporation showed inefficiency and negligence unworthy of men of business, in its complete mismanagement of the valuable borough lands.

The Corporation remained opposed to any notion of its own rejuvenation and in 1830–2, when Parliamentary Reform foreshadowed municipal change, only two of the forty-seven members of its Select Body voted for Reform candidates. Its obduracy was reinforced by its complex, oligarchic constitution. Though Assemblies of burgesses had nominal sovereignty, effective government was by the Select Body, elected by tax-paying burgesses according to procedures which, as events showed, precluded any effective challenge to the ruling group. The Select Body comprised four ascending orders, Common Councillors, Assistants, Aldermen and Mayor. A Common Council vacancy was filled by the burgesses electing two nominees, one of whom was then chosen by the Select Body. The burgesses filled a vacancy among the Assistants by electing an existing Common Councillor to it. An Aldermanic vacancy was filled by the burgesses electing two of the Assistants, one of whom was then chosen by the Select Body. For Mayor the burgesses chose two of the Aldermen, one of whom was chosen by the remaining Aldermen. The Justices, who through the Courts exercised a day-to-day control of the town, were also indirectly chosen. Below the Mayor, nobody had to seek re-election and at no stage was there unconditional election by the burgesses. After 1763 few who were distasteful to the ruling oligarchy reached even the first rung, whereafter prospects of advancement for them were poor. No effective challenge was ever made, not even in the 1780s when the Squire of Berechurch, a Borough M.P., attempted opposition.

The higher orders of the Select Body were slow to change; after 1763 Charles Gray was Alderman for thirteen years and Thomas Clamtree for twenty, and in 1764–73 nine out of eleven Aldermen remained unchanged. Moreover some were Mayor several times each, since only Aldermen were eligible. Though Aldermen were chosen only from among the Assistants, few Assistants were so promoted, for instance only three of those serving in 1769. Innovators would have found it almost impossible to rise from the lower to the higher orders of the Select Body against the solid opposition or mere indifference of colleagues, whose permanent tenure made them unresponsive to criticism or advice from within or without their own ranks. Initiative was rare within the Select Body and attendance at meetings was poor. Critics often alleged that a small circle, manipulated by the domineering Town Clerk, controlled the Corporation and certainly the constitution favoured such a regime.

In Parliamentary politics, too, economic developments exercised decreasing influence. In the seventeenth century the town's industrial character, its strong Puritanism and the bourgeois connexions of neighbouring gentry placed it firmly on Parliament's side, and after 1688 these sympathies were still reflected at elections. They soon weakened and the Whigs were happy to share the two seats with the Tories by an arrangement which annoyed their supporters, mainly because, by diminishing the likelihood of a contest, it made the franchise less valuable financially. The industrial and commercial electorate showed no political preference for the candidates with strong commercial connexions who sometimes presented themselves. These were valued by their backers more because their wealth could support lavish bribery than for any appeal which their commercial connexions might exert in this industrial and commercial constituency. Colchester clothworkers liked candidates of local standing, such as the Rebows of Wivenhoe, who were esteemed more for their ownership of Wivenhoe Park on the hill overlooking the Hythe than because they had long before been connected with the Dutch community. Nor did clothworkers rally to Sir Robert Smyth, the reforming Whig candidate. Indeed, if Colchester elections were, on a superficial level, very lively, it was not the intrusion of political principle or economic argument that produced the excitement. Real political debate began only when, at the end of the Napoleonic Wars, the radical D. W. Harvey took up the Reform cause, which with more persistence than influence had kept itself alive in Colchester since the late 1770s; he began to fashion from it the political party which was to win him one of the Borough seats.

By 1815 Colchester had long ceased to be a major industrial centre and had become instead a market-town for a thriving agricultural district. It was more of a middle-class community, in which the solid working-class of clothworkers had given place to a number of artisans' businesses, the employees of which were often ambitious to have a business of their own one day. Workers were less of a force in local life, partly because they were spread about a number of minor trades instead of being concentrated in textiles and partly because many of them were newcomers to the town from rural north Essex or south Suffolk, as the records of Colchester parishes show clearly. Socially this was no longer the workaday town with only its air of business and its battered churches to impress the traveller, but a more pretentious place, conspicuous with its pretty shops, gay inns, new brick or brick-fronted residences and its street-lighting, thronged on market days by prosperous country people, and on moonlight nights traversed by sedans and carriages taking genteel families to the Assembly or the theatre. An advertisement of 1791 recommended the town in these terms:

> Colchester is a pleasant and healthy town, abounds in genteel company and has a market well supplied with fish [6].

Both the economic and social transformation were illustrated by changes in female employment; whereas in 1700 the typical woman worker was a spinner, in 1800 she was in domestic service. Politically, the town was Tory instead of Whig and very attentive to the affluent classes of the surrounding countryside on whose custom it depended. Municipal government had lost vigour and seemed indifferent to modern needs. Meanwhile wartime conditions obscured the town's economic weakness. When the post-war slump began, Colchester's market-town occupations proved inadequate to support the now increasing population. In 1815–50 and after 1875 it became clear how dangerous it was for the town to have been left dependent on the vicissitudes of Essex agriculture. There then arose the depression foreseen by Morant when a

century earlier he had warned that shopkeeping would give far
less employment than the cloth industry.

REFERENCES

1. *Journal of the House of Commons*, 1715. 'A note on a labour dispute in
   early eighteenth century Colchester' by Dr K. H. Burley, in *Institute
   of Historical Research Bulletin*, XXIX (1956), pp. 220 ff. Essex Record
   Office T/A 214.
2. Francois de la Rochefoucauld, *A Frenchman in England* (1933),
   p. 161.
3. Sophie la Roche, *Sophie in London* (1933), pp. 82 ff.
4. Manuscript Journal of a Very Young Lady, Tour from Canonbury
   to Aldborough, 1805.
5. *Chelmsford Chronicle*, 7th Nov. 1783.
6. *Ipswich Journal*, 16th July 1791.

The chief sources used are as follows:

Essex Record Office. Records of Colchester parishes, miscellaneous
Quarter Sessions documents, family papers, files of *Chelmsford Chronicle*.

Colchester Corporation. Borough records.

Colchester Borough Library. Files of *Ipswich Journal*; files of *Essex
County Standard* for 1963–6 for valuable articles by J. Bensusan-Butt on
Colchester families and houses; poll-books; trade directories; maps.

Colchester and Essex Museum. Boggis letter-book; St Leonard's
rate-books; Michael Hills papers.

Public Record Office. Colchester port-books.

Ipswich Borough Library. Files of *Ipswich Journal*.

Essex Archaeological Society. Journal of John Hanson; volumes of
Essex Review.

Newcomers in Town and Country

R. E. Pahl

In the late 1940s Hertfordshire was referred to by its planners as 'a county of small towns set in a rural background on London's fringe'. At that time I was a schoolboy travelling from a London suburb to St Albans every-day. The post-war housing estates had not yet been started and many of the boys' parents were small local businessmen or farmers. It seemed perfectly in keeping with the local situation that I should be taught geography in a converted straw-hat factory. If I had been more perceptive I could have considered the impact of boys from North London, Watford or Welwyn Garden City on the sons of local burgesses. Did we bring in ideas about different jobs or careers? Were our assumptions any more cosmopolitan? Certainly St Albans seemed a long way from London then. It would be interesting to know something of the present generation's conception of distance; I would guess that individuals' mental maps have been considerably foreshortened.

Yet Hertfordshire had been changing since the beginning of the century. Letchworth and Welwyn Garden Cities brought in many new people and the Watford area was an important centre of light industry: indeed, in February 1930 Watford was practically the only town in Britain with no unemployment. The population of the county had more than doubled between 1901 and 1951, a rate five times that of the country as a whole. The momentum was building up: the New Towns Act of 1946 and the Town and Country Planning Act of 1947 were the instruments which were to do so much to change the character of the county. Situated in the important growth zone between London and the Midlands the county could not escape. At first there were signs that this new wave of change would be welcomed. In 1947 an editorial in the *Hertfordshire Mercury* entitled 'The Old Order Changeth' argued

we have lived far too long on tradition and custom without questioning

Newcomers in Town and Country

even social justice and we have carved our communities into cliques and coteries . . . (but) . . . the self-centred community today simply will not fit into the larger frame of human endeavour.

However, as the months went by a more cautious note appeared as the paper realised that 'the threat of Hertfordshire becoming urbanized is real in the minds of old residents'. The storm over the designation of Stevenage New Town led to a prolonged lawsuit which was eventually decided in the House of Lords. Yet few newcomers were able to come until the early fifties. Various economic difficulties held up large-scale developments, apart from the essential L.C.C. overspill estates at Borehamwood and Oxhey.

National Service and university took me away from the county but when I was able to return in 1959 after a gap of some six years I was struck by the changes. Forced into the east of the county by the impossibility of finding accommodation elsewhere, I found myself becoming interested in the rural areas because I was living in a hamlet myself. I was introduced to a new circle of country-dwelling commuters. Small talk centered on old 'things', carefully polished or renovated and placed about a cottage in which I stooped to avoid the carefully exposed beams, when not blinded by the wood-smoke of the newly 'discovered' fireplace. I lectured on the making of the landscape to men in city clothes in villages over thirty miles from where they worked.

At the same time the world of the New Towns was even more typical of the new Hertfordshire. Among the lawns and flower-beds of the industrial sites were neat little factories producing nice clean things like pens or guided missiles. New shopping centres with new supermarkets were surrounded by acres of car parks filled with new cars. Talk was about money and children. Everybody had lots of children. Schools and libraries were the centres of a booming growth industry. Between 1951 and 1961 Hertfordshire's rate of population growth was greater than that of any other county in the country. Nearly a quarter of a million newcomers, mostly married couples building up their families, came in during the ten-year period.

It is understandable that within this situation people coming to adult education classes should wish to make conscious the processes of which they formed a part. Even if I had not shown a leaning towards sociology before becoming Resident Tutor in the county, I think I would still have had sociology thrust upon me. In this essay I have chosen to describe the investigations which the situations of three adult education classes suggested. In a Hertfordshire New Town class newly arrived wives were interested in friends and neighbours and bringing up children; in a Cambridgeshire village just north of Hertfordshire there was the problem of integrating the established villagers with the new commuters; finally, in a new estate at the edge of a small Hertfordshire market town the new suburban situation created a self-conscious appraisal of the wives' situations within their families. None of these studies has been published before and it is particularly appropriate that they should now appear in this form. They should be seen as the joint work of tutor and students* and I have no doubt that other adult education classes throughout the country have produced a whole mass of similar material, which rarely gets published. Perhaps this essay may do something to stimulate an interest akin to that developed by local historians in the publication and discussion of their material.

The studies which follow may be seen in a broader context. Sociologists are much concerned both with the way existing communities work and also with broader changes in the national class structure. Studies by Goldthorpe and Lockwood and, more recently, by Runciman, stress the importance of values, self-rated class and style of life in an understanding of our changing social structure. Some of these broader changes can be fully understood only by detailed analysis at the local level. Occupational groups are becoming more sharply segregated, not only by residential area, but also socially and culturally. The cultivation of a particular style of life may be linked not only to present occupation and life-chances but also to social origins. That is to say, in any one occupation not only is present salary important but so also is access to capital, however limited. For those without any capital, apart from what they can save, the housing market forces them into a particular sort of house at any given stage in their life-cycle. For those with capital, however, their choice is considerably

* I should have liked to have acknowledged the very great help I had from particular students. However, in order to respect the confidence of the respondents it is better that they should remain anonymous. Nevertheless, the debt to the many who helped is very real.

extended and their style of life may be significantly different. Again, social networks may depend very considerably on the level of education of the wife. Even when the middle-class husband does not commute long distances to work he is still very dependent on his wife for maintaining social contacts.

NEWCOMERS IN A NEW TOWN: THE ENERGETIC LAITY OF THE WELFARE STATE'S PRIESTHOOD

A group of young wives in a New Town felt that they would like to focus the discussions they had been having together informally. Thus, early in 1964 a short series of classes on 'Growing Up in a New Town' was held in the afternoons and was later repeated in the evenings, with some husbands coming as well. I had the impression that this group was particularly lively, yet introspective, and felt that here was an opportunity to gather more detailed information from the group, with the intention of analysing it in a future class. I accordingly devised a short questionnaire, asking for basic information about the socio-economic structure of the household, the wife's attitude to paid employment since marriage, and her husband's reaction to his wife taking a job; there were also questions about children, play facilities, baby-sitting problems and so on, and finally questions about friends and neighbours.

In no sense is this a sample with the slightest statistical validity. It was self-selected, exceptional in that most people do not attend W.E.A. classes, and the class was focused directly on itself. They were all newcomers in a new town with young children. Being in this situation they were self-consciously interested in their own problems. Hence I think they enjoyed filling in the questionnaire: they knew why I was asking the questions and they wanted to help. All this introduces considerable bias: they thought they knew what I expected and what other people thought about the various issues. Nevertheless it would be foolish to dismiss these twenty-eight families as being of no interest. I believe that they are representatives of a more articulate element which may be characteristic of the New Towns. The fathers of the husbands were more likely to be junior non-manual workers or skilled manual workers, whereas the husbands themselves were overwhelmingly white-collar workers. Ten out of twenty-eight were teachers or concerned with education and only three were manual workers. Their wives had been secretaries, teachers or nurses, and although fewer wives than husbands had had further education more wives had stayed at school until sixteen or older. They all wanted their children to stay on at school as long as possible, many mentioning university, even though they themselves had not been there.

The wives are almost too neatly type-cast as readers of *The Guardian* women's page. 'Full-time housewife' sounds degrading to them, but they enjoy their young children and are acutely aware of their responsibilities. 'The garden has sand, a swing and in warm weather a plastic pool, however they prefer the street for skates, pram, pedal car and group play'. Most husbands reflect *Guardian* women's page views about a part-time job for their wives when the children are at school. They feel that the occupation 'housewife' is dull and soul-destroying and they want their wives to be 'stretched', to receive 'mental stimulation' so that they do not get discontented. They are very conscious of their spouse's lively mind, which must not be allowed to stagnate. 'Although she loves being with the children, she is noticeably rather frustrated when there is nothing else to "stretch" her. During the last two or three years she has benefited from the great amount of voluntary social work she has done'. Many men happily acknowledged their wives' mental abilities—as another man put it: 'She is an energetic bundle—mentally and physically —for whom the maintenance of a household would be psychologically quite unsatisfactory'.

There was general agreement among both husbands and wives that full-time work would not be possible. There was also a feeling that a paid job might not provide the social satisfactions and the mental stimulation that was needed. Voluntary part-time social work, or paid part-time teaching or nursing, were the most frequently mentioned activities. These are the energetic laity of the welfare state's priesthood. They are the new radical middle-class, anxious to serve. One husband put it like this: 'Since she had a higher education and is capable of dealing with problems far removed from domestic trivia and cosy coffee mornings, it would be wasteful of her professional training not to apply it both for the good of the community and her own fulfilment'.

Most of the wives know the parents of the children with whom their own children play fairly or very well: those whose children go to nursery school know an even wider circle. Husbands are very much aware of their responsibilities to play and be with their children, two-thirds of them spending two or more hours a day with them and a quarter spending three or more hours. They liked speaking about their children and the problems of bringing them up and it would be wrong to imagine a sharp division between 'men's talk' and 'women's talk'.

Finding baby-sitters was a problem and prevented many going out together as much as they would have liked: some were able to get teenagers to help but a more general difficulty was the expense of paying for them. They would have preferred to work on a reciprocal basis with neighbours but it always seemed that neighbours did not want to go out so frequently. Hence husband and wife were obliged to go out separately. Meetings of one sort or another were very popular: discussion groups, political meetings, lectures and so on. One couple took it in turn to go to the film society, another couple were out separately most nights of the week but rarely went out together more than once a month. Each of them going out once or twice a week separately seemed a familiar pattern. Only one respondent mentioned that she and her husband had personal friends not so well known by the other partner, but it is clear that when husband and wife join separate groups they will move in different social networks.

Entertaining and being entertained in each others' houses in the evenings is popular and there is much emphasis on the conversation which such occasions generate. 'As our cultural, political, etc., interests are wide, conversation is never lacking when we are with friends . . . it . . . moves rapidly and varies greatly'. The emphasis is on ideas and stimulation. 'As so often happens the hostess has to spend too much time in the kitchen, therefore misses interesting conversation'. Wives did in fact enjoy talking about children, but there was a great fear of missing out on general talk. There was a feeling that conversation ought to be varied; for example: 'I find our social circle rather limited. Most of our friends are in education, the majority from comparable backgrounds. I have found our efforts to meet other people rather difficult as many of the sports and social groups throughout the town have a very high proportion of teachers and teachers' wives in their membership'.

This group is not concentrated in any one street or area of the New Town. It is scattered in a variety of houses rented from the

Development Corporation throughout the town. Although they are mainly non-manual workers, the incomes of the group would be much the same as many of the highly paid manual workers. How do individuals fit in with their neighbours and do they have many friends? Nearly a third of the wives knew at least a dozen people within easy walking distance on whom they could call for help such as getting shopping. Such people lived in the same street or cul-de-sac and their children played together, or they met each other when collecting their children from nursery school. Many of them had moved into the housing area together and the common experience drew them together. Only four women had three or less such friends, the remainder having between four and a dozen people on whom they could call.

This socially confident group is not typical of the New Town as a whole; many women were conscious of their distinctiveness and two-thirds of them knew other women who were said to be lonely. Those who keep themselves to themselves were pitied. In this child-centred society working wives were unlikely to make contact with their stay-at-home neighbours: children help to make friends. The situation of the isolated and lonely was discussed with some perception: 'Sometimes they feel torn from their roots and are always hankering to be back in London or "up North". They miss their parents or old friends so much they seem unable to accept new friends'. The secretary of one of the local nursery schools went further; she felt 'some women are rather frightened of others with conflicting views, maybe they are scared that theirs are wrong. Friends I am really myself with, are those I have met through the local C.N.D. Women are very friendly here, one can spend a whole day bumping into them and chatting for twenty minutes at a time. Many seem very lonely . . . .' This woman was in full-time education until the age of twenty. She has confidence and little status-anxiety. She meets like-minded middle-class radicals at C.N.D. meetings. Yet even she does not understand that loneliness is functionally related to class and mobility. 'The more articulate immigrants "join things" —there are any number of associations and clubs in the town'. But this is not so easy for the woman who left school at fourteen and whose family, school contemporaries and the friends she made at work before marriage have been left in London. It is understandable that such people should be afraid of taking a false step. Those who try to be friendly to them complain of 'clannishness' or of aloofness; in fact it is fear and uncertainty. Women without the necessary confidence and social skill withdraw from a situation in which they might be hurt or embarrassed.

It is perhaps the fear of offending a neighbour on account of the children which helps to keep some women isolated: 'A great need of women living isolated lives in New Towns is someone reliable with whom they can leave their young children while they shop, have their hair done, relax, take a course, etc. Why not each other? There seems to be a great fear of becoming too familiar with another family. Some don't want the responsibility even though it frees them on another day. Others can't believe their children would go happily to another woman. Some children's first day at school is their first day away from Mother'. (Thirty-two-year-old social worker.)

Newcomers in a New Town may all be in a similar situation looked at from one point of view, but there is no doubt that some are able to cope with the problem of creating new patterns of social relationships more easily than others. The radical middle-class islands are surrounded by a sea of others: distinctions in values and life-styles are understood and discussed. The affluent manual worker withdraws into his own small family circle and is criticised for his lack of interests (in a middle-class sense). 'The women go out to work for money—they always say they can't manage but they're just bad managers. Some wives go out solely to buy and upkeep the car'. Their husbands are not interested in politics because 'they don't feel it particularly involves them'. Stimulated by this lack of firm ideological commitment by those who may have much more money coming into the house, the radical middle-class minority is acutely conscious of its distinctiveness, despite frequent face-to-face contacts. 'I can never get very far with them', said one thirty-two-year-old mother, 'they just sort of close up when you talk of politics. There's some you almost put off being friends with as they're afraid of what you'll say next'.

Clearly one must be very wary of rash generalisations about 'New Town People'. The articulate minority I am describing is highly self-aware and has some general knowledge of social processes. Social links start with the children but very soon the ideological feelers work out through the various clubs and associations to bring the like-minded elements together. The usual status differentials of home ownership, cars or consumer durables do not work in the New Town where houses are for rent, and wage differentials are slight. Ideas sort out the middle- from the working-class: people very soon move into a social network that links them together. Many of those who are politically Conservative and more self-consciously middle-class leave as soon as they possibly can. Refugees from the New Town are scattered over rural north and east Hertfordshire. They try hard to become integrated with the village and approve of status-assenting, deferential rustics. Since those who do not like the New Town leave it, those who remain are to some extent self-selected. Only the social and political activists who do not mind living next door to the working-class appear to enjoy living in the town. There is a fellowship in the mental activity; they see the same familiar faces at lectures, political meetings and discussion groups. They enjoy the Welfare State and what it stands for, but while complaining of the political apathy of those around them, they were angry when I discussed problems of social stratification. 'Class does not exist in this New Town', they assured me, yet everything they told me confirmed that the barriers were there.

NEWCOMERS IN A VILLAGE

During the 1950s this south Cambridgeshire village had been losing population. Men were not needed on the land and there were good employment opportunities in north Hertfordshire, particularly in Letchworth. Indeed, between ten and twelve thousand workers—nearly half as many as the Garden City's total population—came into Letchworth from the surrounding towns and villages each day. Manual workers are forced to leave the village or commute, while many managerial and professional people choose to live in a village and may prefer to commute. Hence depopulation of one element may be disguised by the immigration of another. However, in this village the arrival of the newcomers could not be thus hidden: in 1959 the population of the village was 610, in 1962, 660, and in 1963 it was 700.

The small cluster of new houses more or less discreetly tacked on to a village is now a familiar sight in many parts of the country. How do the people in these houses relate to the established villagers? Is it possible for there to be a feeling of common interest between the middle-class commuters, whose network of social relations extends widely throughout the country, and those more locally oriented? How do the newcomers become integrated into village clubs and organisations?

The first step was to gather data on the various voluntary organisations in the village. We wanted to get information on membership and meetings; in particular we wanted the names and occupations of all the office-holders (secretary, treasurer, chairman, etc., and all committee members): we also wanted some general information from the secretary on the purpose of the organisation and how successful it was in achieving it. We therefore devised a simple questionnaire asking for this information and explaining that the information provided would be used in the class on 'Our Changing Rural Community'. A class member who lived in the village spent many hours distributing, collecting and editing the forms. Without a local informant the data would have been much more difficult to obtain. For example, thirty-seven per cent of all the names on the electoral roll were divided between five families and their names appeared frequently on the lists of office-holders. Without detailed knowledge of kinship links further analysis would be impossible, as there would be no way of distinguishing between those with both similar surnames and initials.

A somewhat unusual feature in the pattern of voluntary associations was a Welcoming Club, with a membership of about fifty, founded early in 1964 'to introduce new residents to the village—its people, organisations and services'. It was initiated by the Parochial Church Council 'to integrate newcomers' and the vicar was made president, with two other members of the P.C.C. as vice-presidents. New residents were visited and given a diary of village activities—a stencilled sheet with details of the Churches, headed by the Church of England, followed by the Methodist Chapel, and then other nearby denominations, sports clubs, W.I., British Legion, Civil Defence. Information was also given about evening classes, the children's clinic and the nearest doctor. Coffee mornings were held once a month in members' houses and twenty-five to thirty wives attended. Fifty people came to a sherry party in the house of the vice-president and 140 to a Hallowe'en Party in the village hall. Remembering that the stated purpose of the club was to introduce new residents to the village it seemed odd that only eighteen months later it was considered to have achieved its purpose, despite the fact that it was openly acknowledged that 'village people will not join' and few newcomers took an active part in any other village organisation apart from the Church.

An attempt was made to analyse systematically the composition of all village committees. It was clear on superficial inspection that there was a good deal of overlap: office-holders in one organisation having similar positions on various other committees. After a certain amount of trial and error the following method showed interesting results. The eighteen members of the Village Hall Committee were listed in the centre of a large piece of paper and whenever one of these names appeared on the committee or as an office-holder of any other organisation a line was drawn from the names to the appropriate box. Cross-affiliations were such that sixteen out of the eighteen had thirty-eight other positions between them, six having three each and one man having six. Furthermore half of the Village Hall Committee were Methodists and an analysis of all office-holders in Methodist organisations showed that the cross-affiliations of Methodist committee members and Village Hall Committee Members intermeshed very tightly. The summary diagram (Fig. 1) shows clearly the interlocking of village organisations as determined by their most influential members.

Further analysis of office-holders by occupation failed to produce such striking results. The most common occupations were farmer, smallholder and farmworker. It was clear that village organisations catered for like-minded groups, and only in the football and cricket clubs, the Young Farmers and the British Legion was there much mixing between the distinct social elements of village 'gentry', the Methodists, the Church and the new commuters. Both the Conservative and Labour clubs refused to complete the form and so it is not possible to do more than note some association between the Church of England and the Conservatives and between the Methodists and the Labour Party.

This is clearly a Methodist village. Average attendance in Chapel is about fifty and in the Church twelve. The Methodists are a tightly knit group with a very large proportion sharing four or five surnames between them. Non-Methodists are needed to complete the teams in the sports clubs and are accepted on the common ground of the Young Farmers' Club. The newcomers are likely to be both Conservatives and Anglicans and it is hardly

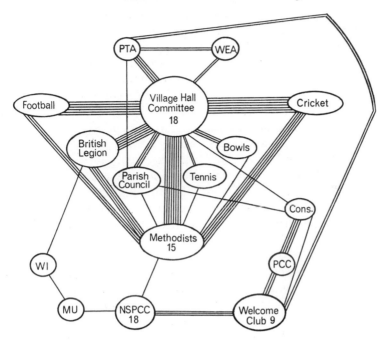

Fig. 1. Web of affiliations

surprising that quite apart from fundamental differences in styles
of life, chances of 'integration' with the village are slight. *Some*
commuters' wives meet *some* of the more elderly village women
at the Women's Institute but because the energetic Methodist
group do not join the W.I. the newcomers are not drawn into the
more important village net.

Eighteen months after the foundation of the Welcoming Club
an extraordinary general meeting was held in the afternoon in the
Village Hall, which I was able to attend. The business was to
decide the future of the club. The vicar reminded the sixteen
commuters' wives present (others were absent at work) what the
club had done. The committee recommended that the club should
be disbanded since there could be no further building and no
more newcomers in large numbers and 'members have all met
each other now'. It was unanimously agreed that the club had
achieved its purpose (presumably of integration with the village?
Or of strengthening the Church of England?). Some discussion

centred on alternative activities for the club: someone suggested a mime group; someone else suggested that theatre trips could be arranged. The vicar interposed a suggestion that the meeting should not forget that 'there are clubs in the village which cater for all interests'. His point was ignored and discussion continued, on the possibility of doing mimes 'for old people at Christmas'. Discussion then shifted to a debate on the coffee mornings, the argument that it would be a shame to disband being countered with the argument that since people now all knew each other there was no need for a formal arrangement. It was clear that certain conflicts were being revealed: some church people wanted the group to continue; other local, more established 'gentry' commuters felt they had done their duty and did not want more work. Someone proposed that a Coffee Club should meet irregularly as announced in the Parish Notes. This motion was accepted by eight votes to six.

The Welcoming Club was thus disbanded; the newcomers were certainly not integrated with the village and, as the above account demonstrates, they were hardly integrated amongst themselves. However, they had become used to a village-in-the-mind, in which they now live quite happily: their own definition of the situation is more important to them than objective reality. The quality of their social life has been improved now that they have met each other, and the mediating links forged by some longer established commuters' wives, linked with the P.C.C., take the place of genuine involvement with the village.

NEST-CENTRED NEWCOMERS: THE MIDDLE-CLASS SUBURB

In March 1966 a Review of the South East Study was published by the Standing Conference on London Regional Planning. The original South East Study suggested that of the 3·5 million people to be accommodated in the area by 1981 some 1·3 million would go to 'planned' expansion, that is new towns or officially sponsored 'expanded' towns. However, in the Review, with a total population to be housed only slightly less than the original estimate, the proportion to be housed in planned expansion had markedly declined. This left 2,480,000 people to be housed under what is known as 'normal' allocations of land in the development plans of the local authorities. This means that a population equal to that contained in twenty-five towns of the present size of

Cambridge will have to be added on to or squeezed between the existing settlements of the South-east in the next fifteen years.

It is thus almost inevitable that the medium-sized privately built estate will become an even more characteristic feature of the South-east. In an attempt to find out something of the style of life characteristics of one of these estates, some time was spent during the summer of 1964 with a group of young wives in a Hertfordshire market town, devising a questionnaire and interviewing a quarter of the housewives in the McManus estate of 200 houses, just over a mile from the centre of the town.

Everyone is a newcomer: of the forty-six women interviewed in the autumn of 1964, thirty-nine had arrived since the beginning of 1962. Most people had moved out from north London suburbs, twenty-five in all; of the remainder, twelve came from other parts of east Hertfordshire and five from elsewhere, the furthest being from south Oxfordshire. A few husbands worked in the market town itself; each of the three New Towns in the area attracted its share of commuters, and the remainder went either to the north London employment centres such as Southgate or Enfield, or right into the City. A few were representatives who had no fixed place of work. The longest journey to work was probably made by the manager of a supermarket in Watford. Most of the husbands could be classified as junior or middle managerial or professional people. In all, eleven were described as an engineer of some sort; this might be prefaced by, for example, aircraft, electronics, civil or development. There were eleven professional people, such as mathematician, physicist, accountant or solicitor, and there were three draughtsmen and four company representatives. A further five were employed at various levels in commerce, insurance and banking, and the remainder included such occupations as a self-employed builder, a supermarket manager, the head of a test room, the owner of a draper's shop and a toolmaker.

The fathers of these men were generally in occupational categories of slightly lower status—junior non-manual or skilled manual workers—but ten of the fathers were in firmly established middle-class occupations. Of their wives, as many as twenty-eight were engaged in secretarial or clerical work before marriage, a further five were in nursing or physiotherapy, and of the remaining ten, three were engaged in professional occupations, and seven were junior non-manual workers such as shop assistant, or manual workers such as a comptometer operator. The fathers of these wives were of very similar socio-economic status to the fathers of their husbands. Inspection of the fathers' occupations of all the couples showed that in only two or three cases were sons of solidly middle-class fathers married to daughters from a lower social status background. Thus we are considering here the lower-middle- and new middle-class (created by the expansion of job opportunities in the new growth industries), which together has common problems in status placement and in learning new patterns of behaviour both within the newly founded family and in relation to others. Any tension is thus common to the group which makes up most of the estate and is not simply related to individual differences and difficulties. In any comparison with the New Town group it is of course crucial to note that these wives are much less well educated: sixty-four per cent left school at sixteen or younger and a further twenty-five per cent at the age of seventeen. The level of education of the wife appears to be of greater importance than the occupation of the husband 'when considering local interaction or assimilation.

The wives who were interviewed were generally mothers of small children since those out at work could not be contacted. Only seven households comprised husband and wife alone; thirty-three had at least one child under five (eleven had two children under five) and twelve households had at least one child over five.

Questions were asked about friends on the estate, how they were met, how many are entertained in the home, how many are 'real friends', and so on. In addition, respondents were asked for their general comments on friendliness on the estate.

It was clear that there was a wide range between those who led a very sociable life and those who were isolated and sometimes extremely lonely. There were sixteen people who were classified as being 'very friendly'. They had all moved in together, and during the first hard winter when water supplies were limited there had been a fair amount of visiting each other's houses. Children also provided a means of effecting introductions. All in this category entertained frequently and there was little discrepancy between those entertained and 'real friends'. It is perhaps significant that *without exception* those classified as 'very friendly' (by the number of friends they had and the remarks and comments they made) were from the highest status level on the estate, the husbands being in established professional or managerial occupations. Of the fathers of the 'very friendly' wives, only three or four were manual workers and where this was the case the husband and husband's father were in established middle-class occupations. Strikingly, the 'very friendly' also had more relatives close enough to visit and be visited, variously described as 'many', 'hordes', 'lots', 'countless', 'hundreds' and so on.

Most of the sample—twenty-five people—were classified as of 'average friendliness' (and of these only three had no children). None of these twenty-five respondents was without help if it was needed, and none relied solely on relatives for this help. Like the 'very friendly', they were seemingly able to accept and integrate a *variety* of friends incorporating different aspects of their lives. Among the 'averagely friendly' group, too, by far the largest category of 'real' friends had been carried through from their previous address. The twenty-five households in the averagely friendly group had between them a total of 297 people whom they recalled entertaining since moving in. Of these, 170 were considered 'real friends' and of these 170, thirty-five were carried through from the previous address, twenty-six were wife's friends before marriage, another twenty-six were wife's local friends and twenty-three were wife's old school or college friends. Husbands supplied fewer real friends—twenty-three were colleagues from work, seventeen were old school/college friends and only six were friends the husband had met locally.

The young women with young children who arrived with the rest during the early days of the estate generally felt the estate to be a friendly place—especially those with relatives nearby to give confidence and to supply a stable background of friendliness on which to draw. However, the old or those out at work during the day might find it difficult to break into the friendly net. For example, when one man's wife was dying no one offered to help, and when she was brought to lie by the window, neighbours complained that she was prying, since she could see into their back gardens. The world of the wives appears strikingly insular, with an outward friendliness, but little interest in people and activities outside their narrow world. For those without relatives nearby it might be difficult to escape from the local mould: 'be one of us or be lonely'.

There was no baby-sitter's club or crèche on the estate at the time of the survey, and it seemed as if mothers did not want to engage in any different sort of social activity. Many wives did not like to leave children with baby sitters at all, and some would not go out without taking the baby: it is clear that the majority prefer to spend the evening watching TV. Money was not mentioned as a factor influencing out-of-home activities and though it may have been important, only eleven couples went out together for pleasure more than once a month.

This is a child- and home-centred society. Respondents were asked how much they looked forward to various alternatives when their children were grown up. The following table summarises their answers:

	Percentage	
	Positive	Negative
Being a grandmother	60	40
Freedom to travel	77	23
Doing a full-time job	20	80
Going out more with husband ..	85	15
More local activities	37	63
More relaxation at home	58	42
More attention to husband	55	45

If the above table is compared with the following, which shows the extent to which respondents wanted their husbands when aged fifty to have various characteristics, some interesting conclusions emerge:

	Percentage	
Husband	Positive	Negative
Wealthy and successful	60	40
Contented family man	100	—
Respected member of local community	60	40
With power and influence but no great wealth	10	90
Pleasant companion to do things with ..	100	—

Interviewers had the impression that wives gave little thought to what a man of fifty might really want. They assumed that being a contented family man, doing pleasant things with his wife and family, would be enough for him, and indeed this may well be true. It is significant that they fear their husbands having power and influence without great wealth, yet one imagines many men would be disappointed if in their various careers they were not able to have power and influence at the age of fifty. Clearly the wives do not want their husbands to move away from the nest on account of their interest in their jobs: maybe they also fear that the job might stretch them beyond their capabilities.

In an attempt to understand the wife's conception of her rôle in the home, a question was asked about the wife's ideas of what importance, in her opinion, a number of alternatives would have for her daughter. This question elicited a most interesting series of responses and the results are tabulated in full:

	Essen-tial	Very impor-tant	Impor-tant	Don't Mind	Not Impor-tant
Healthy, happy children	17	14	9	1	—
Specialist training for a career	4	6	17	13	—
Wealth	1	1	4	17	17
An exciting and adventurous time	—	3	10	12	12
Someone like a doctor or M.P. for husband ..	—	—	8	16	15
A nice house with a kind husband and steady income	10	10	10	5	1
Freedom to be herself ..	21	8	10	1	—

When these results were described to the New Town group of mothers they were very surprised: many imagined that although children would certainly be important for their and other people's daughters' happiness, they would not be *so* important as the replies suggest. Similarly, the more radically minded middle-class mothers expected a greater emphasis on specialist training and were surprised at the relatively high proportion which did not appear to mind about this. The aversion to wealth may also be unexpected. Since this question was answered very seriously, with a deliberate weighing-up of alternatives, it is perhaps reasonable to assume that mothers were imposing their own values and attitude on to their daughters. One might have expected some sort of fantasy, relating 'freedom to be herself' to career or adventure. Instead the 'freedom' leads to *kinder*, *kuche* and the nest. Respondents do not have very high-status husbands, their own careers have been brief and they have found themselves with children early in life; they seem to want their daughters to be the same. Is this because they dare not face the alternative for themselves?

An attempt was made to make respondents face various changes in their lives such as a sudden increase in their husband's income or a possible change in his job. It was hoped that by asking respondents to put themselves imaginatively into new situations they would reveal more of their own image of themselves and their aspirations and ideas of 'the good life'. In a question which postulated a sudden doubling of the husband's income, respondents were asked to choose from a list of fifteen ways of spending the extra money, but were warned that they clearly could not have everything and that some restriction on spending would still remain. Far and away the most important item was felt to be a bigger house; sixty per cent would consider this seriously and a further twenty-one per cent would certainly not disregard such a move, this despite the fact that respondents were new arrivals in new houses. Second in importance was spending money on children's education, which would be considered seriously by half the respondents.

Turning to the wife's attitude to her husband moving his job under various conditions, the strongest feelings were expressed against any form of shift work, despite the increased income this might involve, and the strongest approval was expressed for a better job which would involve the wife in giving more help and encouragement to her husband. This latter is hardly a very valid point, since few wives would admit that they would not help their husbands, although two did say so and a further eight claimed that they would not mind. In general most wives were against their husbands moving. Most strikingly this was shown in the response to the situation where the 'new job would stretch him to the limit of his capacity'. Only seventeen per cent would encourage this, and sixty-nine per cent would discourage it. The other situation which most wives felt they would discourage would be if the new job, although better paid, involved a longer time away from home. Opinions were fairly evenly divided on the situation where the new job was less well paid but the work was more interesting and satisfying. The fact that there was not unanimous approval for such a move may imply that, in this, respondents were being realistic financially, or that they were relatively unconcerned about the work satisfaction of their husbands. When wives were asked what they thought the main purpose of their husband's job was, thirty-two mentioned that it gave him satisfaction, eighteen mentioned the provision of income, and a further eleven mentioned support for the family, supporting the home, and so on. Only two respondents thought that the job should satisfy their husband's ambition. Rather they felt that the satisfaction he should get should perhaps inhibit ambition. As one said, 'If he's satisfied at work he's more contented and satisfied at home with his family', or again, 'He should leave a happy balance for the family', 'He should be satisfied with his job but it should leave a happy balance for the family', 'He should be satisfied with his job but it should not be a be-all and end-all'.

No one seemed to think that her husband was dissatisfied with his job. Husbands, apparently, enjoyed their work, found it interesting and were by no means concerned about more money or status. Wives had to think this, presumably, to give force to their concern that their husbands should not be stretched further. There is clearly some tension here. Many would *like* a bigger house, second car, and so on, but seem reluctant that their husbands should work harder to get more money. Similarly they do not appear keen to go out to work themselves. I get a very strong impression that an ordinary, comfortable existence is the highest goal. These wives seem afraid of too-successful husbands. Many have vaguely idealistic ideas about their husband's work serving the community and so on, but it must be other people's husbands who rise to the top to take the major decisions and responsibility in society. No one felt that her husband was being held back, no one felt he lacked scope. If the export drive meant that some of these husbands would be obliged to work in the evenings, their wives, I suspect, would be against it. The woman who said 'I don't mind what he does as long as he gets a reasonable [*sic*] salary and he's happy' summed up the opinions of many. A fear of 'nervous strain' or otherwise endangering health was widespread—maybe this is due to the sort of studies in women's magazines or on TV—the ideal is 'a good happy medium position'.

Another woman felt 'any great success or interest in his work would inevitably bring sacrifice of family life'. Quite exceptional was the comment 'ambition is a good thing in a man'. It is understandable that wives should wish to discourage their husbands from staying away overnight, from excessive travel and from dirty or monotonous work, which was, of course, the view of the majority. Perhaps more worrying is the statement 'I'd be against anything which disrupted home life and I'd discourage anything too new and experimental'. In the light of these comments the aspirations expressed on behalf of their daughters are much less surprising.

When respondents were asked generally 'In what do you find your chief sense of security?', thirty-three mentioned their husbands, sixteen of these also mentioning children; two others also mentioned children, making eighteen in all. Twelve respondents mentioned their 'home' as providing a sense of security, but all these combined it with other things such as husband or religion; three other respondents mentioned the material security of their own home as their chief source of confidence. Parents as a source of security were mentioned by four women, and three others mentioned their own happy childhood or upbringing. Only two women mentioned 'other people' and 'friends' and only two mentioned education and training; a further woman claimed 'growing experience' provided her chief sense of security.

NEWCOMERS AND SOCIAL CHANGE

In this final section I want to draw on my more extended research on three Hertfordshire villages. Without providing a summary of all my work (which I list at the end of this essay), I should like to make explicit a line of argument which may put the more limited studies described above in a wider context.

I do not want to refer to the villages by name since what I am doing now is to create 'ideal types' which I can fit into a model or continuum of change. In the first village almost everyone is engaged in or retired from agriculture. Apart from the church, the school and one or two other houses the squire owns the complete parish and the estate is run with an efficient and enlightened paternalism. Newcomers may be a shepherd from Yorkshire or a gamekeeper from Norfolk and everyone soon gets to know them. Since in one way or another most men see each other when they are about their day-to-day business, there seems little point in meeting together in the evenings. The women are more isolated—as the gamekeeper's wife said, 'It would seem funny to have a neighbour'—and so the Women's Institute meetings are welcomed for the opportunity to get out of the home. Thus there are two groups: the squire who owns the village and the villagers who are economically dependent on the squire and interdependent on each other. The squire refuses to sell land to potential newcomers.

The second village is in a different category. The squire still owns most of the parish but he does not exert the same sort of influence. Tenant farmers are responsible for the management of most of the land and the squire is more concerned with his strong financial interests in London. The local R.D.C. has chosen the village as a centre for local authority housing and an estate caters for a number of surrounding parishes, in addition to local needs. In keeping with the squire's stronger financial interests, land has been sold to private developers, who have built suburban-style houses for junior white-collar workers who commute. Nevertheless the squire still owns most of the village and exerts influence as chairman of the R.D.C.'s housing committee. For most people, whether as council tenants or private tenants, he controls their housing. However, the squire does not control the jobs of the majority, who commute out to local factories or work for builders, transport contractors and so on: their houses are in the village because they were born there, but their main economic life is elsewhere. People such as the rector or the area youth officer believe there ought to be more local activity—dances, clubs and so on—they do not understand that the community is in transition and sees no purpose in itself for itself. Those white-collar newcomers, who work for a large factory in a nearby town, can get all the social facilities they need in the firm's country club for employees, which is just down the road. Their children may go to the local school but, for them, the village is simply a bus-stop in the country. They have a cheaper house and a larger garden than they could find elsewhere.

It was difficult to know where 'the village' was. The old-age pensioners in condemned houses in the village street? The people in council houses who have moved in from a neighbouring parish and who work in a neighbouring town? The agricultural workers in their tied cottages out near the farms or in tiny hamlets? The newly arrived 'privates' who commute from their smart suburban houses? Only the squire 'is' the village, and he is only interested in it from a financial point of view.

In the case of the third village the squire sold much of the land after the First World War and only the ex-governesses or butlers, who still live in the village, remember the old order. One manor house is a school, another is divided into flats, and a third is smaller and is still used as a private residence (open to the public on Sundays). This village is much further along the continuum of change. During the 1930s the nearby Garden City drew out men to work in factories and they could easily commute by bicycle. An area of woodland, just over a mile from the village, began to be developed by professional and managerial immigrants. Individuals bought two or three plots of land so that substantial houses could be built and remain hidden in the trees. This set a precedent which was continued after the Second World War.

Since the junior white-collar workers were in a very small minority the village was divided between the manual workers at one end in council houses and the managers in privately owned houses at the other. The two broad groups had quite distinctive styles of life and lived in distinct social worlds. The differences between manual and non-manual workers in terms of educational opportunity, conditions of employment (holidays, hours of work, pension rights) and so on have been well documented by sociologists and are summarised by Klein. The village provided an arena in which the two value-systems and ways of life could confront each other. In order to understand each system the sociologist is forced away from the local milieu to the wider industrial situation. Employment and level of wages or salaries depend less on local and more on national or international decisions. For example, the reassessment of an international defence commitment may lead the Government to cut back on an armament contract which may lead to the redundancy of a worker from the council estate as much as a manager. The manager may be obliged to move house on taking up his next job, possibly some distance away.

In the same way that the villages round the towns expand as immigrants move in, so also do the towns round London expand as people move out of the conurbation in search of a cheaper house, from which the men commute back. New towns to provide jobs and better houses for Londoners are just part of a broader process of peripheral expansion. The centrifugal movement out of the cities and out of the smaller towns hits villages which are themselves in a process of change, as I have just described. New industries create new jobs which mean new occupational categories (or status groups) with distinctive value systems. 'Traditional' jobs and values come up against 'non-traditional' jobs and values, as Margaret Stacey shows so clearly in her study of Banbury. The son of a coalminer who is now a tutor-librarian in a college of further education does not see himself living next door to the tea-importer in his wooded retreat, even if he could afford it. Similarly the daughter of a bus-conductor who was a typist for a few years after she left school, before marrying a salesman in the firm, would find the radical, graduate wife too frightening and confusing. Both are doing what is expected of them: the nest-centred wives of the small town estate reflect values which are still typically found in women's magazines of the traditional sort, whereas the radical wives are more self-conscious and read *New Society* and *The Guardian*.

During a period of rapid social change there is a need for many more careful studies at a local level, describing distinctive, normative patterns of behaviour, or styles of life, and the relations between increasingly segregated social worlds. The examples I have given here raise more questions than answers and are limited to a narrow range of the occupational spectrum in a particularly prosperous part of the country. In the New Town study I probed the values of one atypical minority but at the time there was no way of finding more of their pattern of relations with other groups. In the village the introduction of the religious element added a distinctive complication to the local configuration. In a village with a different local status hierarchy, for example, in an area of smallholdings, the response to newcomers would be different. In some places those who have established themselves in the recent past may act as mediators linking newcomers to the local situation. It would be interesting to know more of such people and how easily they can move between social worlds. Is their position in the local social structure ambiguous because of their occupation or because of their length of residence or something else? If some groups expect more from a local place, in the way of active voluntary associations and so on, than others, is it possible to define these more precisely, possibly relating them to occupation or house type, in effect income?

Newcomers in Town and Country

Adult classes in sociology or local studies could perhaps discover the basic structure of their established community and relate it either to their own continuum of change or to the morphological continuum suggested by Frankenberg. Then they might characterise the newcomers in terms of distinctive styles of life and relate these to the local configuration. Local situations of conflict—over schools, local planning decisions and the provision of other services—or the action of residents' associations or local councils provide opportunities for mapping out lines of tension between social worlds. The distribution of power, whether economic, political or social, should be an important part of the analysis, and studies such as those by Vidich and Bensman or Lowry provide readable introductions and give valuable hints even if they are not close parallels to the British situation.

In this final section I have raised certain issues which may not be so familiar to the non-sociologist. I hope that this will not deter readers from following up some of the references and doing work in local milieux along the lines I have suggested. Making conscious the processes of which we form a part is a challenging and yet necessary task if we are to remain self-aware people and not puppets.

REFERENCES

E. Bott, *Family and Social Network* (1957).
R. Durant, *Watling: a Survey of Social Life on a New Housing Estate* (1939).
R. Frankenberg, *Communities in Britain* (1966).
J. H. Goldthorpe and D. Lockwood, 'Affluence and the British Class Structure', in *Sociological Review* n.s. 11(2) (1963), pp. 133–63.
M. Jefferies, 'Londoners in Hertfordshire', in *London, Aspects of Change* (1964).
J. Klein, *Samples from English Cultures*, vol. 1 (1965).
J. Lowry, *Who's Running This Town?* (New York, 1965).
R. N. Morris and J. Mogey, *The Sociology of Housing: Studies at Berinsfield* (1965).
R. E. Pahl, 'Education and Social Class in Commuter Villages', in *Sociological Review* n.s. 11(2) (1963), pp. 241–6.
——, 'The Old and the New: a Case Study', in *New Society* 29.x.64.
——, 'Class and Community in English Commuter Villages', in *Sociologia Ruralis* 5(1) (1965), pp. 5–23.
——, *Urbs in Rure: the Metropolitan Fringe in Hertfordshire* (1965).
——, 'Commuting and Social Change in Rural Areas', in *Official Architecture and Planning* July 1966.

Newcomers in Town and Country

R. E. Pahl, 'The Social Objectives of Village Planning', in *Official Architecture and Planning* August 1966.

——, 'The Rural-Urban Continuum', in *Sociologia Ruralis* 6(3–4) (1966).

W. G. Runciman, *Relative Deprivation and Social Justice* (1966).

M. Stacey, *Tradition and Changes: a Study of Banbury* (1960).

A. J. Vidich and J. Bensman, *Small Town in Mass Society: Class, Power and Religion in a Rural Community* (New York, 1960).

Index of Names of Persons and Places

Index

Index

Index

Index

Index

The editor wishes to thank Mrs D. Bicknell and Mrs B. Horne for help in preparing this index, and Mrs Bicknell for typing it and many other sections of the book.